THE ENSLAVED QUEEN

THE ENSLAVED QUEEN
A Memoir About Electricity and Mind Control

Wendy Hoffman

AEON

First published in 2014 by Karnac Books.

This new edition published in 2019 by
Aeon Books Ltd
12 New College Parade
Finchley Road
London NW3 5EP

British Library Cataloguing in Publication Data

A C.I.P. for this book is available from the British Library

ISBN-13: 978-1-91159-783-4

Typeset by Medlar Publishing Solutions Pvt Ltd, India
Printed in Great Britain by TJ International Ltd, Padstow, Cornwall

www.aeonbooks.co.uk

*To the living children whose lives were twisted and thwarted
and who were forced to do things
that no child could do without being split into many pieces
and in memory of the dead children
and for those struggling to know who they are*

PART I

THE SPLIT MIND

ONE

The sell-off

If you have a single, undivided mind, it must be difficult to fathom how people could walk around with splits in their mind; how one part of the mind could take over and all the other parts would know nothing of it; how one part of the split mind could make the body do something that none of the other parts would want or remember.

I had already had mountains of therapy and thought I was finished with my memories of my childhood and adulthood as a victim of mind control and ritual abuse in a multigenerational family, and the obliteration of my memory by criminal groups. Traumatic remembrances still dribbled out, but my concept of myself held a steady course like a vessel sailing through a fogged night.

I had long suspected that my sister and I did not have the same biological parents. Perhaps we had the same father but not the same mother, I thought. We don't look alike but there is something familiar about us. Marlene is stunning with her long straight hair and I'm not. But we have the same overly narrow wrists, one of our eyebrows is almost identical, and we share the same inherited talents and interests. And now that we have aged, we look even more alike. I ignored all that and thought we were too different as people to be full sisters, though I knew this disparity to be common. How could one sister be interested in the recovery of memory and being, and the other adverse?

A couple of years ago, Marlene visited her married son in a nearby state with her new boyfriend. They slept over at her son's house. I was invited for the afternoon. I went into their guest bathroom and saw my sister's hairbrush filled with her luscious long hair like a bird's ambitious nest on the sink. With my fingers I combed most of it out and placed it in a plastic bag I happened to have in my purse. I left enough hair in her brush that Marlene wouldn't become suspicious. None of this was premeditated. Once I got back to my home in Baltimore, I called laboratories that specialized in DNA testing. I mailed it and a sample of my saliva to a lab. The DNA report said we were full sisters with the same parents. I was shocked. I had been so sure. I started doubting all my memories.

Meanwhile a towel fell off my shower door onto my right little finger and tore a tendon. I went to a hand specialist. While I was in his office, I said, "Would you look at my left little finger and tell me what made it like that?" My mother had told me I was born with a deformed left little finger. There was no reason for me not to believe her, but I didn't. The doctor examined the tip and said in an instant with certainty, "It's an amputation that happened before you were three. How did it happen?" During the years of therapy I received, I had already remembered my paternal grandfather's chicken farm in upper state New York and the initiation ritual with me wearing a white ruffled dress, a hatchet coming down not to my neck but to this finger. The hatchet aimed at my neck swerved at the last moment. I was under three years old. I didn't tell the doctor. He said, "You probably caught it in a door by accident."

"It was no accident," I mumbled as he hurried to another patient. So I was wrong about my sibling but right about the initiation ritual.

Starting over

Over a decade before this, I had finished ten years of intense therapy, and now I was in another crisis. Confusion makes people desperate, and there weren't many people I could talk to about memories of mind control. I contacted a therapist and writer friend from the past, E. Sue Blume. She is a specialist in dissociative memories. I told her I doubted myself. E. Sue said that while I had been retired from this field, others had been galloping along. She greatly respected Alison Miller's safe and competent, innovative work. She arranged for me to talk with Alison on the phone.

It was as if a voice without a face fell from the skies. I wanted to know whether all my mind control programs had been removed by my previous therapist, Ann, or whether any were still active. During the phone evaluation, Alison asked me what my internal structure was, who my gatekeeper was, whether I had memories of snuff films. "Snuff films!" I was getting more and more overwhelmed, dismayed, and frustrated. Wasn't the abuse I remembered bad enough? I kept saying, "No," and "I don't know". She asked whether I was in touch with my family. I said I was. Alison explained to me about safety precautions. She was especially concerned that I not report what was going on in me to anyone in my family or who could potentially be involved with the abuser group.

Alison told me that my programs were still active. How could this be? I'd had so many memories, and so many years of therapy. She said I didn't know the fundamental and important things I should have discovered. My brain galloped within. Underneath, some people in me panicked, and others had headaches, as if a vise were around my skull. I hadn't yet recognized that feeling as a body memory. Every one of my nerves was in anxious distress. The voice over the phone implied that all the recovery work I had done for decades was for naught. That work had been my life. Despair mixed with fear. A chorus of internal, indistinguishable, indistinct voices sung out to me, "We are here. They will kill us. Don't tell." I had body memories of electroshock. Fear, hope, despair, worry whirled around uncontrollably. I was filled with too much unrest to sleep.

Right there, my world changed. The queens in me slipped out wearing their crowns and ice blue fur-trimmed capes. They sniffed. They smelled hope. Was there really someone in the world to help? They watched and quickened in expectation. Word went up and down the ladders in my system. This exploration into retrieving my frozen-over soul began. In therapy a decade before, Ann, my Christian therapist who was also a plant, had taught me that forces in the universe harassed me, and that when I became anxious and depressed and had "visions" of abuse, it was from spiritual warfare, from Satan and his forces making me uneasy. A plant is someone who pretends to help you but really works for one of the mind-controlling groups. "They are all parts of you; they are not spiritual forces from outside of you. So you need to listen to them, not banish them," Alison said. I grappled with what was outside of me and what was within. Neither one of us initially suspected that Ann was a plant from the abusers. But one day I described the hand signals Ann used during my sessions with her. Alison knew what that meant. Ann was busted, which meant my process was just beginning.

Alison continued to provide long-distance guidance. One day about half a year later, she wrote that she cared about me. Did I want to start this process again, did I want to spend myself finding out what my past is? No, then yes. I do. No. I had held my life intact. I had a simple, comfortable enough house, a job. I could save a little for retirement. I didn't need to open the whole thing again. I didn't need to talk to another of these therapists. Alison was on the other side of the continent and in another country. No. I went to sleep, if what I do can be called sleep. I woke up. I would re-open. I could take out stitches that my skin had grown over. I would begin again.

A therapist who is a good person is an antidote to the people filled with hatred, the people who abused me. It is easy for the tortured to believe that all people are harmful, so it is especially important to be in touch with genuine, wholesome humans. Previously, I had been alone in this world of horror. Now I had an interested companion as I re-entered it. Support also contradicted my low self-esteem. If someone is helping me, I must be somewhat worthwhile, I thought. Alison's targeted questions kept me on track. She spotted the blanks in the narrative, what Ann had deliberately taken out. She probed for the training memories, the first instances of them, pointed out any incongruities and inconsistencies in my story, and reached out to my insiders who held the emotional and physical pain of each memory. She would also ask, "What words did they say?" I might have missed much of this if I were just working on my own.

A life lurked behind and underneath my brain, a life I didn't know about yet but could smell. How could I have spent so many years in therapy and know hardly anything about myself? Now I know it is because I went to therapists who were plants.

If you think the world is pure and innocent and that almost all of our political leaders mean well, then you may not believe what I am about to write. Some of the public has to be interested in the below-the-surface webs of duplicity, why a stench of evil permeates ordinary life.

This story is really about electricity.

The Nazi purchase, 1947

In my normal life, I thought I was a regular Jewish child from Queens, New York, far away from the East European world my grandparents came from and far away from Hitler, about

7

whom I had heard only the vaguest things. I was not face to face with the horrors of the Holocaust, and my family never talked about their escape from Europe.

I think the letters began around when I was born in 1943, but I of course didn't know about them until later.

The memory of the letters came to me in a dream. I saw the stationery, insignia, signature. At first, I couldn't believe that our government was that corrupt. I remembered Mengele's smell in my conscious life, and the black machines, and all the children in the hallways, and the frozen eyes.

A letter arrived which caused great excitement, and Mrs. Twartski called for a special meeting that took place in our living room. Mrs. Twartski was my handler. A handler, also called a trainer, is the person who controls you and makes you do things you never would choose to do. Handlers start by breaking a child's mind into pieces and in cults like these, try to control the mind for the person's whole life. They administer programs and their cues or triggers as they take over a life. All the leaders of our community were present. Children did not attend this family meeting, but we were excellent eavesdroppers.

Uncle Harry and Mrs. Twartski sat on one of Mother's curved sofas. Uncles Richard and Sidney sat on the other sofa. My mother sat on the piano bench by the window that overlooked the waterfall. She wasn't supposed to be at this meeting but since it was her apartment, they let her stay. Maybe that's why she chose the worst seat and was trying to be inconspicuous. Usually she liked a lot of attention. My father was in his wing chair and Wiezenslowski sat in Mother's wing chair. He was very short and always wore a mask. People said he was the master programmer who knew the most. In mind control, programmers divide victims' brains into sections, one section not knowing about another, with each section blindly following commands that are to that person's detriment. Mother had taken the pale blue slipcovers off the wing chairs for this occasion, and their chartreuse silk looked clean and shiny.

Aunts Mimi and Eileen led my sister and me into the kitchen. Grandma and Aunt Bea were there already. We all listened through the walls. Mrs. Twartski read:

The great country of Deutschland is delighted to accept your invitation to have our revered Herr Doktor Josef Mengele visit your United States of America and instruct selected communities on the current state of our advanced knowledge of mental development, stimulation and management.

Our officials will be in contact with you concerning schedule and reimbursement.

Very truly yours, Felix Hofstadtler, Assistant to the Secretary of the Interior

October 17, 1947

This meeting was a big happening in our family and there was a rosier excitement than when they talked politics. I was aware letters were arriving from Germany shortly after Daniel died. Daniel was the boy who loved me and whom they killed. My father kept some of the letters in his safe in his hall closet. He was the lawyer for our group and had been corresponding for years. Germany first wrote to President Roosevelt, then President Roosevelt and Mr. Truman, then President Truman. This letter came after the war had ended. Which part of the German government, undercover government or group impersonating a government, had sent the letters is unknown to me. I might be wrong about the date and the spelling of the name. In their ordinary lives, my Jewish family hated the Germans but in their cult-robot lives, they cooperated with the Nazis. And also their own American government. The United States government was the conduit to Mengele and his entourage. The United States wanted to learn the Nazi mind-control programming techniques and not be left behind. What better weapon than the human brain? The human brain was Mrs. Twartski's and Wiezenslowski's domain. The children who were used were the castaways of the United States government, like dogs abandoned in a vet's office. Mrs. Twartski read the letter out loud, slowly and carefully enunciating every word in her thick Polish accent.

The German research scientists were looking for children who could learn quickly, were between ages four and twelve, and could withstand being famished without dying. Deutschland was paying $50,000 per subject. Everyone in the living room except Mrs. Twartski and all my aunts let out a huge "Ahhh". My sister's and my eyes grew wide because we had no idea what this meant or why the adults were so excited. Then my sister's eyes narrowed as if she knew something that I didn't yet, as if she had just figured something out. She was very smart even though she got bad grades in school.

Mrs. Twartski continued: "Every selected community that receives this letter via the United States government should nominate two children to begin with. The great Herr Doktor Josef Mengele will visit New York, Boston, Philadelphia, St. Paul, Duluth and other Midwestern cities, Dallas, San Francisco, and Los Angeles next month."

UNCLE HARRY: "It's like magic. They do things and don't remember they did it!"

MRS. TWARTSKI: "How is that different from what we already are doing?"

UNCLE RICHARD: "They're refined techniques, much more advanced than our methods. The Germans know."

MOTHER: "But what about the children?"

UNCLE HARRY: "They won't remember anything. Children never remember."

UNCLE RICHARD: "It will be like it never happened."

WIEZENSLOWSKI: "That's why the government brings Nazis over here, so they can learn from them,

                    so that we know how to manipulate people's
                    minds better."
MRS. TWARTSKI: "We are already expert on manipulating
                    people's minds."

Purplish crows outside the windows screeched harrowing cries. It must have been late autumn by the time this letter reached us.

Mrs. Twartski said, "We have decided that Marlene and Wendy Hoffman will be the first subjects. If Dr. Mengele requests other children in the months to come, then Rhonda Jacobs and Sheila Goldman will be the next set, and Michael Jacobs and DeeDee Goldman will be after them."

"Well, children, now that it's settled, I'll be leaving," Wiezenslowski said.

"Aren't you going to stay and eat anything?" Grandma said.

"No, I have business to attend to."

A short time later, my grandfather with his mean beady eyes entered wearing the same kind of coat and shoes as Wiezenslowski, but I didn't think much of it then.

In the kitchen, my Aunt Eileen and Aunt Mimi stared at each other. "Why my children and not yours?" Eileen said. Marlene and I looked at each other. Her features blurred and she breathed sharply. At first, I felt proud. It's always good to be chosen. It was an honor. The letter said so. Although I didn't know what it meant. And why was Aunt Eileen unhappy and angry at Aunt Mimi? Aunt Mimi's children were under four; one was just a baby. But I would be with Marlene. I wouldn't be alone.

My father came into the narrow, pink and green kitchen. His face was glowing. "You can join us now," he said. He was so wrapped in radiance, he forgot to suspect that we were eavesdropping. We all walked into the living room. The letter with its thick veined paper and insignia lay on the table with its envelope next to it. The gold insignia looked like a sunburst with ripples. Children in my class drew suns that looked like the insignia. Fancy stamps were on the envelope.

"Can I show it to my friends?" I asked.

"No," everyone screamed. "Bad child!" All the adults sipped ginger ale and ate cocktail franks, chunks of Daitch's Swiss and muenster cheeses and a wheel of gouda cheese wrapped in shiny red plastic the color of the women's nail polish, different kinds of crackers, pineapple chunks that my father had cut up, herring. Uncle Harry and my father had shots of hard liquor. Uncle Harry slapped my father on the back and said, "You're rich."

It was a big party, filling all the living room and dining room space. People were gathered around Mrs. Twartski, the star of this community. My grandfather also liked being near Mrs. Twartski. He kept bringing her platters of cakes and cookies that Grandmother baked that morning, and smiling his crooked smile and pushing his body a little closer to hers. Grandma glared at her, which didn't stop Grandpa Max. Mrs. Twartski preferred the cheese and crackers.

After everyone left, my parents cleaned up the living room, dining room, kitchen, and bathroom. My mother was angry that someone hadn't used a coaster and had left a ring on the side table in the living room. Marlene would not tell me what the experiments meant, and I sensed it all meant something terrible for Marlene and me. Mother kept banging dishes and seemed angrier and angrier even as my father appeared more and more pleased. My heart was becoming a rope that left my body and twisted itself tight. Around midnight, my sister and I got into her bed together and listened to our mother's ripping screams and deep moans coming from across the apartment. It sounded like something coming from the depths of the forest where Bambi's mother was shot. Marlene and I clasped each other's hands. Around two o'clock in the morning, we heard the front door slam. With our father out of the house, we were able to sleep. I didn't know when he came back, but when we woke he was in his bed.

Mengele in America

A month after my family's meeting, Mengele entered our living room. It is generally thought that Mengele fled to South America after the war and remained there for the rest of his life. He may have used South America as a home base, but during that time he traveled around the world experimenting on victims and informing and teaching other countries about his mind-control discoveries, which the United States wanted to learn.[1] Mengele's face was lined and often had beads of sweat on it. He was like a dead, thinner version of my father. His piercing eyes devoured you in a cannibalistic way. Only my parents were present, and Marlene and I were expelled to the kitchen. Marlene held a glass to the wall and listened through it. She said I shouldn't because I might drop it and then our parents would know that we were eavesdropping.

"Then we'll have to do double experiments on her and it may be too much for one girl. I don't want to have my experiments ruined or falsified," Mengele said.

My heart stopped throbbing and calcified in my stone body. I ceased being a breathing person. I knew what this meant, that Mother had got Marlene out of it and put the whole thing on me. Marlene looked relieved. She let the breath out of her body and her face spread out. I would be alone there. My father was talking to Mengele in that oily way of his. I couldn't decipher their words, something about payment. After he left, no one talked about it.

A season passed and it was cool outside. Mengele was in the foyer of our apartment. He wore a blue overcoat. The man with him wore a cap and ran in and out of our apartment to the driver outside in the parked limousine. My sister wore old clothes. I was dressed up and scrubbed. Mengele glanced at the portrait of my sister in an off-the-shoulder white blouse with braids piled on her head. She looked like a Greek goddess.

I could see Mother killing herself for not having removed the portrait. They never hung a portrait of me.

"I want to see her naked," Mengele said pointing to Marlene. She froze and shook. My mother flung her body in front of Marlene's and said, "You can't have her. I love her, my daughter."

My father said, "Take the younger one. She's smarter," as he pushed me forward.

Marlene cried because our father said I was smarter even though he was just trying to manipulate Mengele. The doctor's chest grew large.

"All right, we'll take her. She'll be back on Sunday or Monday, depending," Mengele said. It was Thursday. He slipped a check on the dining room table in the foyer. It was a pale blue check that contrasted with the dark wood. Morris S. Hoffman, the date and the dollar amount were written in faint, careful script. "Mengele" was in thick black curving lines. I could read everything but the amount, which had many zeroes.

Mengele slipped his rough arm under mine and dragged me to the front door. The top of my oxfords scraped against the pale gray carpet. My mother pulled out a small suitcase the size of a briefcase that she had packed for me the day before and hidden in my father's hall closet by the entrance. I was too afraid to cry. My body was stiff, dragging and not moving on its own. My clothes seemed to follow me. Betrayal is a more subtle, twisted feeling than terror. It burns and eats, but terror stabs right through.

"She won't need anything," Mengele said, pushing my mother and the suitcase away and pulling me through the front door, up the three steps, out the side entrance and into the parked limousine. Mengele got into the back seat with me. Two men were in the front. It was 1947. My sister was almost nine. I was four and a half. The car doors locked.

The limousine drove up 68th Road, turned right at 108th Street. Before we reached Enterprise Avenue, Mengele whipped out his white handkerchief and pressed it against my nose. I fell unconscious. It was past midnight anyway and I was usually asleep by eight o'clock. Even in this heavily drugged sleep, I felt my body spasm and saw iron cages opening and closing.

When I awoke, I was at the Montauk Point Programming Center on Long Island. I had been here before under Mrs. Twartski's care. The Center was part Bauhaus sleek and clean, and part dungeon filled with children. The building looked white, and had an outside overhang where cars dropped people off. Water, the Long Island Sound, and towers with machines on top were outside too. The machines were spinning like windmills. The inside had a central open staircase and programming rooms upstairs and in the basement levels. I was probably in the group of American children Mengele first experimented on. Construction in the basement had not been completed. I don't know why I thought there would be an adjustment period. Attendants strapped me to a stretcher and wheeled me roughly into an inner room. At this Center, there wasn't morning, afternoon, and night. It was twenty-four hours with no sleeping and no eating. Mengele only worked on hungry subjects, like a dog trainer. I heard the staff ate in the cafeteria. We wore only the oversized helmets that shot electricity into our brains, and electrodes all over our bodies. The staff kept us in a drugged state from injections into our bodies and scalps.

Terror is so sharp, you wouldn't believe it could be turned up a notch. When it reaches its crescendo, it transforms into a watchful passivity. The insides are running while the outside is both immobile and levitating. The heart is breaking out of the body while the bones and skin invert.

Our government built the Montauk Point Programming Center for experimentation in mind control. Mengele was a guest there. The workers, including Mrs. Twartski, bowed down to him as if he were a god. Mengele thought of himself as God. These groups' first concern is that none of their victims

15

spill the beans. Mengele adapted his mind-control techniques for America and probably other countries. Children like to talk about what happens to them. Some of Mengele's first experiments were to trick us into believing we would self-destruct if we told. He wanted young children as subjects because young children readily believe lies and their minds are still malleable. I believed almost all the lies they told me.

The mental surgeries took place in the basement chambers. I had already been drugged, my wrists and ankles were clamped, a huge helmet with wires was on my head and electrodes were on my body. Mengele said, "Mrs. Twartski, please notate that these are experiments twelve to twenty-four," as he pushed a long needle into the nerve of the first tooth.

"We are doing a new kind of surgery. It is experimental. We are implanting cameras in you. They are tracking devices. They will follow you forever and record everything you do, everyone you talk to and whatever you say. With these cameras, you will never be free of us. You will never be able to escape. You will always be our prisoner. Only very special people get to be our prisoners. These are the first ten to twenty cameras, telescopes, tape recorders, and other devices that we are sealing in your top row of teeth."

Another day or night in a basement room at Montauk Point, Mengele put a knife on my chest, and told me he was taking out my human heart and inserting a bomb instead. The cut felt like a ragged line.

"If you ever try and turn away from us, it will explode and you will blow yourself up and the people around you. It knows your thoughts and moves. It is in you now and will be in you forever.

"Close it up now, Mrs. Twartski. Seal her chest back. Now we are making the hideous scar invisible only because we are being kind to you. We leave it showing for some girls and boys," Mengele said as he administered intermittent jolts of electricity. Mrs. Twartski put a black glue, then a black tape on the pretend scar, then peeled the whole thing off. The child parts of my brain that Mengele addressed believed there was a bomb instead of a heart in my body.

Also while in the lower levels of Montauk Point, Mengele said, "I am taking out your womb and putting in a cow's womb. I've done this hundreds, thousands of times in the camps. You will only give birth to animals from now on."

I spent my childhood looking down at my chest to see if it was growing. I prayed and prayed that it would not grow. I could never understand why I had this fear until the girl entrapped in the Mengele section of my mind's internal structure said, "I don't want to give birth to an animal or to a half person and half animal. If I have breasts, I could get pregnant."

"We have a nice little girl, let's slice her in half and I can have half and you can have half. Which half do you want, vanilla or chocolate?" I felt my fear rising even though I realized he was trying to make me afraid. I thought of the half chocolate and half vanilla cookies my grandmother brought from the bakery on Paradise Boulevard.

Mrs. Twartski answered, "Vanilla." I was surprised. I thought she liked chocolate.

Mengele said, "I'll get my saw. We'll put this vise on her head to hold her still. Tell me when her brains come out, then I'll know I squeezed too tight." That started my terror despite myself. I could feel worry becoming a mountain with ice on top.

Mengele said "You're going to go to a dentist who'll put very sharp needles all the way down your throat. You have that to look forward to too." Then they spun me, saying "Who wants to remember what's going to happen to her?" They were trying to bring out an internal part that would always do what they commanded.

MENGELE: "It should be a boy and not a girl."
MRS. TWARTSKI: "Why?"
MENGELE: "They're more controllable."

17

I liked to spite Mengele even more than I liked to rebel against Wiezenslowski, the other big shot. I felt my inside people think, if he wants a boy, a girl will come out. That was the only way I could think of to fight back.

I said, "I'll remember and I'm a girl."

Once a part of the mind comes out to accept a task, it's too much trouble for the mind controllers to put that part back in and coax out a more suitable part. This part's name was Annie and she had a Raggedy Anne doll look. Mengele was angry that I popped out. "Maybe I should whip you."

Mrs. Twartki said, "Let's get on with it." Mengele wore a devil costume with a tail. Mrs. Twartski wore her floral dress. She was heavy and square looking like both my grandmas. He went right up to my face and roared and scared me. That made me want to fight him harder. He was like an eight-year-old and I was four.

"Let's take her and flush her down the toilet," he said.

My head was way too big to flush down the toilet. It was silly. He raged at me. "We're going to throw you in the ocean. You deserve to feed the fish. We'll take you to the top of the tower and throw you out the window. Whenever you see a shadow or a Negro man, you'll be afraid, you'll even scream. Whenever you see a Japanese man, you'll be afraid he'll cut you with a sword. Whenever you hear a bell, you'll be afraid I'm going to come and get you. And if you don't get afraid, then know I will take this knife and cut all the way from your chin down the center of your body and Mrs. Twartski will scoop out your insides. So it's better to be afraid, if you want some advice."

He threw me onto a cot. "I'm getting bored."

Mrs. Twartski said "Me too."

"We'll come back later." They didn't come back that day.

The information about all these "experiments" was held in different sections of my brain. When all the distinct parts come together, the memory can crystallize. All divisions need an internal leader to control them when the outside cult leaders are not present. The mind controllers torture the body with spinning, alcohol, drugs, and electroshock until one aspect of the mind steps forward only to spare the others and stop the torture. Usually there were many failed attempts and then a part of me relented. For the internal leader of this section, they ended up with a seven-year-old girl who was alternately raped and strangled while relatives chanted, fusing the names "Mengele" and "Wendela." This girl then thought of herself as an internal replica of Mengele, who kept the other parts obedient. The parts that jump out to do this dirty work are the real heroes because they save the others.

Mrs. Twartski gave Mengele the "black book" on me. Cult handlers record everything that happens from conception to death in the black book. She recorded all the mind-control procedures that were used to separate my mind into sections with purposes. All the victims have a black book on them. Mrs. Twartski hand wrote her entries, but now the black books are computerized. The German scientists would know how to go right into my already created parts, chambers, and structures. They would know how to build from my foundation. People call this mind control Nazi programming. Until Mengele, I had dealt only with my parents and handlers. All of them had a drop of compassion in them, except for Wiezenslowski. They probably had programming in them to force them to control children and believed something worse would happen if they didn't. My parents and handlers flickered in and out of evil, but Mengele stayed consistent.

In that moment, I could have signed up for evil to make my life easier, the way my relatives had, but something in me recoiled sharply. I made a vow and all the morality in me shot out like a missile. From the many parts of my brain that took the Mengele hit, this seven-year-old girl, the internal leader older than my biological age, became the most ethical. I thought hard about whether there could be a God. Mengele's world was sticky and cloying, dense with meanness. There was no God there and no space that I perceived where God could even creep in. In the other world, there was often something of comfort, like eating chocolate pudding with no drugs in it; like my friend's eyes which I remembered clearly even though he had already been dead for over a year; like the breeze, the slope of the hills, when the sunshine leaned on me; like when I could learn something in school; like cantaloupes and honeydews. These might be what other people call God. When you go deeply into the jaws of evil, you have to go one way or another. When you take something to a total extreme, it turns into something else.

My father drove me to Montauk Point many times. He stood by the driver's side of the car while the attendants took me to Mengele's programming chamber. Sometimes a sign said "Advanced Programming" or "Special Programming". I was a rat in a maze. My betrayer went home to my other betrayers. I hoped they would all suffer an agonizing death, that my sister would have a plague of pimples, my mother's mink coat would get wet, my father would have his pocket picked.

I felt only the knock and throb of terror. Later when I relaxed a smidgen, a tidal wave of worry flooded me. The betrayal gnawed me to pieces. So many children here were like the children behind barbed wire I had seen in photographs, children from different countries, child faces frozen into those of the aged. Some of the faces I recognized: my cousins, neighbors whose eyes had become hollow. Hopeless faces that knew drudgery and every kind of pain. Children of parents who were not parents. We had all steeled ourselves. We all wanted to die. It was not so easy to die but he did kill some of us. Closed doors covered many child-screams. The walls were ice. Ice formed around my bones.

Mengele wore a white shirt and black pants. Mrs. Twartski was at the side of the room watching and studying and wore a dress and thick medium heeled shoes like my mother's.

With a vise squeezing my head, I was naked, strapped in a chair, when he injected my arm and I had to drink something like orange juice. He plugged all my orifices during these mental surgeries. Everything got blurry as I watched Mengele reading from my black book and the document my father had prepared which told him crucial things about my programming, history, and general personality. Mrs. Twartski also coached him and kept handing him slips of paper. "This is an experiment to see if we can separate and store emotions," Mengele said into a microphone. He pointed out the window to a line of nine tall towers and told me each emotion had to become discrete and go in a specific tower. He considered this experiment one of his best innovations. I knew some of the towers he showed me were an optical illusion, because a bird on them looked painted and because I was used to my handlers using pictures to fool me. A pile of records played on a phonograph.

"Didn't your mother just keep your sister home and not you!" he said. When my feelings came out, he directed them to a tower that he identified by number, Tower Number One, hatred of my mother.

"Your mother doesn't love you because you have dark skin. Hitler would have exterminated you for your dark skin alone. I'm going to make your skin dark." He had a pail of someone's shit (probably his own) and put on rubber gloves and rubbed it all over me. He put shit through my hair.

"You will never be able to rid yourself of the smell. Now put your shame in Tower Number Three. You're having trouble finding shame. Let me tighten what's around your head to help you." I squeezed out some shame and hopelessness to the tower though I thought he was the one who should be ashamed, but I'd do anything to get him away from me.

"They use your hands to do the sacrifices, don't they?" Mrs. Twartski nodded her head. Now I knew what was on the slips of paper she handed him. I remembered my friend's mother telling me that it wasn't my fault, that they were just

21

using my hands and I couldn't do anything about it. "That makes it your fault. Why does it have to be your hands that kill? They never use your sister's hands. Put your guilt in Tower Number Four. We will keep it there for you and you won't have to suffer so. Let me tighten your headband to help you.

"Your father tells me that some days you can't get out of bed and you can't eat. You're sad because your friend is dead and you have no other friend. Put your sadness in the depression tower. We will tell you when you have to kill yourself. We decide that, not you.

"You're lonely since your friend died. Maybe he didn't love you anyway." I knew he did. Mrs. Twartski cleared her throat. "Maybe he didn't like you." Mrs. Twartski made a noise. She talked to him in secret. I knew some of the things he said were untrue. For example, I knew that they did sometimes use my sister's hands to kill. All the children are used at one time or another. Mrs. Twartski didn't like it when programming held obvious lies which interfered with the potency of the programming. I could see that Mrs. Twartski was much better at this than him. The drugs took away some of my will. I felt sick but then realized it was the emotions from the towers. The towers had a life of their own. They moved inside me. He said to imagine a little rowboat going from a tower to the mainland and back and forth. My body was the mainland.

Mengele got angrier at the little boys than at the girls. He roared, and his white shirt became wet under his arms. He screwed a sharp claw onto his baton and pushed it into a little naked boy's chest. "That's not enough anger," he roared. "How are you going to kill?" he screamed. The little boy was supposed to be experiencing the feeling of Tower Number Six for assassins. Mengele became more agitated and erratic. Mrs. Twartski touched his arm and said "Maybe that's enough for today." He screamed "How dare you touch me!" and sobbed.

His towers were Number One, Hatred of Mother; Number Two, Anxiety; Number Three, Hopelessness; Number Four, Depression; Number Five, Oblivion; Number Six, Assassins; Number Seven, Anger; Number Eight, Physical Pain; and Number Nine, Terror. The prostitutes he trained came from Tower Number Eight, and the spies from Tower Number Five.

If we learned the hand signals for the towers and memorized them for all time, then we could eat something. Mengele was careful to time the offer before the beginning of starvation, when we would no longer want to eat.

The attendants took us away at five in the morning. The maids cleaned me up and gave me a bowl of Rice Krispies with regular milk. They bathed us and dressed us in our original clothes—for me it was a dress and oxfords. The attendant walked me out to my father's car at six thirty in the morning. Father wore his usual coat and hat and had placed a pillow and blanket in the back seat. Mother had cut up raw vegetables for me to eat on the way home, but my father stopped in a restaurant and brought me a vanilla malted, chips, and a hamburger. "Don't tell your mother," he said. She didn't like us to eat that kind of greasy food. In our ordinary life, Mother gave us Walker Gordon non-homogenized milk, baked bread, and didn't allow us to eat junk food. I ate a little of the hamburger and fell asleep in the front seat. I couldn't get rid of the headache or the smell of shit on me.

Why Americans thought they could trust the Nazis is curious. Mengele reneged on part of the deal to show Americans what he knew about mind control and wouldn't let Mrs. Twartski into some of the Montauk Point programming rooms or even her own programming classroom in Pleasant Hills. At least sixty-one of the two hundred fifty-six experiments Mengele performed on me were about suicide. Mrs. Twartski did not know that Mengele would try to make Jewish children kill themselves.

The bridges

"Jews are polluting the universe and you are one of them. Jewish girls are not allowed to have babies to further pollute the world," Mengele preached at a subsequent time at Montauk Point.

I was tied to a large black chair. Mengele used the oldfashioned hypnosis method of moving a gold watch on a chain back and forth, the same way Mrs. Twartski and my Hungarian grandfather did. A large helmet was on my head. Electrodes were all over my naked child's body. How can I still be alive after so much electricity?

"You remember your friend," Mengele said. He showed a film of this boy, his face, him riding a bicycle, him walking his bicycle down the bicycle ramp in our building. I cried. I was naked, sleep deprived, and hungry. Before I left that night, Mother had not let me have dinner. My father had slipped me some oatmeal cookies.

"You remember how sad you felt when he died. The entire Jewish people have to be exterminated. They are polluting the universe and you are one of them.

"Now I will show you pictures of the bridges you will have to jump off to improve the world and rid it of the evil you Jewish people bring into it," Mengele said. "Your father will drive you to the George Washington Bridge, or the Triboro Bridge. You will open the car door, get out of the car, walk to the middle of the bridge, and jump off, plain and simple."

In another room at Montauk Point, he set up several yards of planks with a railing attached to simulate a shaky bridge. I had to walk on it, crouch down, and slip through the bars. If I couldn't, then I had to fling myself over the railing and jump. Beethoven played while I practiced walking along the fake bridge. Mengele made a clockwise circle four times on the tip of my nose and said "Jump." He caught me. He made the planks move as if swaying in the high wind, played sounds

24

of water and wind, and opened a window so that I could hear and smell the water. I felt like I was walking blindfolded on a plank into an ocean.

"Reach over and throw yourself down, you slimy, disgusting Jew. Feed yourself to the birds and the fish. You are good for nothing else. Redeem your people. You must all die," he said. Hunger pains gripped my stomach like claws. It was hard to stay awake. He placed me back in the electric chair.

"Now Heil Hitler! Heil Hitler! Heil Hitler!" he screamed as he leaned on the electricity button, my body now nothing more than a marionette.

"The two worst things you can be are Negro and Jewish. You are both of them. You have no place in the world. You are only fit for killing yourself. Rid the world of your odor, your look. Walk over this bridge and jump, jump to your death. You owe it to the world." He showed a Nazi propaganda film of rats crawling all over one another. The film described the Jews as rats. He spoke as if he were singing to the music. Beethoven reached a crescendo. Mengele's rage subsided.

A few days after I returned home, my father drove to the George Washington Bridge. My parents were in the front seat and I was in the back seat. My mother said, "Get out of the car. Walk to the middle of the bridge. You know what the doctor wants you to do."

The contract with Germany said there was an extra $10,000 for the parents of any child who killed itself. I know why this is happening to me, I thought. It's because I'm ugly. If I were pretty, I would be home safe and sound with my sister, coloring in my coloring book. I am dispensable. To be dispensable is not to be human.

I walked along the pedestrian part of one of the bridges, suspended in space. It was night, black. The wind swept around me like a twirling skirt. I had heard Mengele tell my parents, "No identifying information. No name tags in her underwear. Some fisherman somewhere will find the body. I want no way to identify who she is or where she comes from. Let her wear her heaviest shoes. They weigh the body down." I don't think my parents told Wiezenslowski.

Cars drove by. They didn't see me. I approached the middle. I sat down in the right spot. I brought my knees to my chest. If I jumped into the water, no one would know who I was or match me with my parents. I was shaking and sobbing when another me took hold. I would not do what they wanted me to do. I got up and walked carefully along the railing.

When the wind grew strong, I put both hands on the outside handrail and held tight but I kept walking, one foot, then the other foot, always feet touching each other. I stepped over the rods with my left foot, leaving space for my right foot, and resumed walking. My skirt flew up. I wondered what my best friend who had died would say if he saw me now. I could almost hear him say that he was with me. I could feel his long arms around me balancing me. No, I wouldn't think of him now because I couldn't afford to cry. Focus was everything. I belonged to the universe now, not to people. The moon and stars were out. I pretended they were my friends. My heart was drumming into the world. My heart was making a dent into the night sky. *Did the stars feel the knock?* My bridge was swaying. *Hold on tight. Don't let them win.* I was on the tip of the universe. No one knew where I was except my enemies. I was the mist, the thinnest smoke. I crept along like a turtle, definitely not a hare. Oh, how I wished I had a turtle's shell to protect me from the wind, and parents, and scientists. I would not be blown away like the light branches of a tree or the red balloon. I bent my knees to make my body more like a tree trunk. I took one step after another in my heavy brown corrective oxfords. One foot touching the other. I saw boats going by. They didn't see me. If I jumped into a boat, I would be killed. If I jumped into the water, I'd be killed. I wished the moon would shine on me so that people could see me. I wished I could fly. The pedestrian walk was going up and down like the waves at Jones Beach. I wished I were a clam living in a shell.

I felt Mengele, this Dr. Faustus, on the bridge. I felt him peel my hands off the railing, hurl my body over it and my body spin and spin down fast through the frigid air. Twisting, chopping. His face roared at me like the lion in the MGM movies. He said my neck would snap during the fall and I would be dead before I hit the water. I felt his insistence that I release my hands and bless the world. I heard his incessant music.

A feeling of despair pulsed out of me. I wanted to leave my family and I was afraid that if I left something terrible would happen to them. I felt trapped in conflict so overwhelming that I became hopeless. This was a moment when I needed someone to intervene and no one did. It was September 15, 1947.

The wind roared, the moonlight pierced. I felt a silvery terror but also a strength from outside me—gathered from the waves or the stars—a strength that was not me but infused me. And with my corrective brown oxfords, I kept my progression towards the other end of the undulating bridge. Something from the moonlight went into the pores of my skin. My spine straightened. My heart anchored itself in my body. The wind helped me along like a dog that pulls on the leash. I believed I was going to make it.

I held my stomach close to the railing so that no space was between it and my body. I arched back slightly. The important thing was not to look down. *Look outward. Pretend the vast darkness is a carpet.* I was secure on my velvet carpet. *Do not feel.* When I felt, I spun with dizziness. *Pretend the bridge is my horse, the waters my chariot, the sky my kingdom, the stars my friends, the moon my fairy godmother.* Here on the bridge I had a family. There were moments when it was fun. I never relaxed into the pull of it—I was always fighting not to be overtaken—but sometimes I felt myself in the middle of a momentum. I was taken off the earth and given an experience of nonhuman life. I could have been a seagull or a hawk.

I cemented my fingers closed. I would not let Mengele, Germany, my community, or my parents win. I was alone in the world but I would fight back. I felt my bones, muscle, ribs disintegrate. It was as if I had a hole in my body that the chill air passed through. I neared the end of the bridge. The anger started when I was out of danger. I felt it mostly in my face. I hoped Mengele and Mrs. Twartski would be chopped into pieces. I hoped my parents would die a gruesome death.

My parents' Packard drove slowly across the bridge. They saw me. The car waited at the other end of the bridge. I got in the back seat. I couldn't tell whether my mother was happy or sad but she said, "I'll be punished for this," and sighed heavily. *By Mengele or God*? I thought. My father said, "She's a cat." I didn't know what he meant until years later.

When I got in the back seat of my parents' car, I realized how tired my legs were. The muscles in my thighs crumbled. I lay down in the back seat, my body shaking like the milk in the malted machine in the candy store at the corner of 68th Road and Paradise Boulevard. I shook until I plunged into sleep.

Each time I walked the bridges, my father carried me into the apartment. I woke when he bumped my head on the outside door, entrance, and our front door. If he was careful, then my mother's voice would wake me: "Take her shoes off before you put her on the bed." My father dropped me on the bed anyway and gave my mother a snide look. She ran over and pulled my shoes off. "I don't want the sheets dirty," she said, her voice strident, eyes bulging, the veins on her neck like a dulcimer's tight strings.

My mother would warm up a can of Campbell's Vegetarian Vegetable soup and I would eat all the portions. If I were still chilled, she would warm up Hershey's cocoa for me. I would drink it scalding and eat all the Graham crackers and all the Mallomars I wanted. One day, I woke up early and ate a whole bar of Velveeta cheese and vomited.

In the morning, the parts of me that walked the bridge receded and the rest of me remembered and knew nothing. I didn't know why I was so tired and still felt chilled. My mother's awareness of the bridge walk also vanished in the morning. She thought I was getting a cold, squeezed oranges for me, cooked chicken soup, and kept me home. The brain has infinite divisions and each section can hold a whole life that the other parts haven't a clue about.

In the hidden programming room in my apartment building, Mengele performed other experiments to make Jewish children kill themselves. He used electroshock to teach me how to slit my wrists. The electroshock obliterated the hunger pains.

"It's the only thing to do when no one loves you. You hold out your left arm and with the razor blade that will wait for you in the lower shelf of the medicine cabinet, you slit like this: a long line up like the tree trunk, short lines across the wrists. Anyone can do it. Even a girl like you. It's the obligation of the Jewish people to exterminate themselves," Mengele said. "Let's see you practice with a lipstick. When you draw the tree, the electric shocks will stop. You don't have to draw the tree. You can stay shocked like this. Now let's pretend you're dead," he said putting a cloth soaked in something over my face.

Mengele's words formed a caul that encased me most of my life. But when I peeled the scab off these memories, he fell away, word by word, electroshock by electroshock, hypnosis by hypnosis, rape by rape.

After Montauk Point, I walked down the blocks around my home. The hills sloped gently, the air was clean, and yellow and pink flowers bloomed all around the backyards of the buildings. Adults smiled. Women pushed carriages and strollers. Men rushed to and from the subways carrying briefcases and folded newspapers. Girls walked home from school in herds. Boys shouted and climbed trees even in their good schoolclothes. Everything seemed normal. This was ordinary life. But I felt that in less than a second, as fast as a hunger pain or the space before the next breath, the world could change and all these pleasant faces could turn into roaring monster heads that would devour me. While I walked like this, I remembered nothing of all the procedures done on my mind, and nothing of the endless torture, and the sharp betrayals. Emotions leaked out into normal life, but not the narrative. The world appeared as a spinning disk that I couldn't quite slow down or step onto.

In July 2013, I drove over the George Washington Bridge on my way to Connecticut. As I approached the bridge, I felt a terror inside and discovered it was from the children who had walked this bridge. My strong inside adults surrounded these children and held them close as if they were the jelly inside a doughnut. The traffic that morning was fierce, almost stand-still. A few peppy pedestrians walked along the outside path and seemed to enjoy the air and sunshine. As I drove at about five miles per hour, I noticed the slats under the outside banister were about one and a half inches apart. I had remembered about five inch spaces. I wondered how I had been able to take these steps in the early morning darkness and wind, so small and alone.

In 1962, the movie *The Manchurian Candidate* told some of the story of government mind control in a very mild form. The breaking of the parent–child bond, allowing mothers to have one child so that the mothers can be controlled; government creation of assassins who kill on command and remember nothing; the victim's desire to kill the perpetrator and spare the innocent target; idealization of the villain; mind-control procedures such as drugged states, hypnosis, post-hypnotic visual cues; and the destruction and consumption of a person's mind, will, behavior, and soul are all in this popular film.

One fallacy of the movie is that it depicts adults brain-washed to be assassins without the early splitting of their brains. Children's minds have to be separated into pieces and fragments very young, usually in infancy, sometimes in the womb. People who managed to escape programmers before they turned seven, eight, or nine cannot be mind controlled to do criminal acts and not remember.

Waterfall

At times, both sides of the family joined to administer initiations. This primitive initiation rite occurred eleven times, when I was between the ages of two and thirteen, always in August at three a.m., in the tiered waterfall. Four nine-storey red brick apartment buildings surrounded the falls like giant outstretched wings. On the left was where I lived with my parents and sister, on the right was where my handler, Mrs. Twartski, lived. The time I remember most clearly was when I was six years old. My paternal grandfather stood on the balcony off the lobby of two of the main buildings. In his black robe, he lifted his hammer, struck each child over the head, carried each concussed child down the steps, and threw us all in the water. My father, also in a black robe, lifted us up and placed us on the shore, near the berry bushes. Then each child's parents, in black robes, ran carrying their offspring to the base of the waterfall and laid them on the ground, like dead fish. We all lay there drenched with fear and concussions. They separated one child, and the executioner held a knife to that child's throat. The programmer said, "If anyone cries, this child will be killed."

Portable rods held up an outside curtained area at the bottom of the tiered waterfall. Children of different ages sat there where my other grandfather, Grandpa Max, officiated. He had hung a boy named Donnie from the branch of a tree. Donnie was suffering terribly. All the children cried. In a second, my grandfather slit the boy's throat. Grandpa came to me raging with the bloodstained knife. I was now ten different people. He put the knife on my throat and said "It's your fault the boy died. It's because you cried." Some parts of me stayed in my numb body, and a few flew in my mind to Donnie, who was rising in the air. The bushes were far below our feet and the people with black robes were like dots on the grass. We went up as I pressed my stomach into his spirit-body. Donnie said, "It's not your fault. Go back. They would have killed me anyway." And then he was out of reach. He didn't know my name. He was older and lived on Cobblestone Boulevard. Parts of me still wanted to follow him. Even though Donnie had said it wasn't my fault, I decided not to cry and the other parts of me toughened and steeled themselves.

The programmers installed a reservoir and waterfall inside me, where concussed children sit and feel guilty, afraid to cry or leave their families. The waterfall initiations also became the model for inside rivers that would dominate my internal structure.

Learning and unlearning, 1948

When I started first grade, my world opened. I was with all sorts of other children, had an opportunity to learn something and was aware that I was walking the same path that I had watched my dead friend walk for one year. Feeling that I was in his footsteps made me happy. Only television would open the world as much as school. I was one of the youngest in my class because my birthday was one day before the cutoff. My sister walked me to school on the first day. Getting me and my sister ready for school was all my mother could manage so she stayed home. Our front door would close and she would go back to bed. She got up shortly before we returned. But she always made us lunch, braided my straight hair, and dressed us well, and she too was interested in learning.

It was September but it was still August warm. My sister held my hand as we walked up the hill, across the street and down the block. She left me at the entrance for first graders and my heart pounded through my pink and white ruffles.

The boys who were monitors lined us up and we had to be quiet. No one dared talk. My new class filed up the metal steps. We held ourselves narrow. Each floor had a boy monitor.

"Did you catch any fish?" the second floor boy shouted.

"None yet," the first floor boy screamed back. I continued up the steps to the third floor thinking of myself as a fish swimming in the rough Atlantic about to be swallowed by a hungry whale that was trapped near the shore. The momentum of the crowds pushed me on even though my legs had frozen in place. My teacher looked like a regular fat old woman. I liked the inkwell in my desk. I practiced not listening, because I wasn't allowed to learn. One day, the teacher brought in a mix master machine and made butter, which fascinated me. Another day, I was painting at the easel, peed, and told the teacher I had spilled the jar of water. No one hit or yelled at me. In arts and crafts, I made my mother a brooch out of an oval shape, glue, and little pieces of pink glass. Even more than the delight of pleasing her was that of creating something with my fingers. I fell in love with arts and crafts, as well as letters and numbers.

Using a whip, Mrs. Twartski taught me how to be learning disabled in the special classroom underneath her apartment building. I had learning disabilities put in my brain before first grade was over. For example, I had to reverse numbers and letters, not concentrate, give wrong answers, and especially not create anything. First I had to know the right answer, then figure out a wrong answer. My intelligence could only show in the cult life my family led. But still, I got away from home for hours each day.

Mathematical minds

Various groups contribute to the industry of creating slaves by usurping their victims' brains. Some groups are governmental and power hungry; money or spiritual dominance motivates others. They all use an imaginary geometric structure for mind control, and the trained parts of the mind are located within this structure. Mine was shaped like a layered pyramid that looked a bit like a bridal cake. The section on the bottom was the Reverse Kabbalah group; on top of that the Luciferian group; then the Illuminati, composed of people whose bloodlines made them rulers with aspirations for world dominance; then the Mafia with their criminal deeds; and lastly our government, or MKUltra, with their political interests. The MKUltra Project did secret experiments on people's minds and behaviors. A globe where the soldiers trained in security lived on top of my internal structure. Behind this main structure were smaller inverted pyramids that held different kinds of programming and experiences of torture. Mengele, with his money and prestige, bribed the committee to embellish my structure. The mind controllers put the Mengele child parts of me within the roots of the Kabbalah tree, underneath the structure, driving it, breathing into it. With its spider web structure, it became an avenue of evil.

Note

1. These sources have further information:

    New York Times (2010). Nazis were given "safe haven" in U.S., report says. November 14, p. A1.

    O'Brien, C., & Phillips, M. (1995). *Trance Formation of America.* Las Vegas, NV: Reality Marketing.

    Ross, C. A., M.D. (2006). *The CIA Doctors: Human Rights Violations by American Psychiatrists.* Richardson, TX: Manitou Communications.

    Rutz, C. (2001). *A Nation Betrayed.* Grass Lake, MI: Fidelity Publishing.

    http://www.wanttoknow.info/mindcontrol10pg#ciadocs [accessed January 20, 2014].

TWO

Betrayals

Child labor

Starting in 1947, my parents and I drove through the outskirts of the Bronx, New York, into sections that housed dilapidated factories and warehouses. A few dingy stores that closed early were on isolated blocks. My parents dropped me off at the half-hidden side entrance of a dirty, moldy, flat building. Brothel 8 had eight floors and was the eighth brothel of the network of two hundred fifty-one that existed in the U.S. and Canada at that time. Attendants recorded the number of the drop off. Sometimes I was number fifty-five or fifty-seven or sixty-eight or even seventy-three. That meant there were that many other children who arrived before me. They put my clothes in a locker with the same assigned number. The matrons said, "The parents get uppity if all the clothes aren't returned, though with all the money they get, they shouldn't mind." They gave me a pastel shift to wear, and bedroom slippers. The women watching the girls also wore bedroom slippers and shifts but theirs were floral. They weren't allowed to use any cosmetics or put anything in their hair because the owners didn't want anything detracting from the children. The women especially grieved for their toenail polish. The men who visited the brothels mostly liked children so I didn't know what the managers were worried about. The lines for the boys were the longest. I thought maybe it was because they had more to their bodies on the outside than girls our age, though some girls already had breasts. The boys came from all over the world.

One of the younger children inside of me is talking:

> I was one of the girls standing on the stage at the Brothel 8 lower level theater—standing on a stage in a littered room in front of a jeering audience of men hooting, throwing objects, blowing on party pipes; men—smelly men with unshaved whiskers, beer bellies, and cocaine noses. The other girls who were just like me pushed me forward to represent them. The other girls wanted to hide behind me—they were ashamed, too ashamed to come forward themselves but they want to be known as well. (The girls she refers to are all inside me, all part of me and my experiences there.)

We were naked. Our skin was darker than many of the girls there. The men preferred the lighter skin, especially the dark-skinned men. Some were throwing coins at us, others beer cans or just pieces of damp paper. Some were jerking off as they watched the line of us standing naked on stage.

"Pull your pants up," a guard screamed at the low-class men. "Get your hands off."

We were trying to shrink. We felt our body crumbling. Our soul was twisting out of our skin. But there was nowhere to fly. We were trapped in this stifling, perspiring, tiny room. A guard was at each side of the wings. The men who finally got me were angry and rough. They threw me against the wall, which wasn't allowed. One time I was in a leg cast and they paid my father extra money because I was hurt more than the contract said I could be. They also rubbed me against their penises. Some girls were raped all the way. The blond, fair girls were raped the most. One of the older girls bled to death.

We saw them roll people out on a stretcher. When someone was killed, they put a purple lily or tulip on the covered corpse. It was a warning, but these girls didn't do anything wrong.

Once I had pubic hair, I would not have to be on the bidding stage, but then life would get worse because they could impregnate me.

"Hey, ugly."

"Hey, fat legs."

"Hey, skinny thighs."

"Let's see your ass."

"Hey, gawky, turn around," the men screamed at the scared girls.

Shame like boiling syrup covered our bodies. Shame became a barricade between us and the men. Shame became a tight home we lived in and did not exit. Its windows caved in on our eyes, its door pushed into our vaginas.

My parents didn't really need this money. My father was a bad lawyer but he brought in enough to pay the rent and clothe us. My mother's father was a millionaire and could always lend him money in an emergency. He gambled the money away anyway.

Shame can burn, like a stove left on overnight. Shame can burn through the layers of skin. I wanted to stay hidden, shielded, tucked in a safe person's body. I didn't ever want to be looked at or touched again—ever.

My heart folded into itself. My heart slipped down my vertebrae bone by bone. My blood could not hold my body up.

"Turn that ass around."

Grownups who use children and only care about themselves are bad people. When children were killed or just died, grownups didn't care. There were always more children they could make money off.

The world seemed all dirt and filth like the littered floor and stage. I didn't like the overhead lights shimmering on my skin. I didn't want light to touch my skin. No, this was not a good world for children. And all these mean adults were once children.

It would be easy to say that money motivated this kind of abuse but that's not the whole story. The parents who sold their children must have been programmed, which means that one part of their minds had been separated through torture and did what they had been instructed to do. These parents were programmed against their will until they didn't know consciously what they were doing. They hadn't an idea that they were acting against any instinct for decency, or perhaps they thought their children would be killed if they didn't cooperate. The parents who dropped their boys and girls off at brothels and warehouses—most of these parents would not have done so if they were living in awareness of the other parts of their minds. The customers who frequented these brothels were not programmed. They were simply criminals and perverts. When I returned home, I remembered nothing of being a child sexual slave.

The school yard

Back in my ordinary life, it was a sticky, cloying August in 1949 Queens, New York. My big sister was in charge of me. I was six, she was eleven. She had begun menstruating and had breasts that pushed out from under blouses and sweaters and said "Look at me, I'm swelling." I had no breasts, just nipples that squeezed together when they were cold or wet. I was glad I didn't have blooming breasts because that meant I wouldn't be pregnant. My sister was glad she had blooming breasts because they brought her attention.

It was hot in our family's small apartment. The walls were sweating and curving from the heat. My sister said we would walk to the playground of Public School Number Three—that was up the hill to 108th Street, down the block to 67th Road, across the street, down another block and there was the schoolyard on the left. My sister had soft black hair in a loose pageboy. We both had dark eyes. Hers always looked in the mirror. Mine looked around to spot dangerous people.

She said we would go to the schoolyard and stand under the fountain. I don't remember where my mother was, probably shopping or going to a doctor's. My father was at work losing money.

My sister put on a green one-piece bathing suit. She looked in the dresser mirror this way then that way. She looked this way and that way again.

"Just wear your bottom part," she said.

"You mean go out naked?" I asked.

"You're not naked. You're so young, you don't have to wear a top. You don't have breasts yet."

"But people will notice," I said.

"No one will notice. You're just a little girl," she said. "You'll be cooler."

I wore my yellow bathing suit bottom. She took my hand and walked ahead. Her arm was stretched backwards, mine forward. She walked eagerly, rushing. She seemed to be rushing to meet someone. I looked from side to side trying to see if anyone was looking at me. When she got to the schoolyard, she ran to the back where the sprinklers sprouted water and where a group of girls congregated. They laughed and jumped up and down looking at one another's bathing suits. Then they pointed to me. I don't know what they were saying. Other children were playing. Their happy shouts formed clouds above the cold blue water.

"Look at her. Look at those nipples," a boy pointed.

"Right out of a pin-up calendar."

"Little girl forgot to get dressed," a freckled boy shouted.

"I caught a fish and the fish is naked," another boy laughed.

They circled around me. My sister was on the other side of the fountain standing this way and that way for all to see.

I cried and covered my chest with my crossed-over arms.

"Cry baby."

39

"Go suck your thumb."

"Wa, wa, baby wants to go home."

I wasn't sure of the way home. I wasn't allowed to cross the street.

"Bye bye, baby, cry baby, bye bye."

One of the girls near my sister yelled at the boys, then yelled at my sister, "Don't you care about her?"

My sister finally came back and took my hand and we walked home while I cried and shivered.

"I'm not responsible for what boys do," she said. "Don't tell Mommy."

"I hate you," I said.

She pulled up her bathing suit and wiggled around in it. One of her breasts moved around.

The Hansel leading me by the hand pretending to be a friend and big sister—this Hansel is an enemy. "I must be careful of people leading me by the hand," I thought.

Shame burned within me. It started from the inside, forced its way through my ribs, and crawled up my skin, lodging on my cheeks. The boys had seen my chest. I was branded.

Alison thought my sister may have just returned from being used in a brothel, where men had jeered at her, and that she was acting that experience out on me.

Mengele's return, 1951

Mengele wore an overcoat and entered our living room in his fast, demanding way but sideways, hip and shoulder first, not straight on; the way people enter a sick room when the invalid is contagious. He demanded Marlene, who hid in our bedroom. My father told her to come out. Mother had dressed her shabbily on purpose in play clothes and old shoes. Her idealized portrait had been removed. My mother again threw herself in front of Marlene, and this time thrust out a large kitchen knife that she held behind her back.

40

"You can't have her," she screamed.

Mengele twisted away as his fingers squeezed my left shoulder and he dragged me. I vomited.

"Jewish vomit," Mengele said.

"I'll clean her up," my father said.

"We'll take care of it," Mengele said. He grabbed my new Tiny Tears doll dressed in a pink and white checked pinafore that I had got for my birthday. I had seen my mother put Baby Jane on the loveseat in the foyer that morning and hadn't understood why. Mengele shoved me into the limousine, handed me Baby Jane and wiped the vomit off with a towel. I felt no better than the yellow vomit all over the front of my pink dress. I pressed Baby Jane to my body. I was in the second grade. We drove for a long while in the night.

Inside the Programming Center, two black programming chairs sat side by side. My cousin, DeeDee Goldman, was already buckled in her chair. DeeDee was one year younger than me with a November 11th birthday. She clutched her teddy bear. "If you resist, we will squash Baby's legs with this hammer," Mengele said.

To DeeDee he said, "If you resist, we will pull off Teddy's legs."

He showed us alternating photographs of our mothers under strobe lighting. Aunt Gertrude looked angry. My mother looked beautiful and in love with herself.

"Your mothers hate you. They sold you to me." My father got my mother to sell me. "They love your sisters, not you." Uncle Paul may love DeeDee. "It's best for you to eliminate your mothers. Your father will wake you up and show you the jack of clubs. At three in the morning, you will go into the kitchen and get the sharpest butcher knife. It will be on the kitchen table where you usually sit for meals. You will sleep-walk to your mother's bed and stab her in the heart. Just like in the rituals. You will leave the knife by her body, return to your own bed and sleep. You will do this Thursday night,"

Merkel said. Mengele used the names Dr. Black, Dr. Schwartz, Merkel, or Menkel when he was programming us to kill, and Dr. Faustus when he wanted us to kill ourselves.

DeeDee loved her family and may never have even picked up the knife. On Thursday, I made it all the way to my mother's bed. I looked down on Mother's head. She had set her hair in curls with bobby pins holding them in place. Some curls took one bobby pin on a diagonal, others crossed like a pair of swords. Mother, a light sleeper, turned, woke and asked with a groggy expression on her confused face, "What's going on?" She probably had just fallen asleep an hour or two before. Her little pills took a while to work. I dropped the knife and raced back to my bed. It was as if I galloped breathless over clouds. My father followed me out; I heard him put the knife back in the kitchen drawer.

That weekend at Montauk Point, Merkel said, "I'm disappointed in both you girls. You did not complete your task. You will have to be punished." We received double the electricity and harsher drugs. I couldn't think.

"Never disobey Dr. Black. Whatever he says, you do. Dr. Black is your master. You are his concubines. All little girls have to kill their mothers. Mothers are bad people. If your mothers loved you, they wouldn't have sold you to me." Enthusiastic Bach music played in the background. Sometimes he played along with his violin, especially when DeeDee and I screamed. Our screams became part of his symphony.

One day, the female doctor, Dr. Lillian Kraus, administered the shocks and in her lust to hurt, she upped it too much for DeeDee. A harrowing scream ripped out of DeeDee; then she faded. Mengele pulled off her helmet, did artificial respiration and put an oxygen mask on her. He yelled at the woman, "We have to pay $50,000 if you kill one of these." Our programming ended for that day. I felt glad that hadn't happened to me but also guilty. If I had somehow taken more of the electricity, it might not have happened to DeeDee. I pictured twins where one is born larger and healthier than the other. One took too much and the other not enough. After that day, DeeDee couldn't remember anything, not even where the bathroom was. Merkel dismissed the female doctor. "She's too dangerous," people at the Programming Center said. Our screams. I can still hear our screams. Her scream.

Mengele had access to my foundational homicidal and suicidal programming. Earlier, he had worked up some homicidal programming while in Mrs. Twartski's schoolroom in Pleasant Hills. Mrs. Twartski was not permitted in while Mengele showed us children a cage filled with parakeets, fluttering green and blue birds with busy beaks. Mengele wore his preferred devil suit. As he wielded his whip, we had to jump. If his whip hit us, he took us to the altar where a little bird was pinned down but still fighting for its freedom, its wings thumping. There was a difference between killing a human who was already dead or drugged into a lifeless state and killing a fighting bird. Mengele—he wanted to be called Menkel for this display—held our hands over the knife and stabbed the little bird. "If you tell your parents or anyone at all, all the birds will die and it will be your fault. All the birds will die." He reinforced the don't-tell program with his gold watch, which we had to follow with our eyes. "Never tell what we have together here," Menkel said.

We had to choose the weakest child in our group and kill that boy or girl. If we didn't, they would; but they would do it slowly, first skinning the child alive, then in slow motion pushing a knife into the solar plexus but so slowly—it was more than death, it was slow-torture-murder. We saw that happen to a girl named Nancy and a boy named Richard. After that, we stabbed as fast as possible to spare them. Mengele's hands always covered ours. Most of the children wanted to be chosen to die but a few of them wanted to live. The meanest children wanted to live. Our group had thirteen children, six girls and seven boys. If a child was killed, the parents got more money.

A child who didn't learn the programming fast enough would be chosen.

Mengele was interested in the mixture of pain and pleasure, always raping while he performed his experiments. He clamped a vise around my head to see whether the brain would squeeze out while he sexually abused me. He measured the pain and sexual response with a little clicking machine like a metronome. He loved machines, but I suspect many of them were just for show. The bones in my neck popped.

In 2012, I had an ultrasound. When the technician put goo on me, and wheeled the table, my jaw clenched so hard it could have broken. She moved the wand over my neck testing the blood flow in my carotid artery. Then my memory transported me to Montauk Point with Mengele and Mrs. Twartski. Mengele shone a red light on my young, closed eyelids.

"This is how you do it, Mrs. Twartski. You slowly move the little red light back and forth tracing the orb of the moon. Start with the right eye on the top and work gradually down to the bottom. Then do the left eye in the same manner, tracing its contours, slowly, excruciatingly slowly. Children will be eternally confused." Before Mengele began, he called out two of the original infants whom Mrs. Twartski had created in me, and gave this confusion-training to them.

I was shocked to see my mother on a stretcher at the Programming Center. I thought Mengele only worked on children. I felt bad for her lying there immobile as if she were in a coffin. I wondered how she would be changed. Her gray hazel eyes stared wide, unfocused. She had a white turban wrapped around her head. Underneath the turban, her scalp was shaved down the middle. My father stood in the hall. He looked guilty for a while but he shook it off quickly. He once said he had a moment of truth around three every morning, but it was gone by the time he woke up in the morning. He didn't say what he meant by "a moment of truth" but I supposed he was talking about having a conscience.

Hours later, Mengele came out and said about Mother, "She was an easy subject. Very little fight in her." After that, Mengele used Marlene, and Mother spent hours in bed too drugged to move. She never woke before noon. I noticed that she had no reaction when he took me. I saw my sister at the Programming Center often, though we were not always there at the same time. Mengele brought Marlene home one time with bandages on her breasts. He or his assistant had given her nipples too much electricity. They no longer had feeling. Mengele must have gone after her sexually more than usual. My mother turned sharply to me and spit out, "Why did this have to happen to her? Why not to you?" I knew she was thinking that but was surprised she would say it. DeeDee came home without her intelligence, my other cousin Rhonda with epilepsy, my sister with dead nipples, and me not able to trust anyone in the world. Rhonda's parents said Rhonda had given herself epilepsy by banging her head against the wall. I believed their explanation for decades until I remembered Mengele's experiments on us. Rhonda probably still believes it.

The early morning after Marlene returned, Mother came into our bedroom, ripped off my covers, tore open my pajama top and made four slashes on my nipples with a double edged razor blade. The sting kept me in my body. Perhaps that is why I remembered this assault before I remembered the mind control and Mengele. I don't know whether my mother's violence and favoritism were from programming or whether the environment and abuse drove her crazy. Had my mother been born into another family, she might have had a little life in the real world like other people.

My father drove me to the hospital. The doctor looked at my nipples under a magnifying glass similar to the one Mother's jeweler on 47th Street used. I told the doctor everything because I wanted the world to know what happened. He said, "Parents can do whatever they want with their children." It was 1951. I had never seen this doctor at rituals.

Mengele spent days programming me to be a spy, thief, and prostitute at Montauk Point. He began these procedures with injections going into the side of my nose outside the right nostril, which is now discolored.

"We are giving her the civilian treatment. In the camps, we didn't have to worry about this. We could put needles in them absolutely anywhere," Mengele said to Mrs. Twartski, who assisted him for this round of programming. "We have multitudes of *frauleins* like her entertaining our boys in the cafés in my country. They have no idea what they are doing and do it so well. I tell you, Mrs. Twartski, the less they know what they're doing, the better they do it. Let that be a lesson to you."

In the present, as I retrieved these memories, my sleep fell into the pattern of sleeping for several hours, then waking in terror. I tried to store the terror in containers and breathe it out. I would fall asleep again and wake later in a daze.

"Now, Mrs. Twartski, I will show you how to construct a government puppet. For males, we build on their capacity for violence. For females, we build from their capacity for sexuality and seduction. The formula is sterling and simple. We divide these programs into age categories: sixteen to twenty-two, twenty-two to twenty-six, twenty-six to thirty-one, thirty-one to thirty-seven, thirty-seven to forty-four (especially if the girl looks young). Each girl will go once every seven years on these particular kinds of adventure. After that, we close the program down. No age group knows about another. No function within a category knows about another. Ingenious, isn't it?" Mengele said.

"Brilliant," Mrs. Twartski said.

"We will make her a sexual robot. She has a good body and we will use it. We use the obedience drug. We show her the card. We tell her to sit in the chair. We tell her to put her own helmet on. We strap her in."

To me, he said, "You are now being made a criminal. Do you agree?"

"Shoot her with electricity."

"Nod when you agree."

"Keep shooting her, Mrs. Twartski."

"That's all for today. We want to make her agree, not kill her," Mengele said. This went on for consecutive days until I started to die. They gave me no food or water and didn't permit me to sleep. On the fifth day, some part of me nodded and I agreed.

"When you are beckoned, you come out. The *maitre d'* will point to where you go. The next person inside sits on the designated man's lap. The next person dances on his lap. Next person gets two pills from your purse. The next person leans her breasts into the designated man's face, covering his eyes. Next person drops both pills in his drink. Next person slips out documents from his pocket in his jacket. Next person slips in replacement document. The man should have already passed out by now. Next person slides away from the man. Next person exits room. Exiting, next person hands *maitre d'* in doorway papers taken from passed out man.[1] The assistant will help girl take off her costume. She will return to her home and remember nothing. No person will feel anything—no fear, pleasure, shame, victory—nothing. She will perform her sequence of tasks like a puppet with no emotion, an emotionless puppet. A puppet of the state. Herr Hitler wanted a country filled with these people. Controllable people doing the right thing for the welfare of the government."

Mengele was in a frenzy of ecstasy. All the people he referred to were internal parts of me that he and my grandfather had put in. He instructed me on which fingers to use to retrieve the pills from my purse. "If you drop one of the pills, you discreetly pick it up. If you can't find it, you motion with your left arm to the *maitre d'* who will be watching, and he will deliver one to you."

When I look at the faces of some of the assassins of political leaders, I think that they are programmed because of their

47

wide-eyed stare that seems to go back into their own brains, and the hyper-determined look of a person acting on a program. When they say they don't remember what they did, I believe them. The part who assassinated recedes, and the other parts of the person's brain don't know anything about the crime.

Elise brings down Mengele

Mengele used Mrs. Twartski's musty schoolroom. Sometimes he permitted her to observe his practices but often he didn't. This day, he permitted her to be present along with almost every child in the immediate neighborhood. He sat us in orderly rows with the youngest in front and the older children behind. Elise was one of the youngest, sitting third from the left in the front row. She had red hair and an open face, and wore smocked dresses that her mother probably bought in a fancy store. Elise was small and looked younger than her four-and a-half years.

Mengele, naked from the waist down, stood in front of us on a little raised wooden platform. He preferred being naked on the bottom during his teaching times, but wore a tuxedo with tails on top or a devil outfit. Sometimes he wore plain black slacks without a single crease in them anywhere. My grandfather Max, also obsessively neat, admired his ironing. Mengele used hand signals to make us take our seats and be quiet. We were all so afraid, we didn't want to make noise anyway. He could even make us all go to sleep by moving his right arm down from the elbow. Mengele instructed Mrs. Twartski on his methodology, right in front of us:

> Step one, destroy their sense of self. This is foundational, Mrs. Twartski. It's easier to take it away from boys, but we can get it away from everyone.

We didn't know what he meant by a "sense of self".

48

"Dr. Black, we have already done that by dividing them at birth," Mrs. Twartski replied. We didn't know we had been divided at birth. She had done that by torturing us as infants until we split away from our body.

"You will see," Mengele said tossing his head. "We can take it further."

"Well, I'm certainly not going to stand in front of them naked," Mrs. Twartski said. She wore her blue and white flowered dress with buttons down the front. Shocked that the great doctor preferred to be naked, I overheard her tell grown-ups that he disrespected her and was a pervert.

"Children," he said, turning his full attention to us and pushing Mrs. Twartski aside, "take your assigned seat." We were already in our assigned seats. Mengele spread the tails of his tuxedo out like a peacock spreads its feathers. He liked performing for Mrs. Twartski and also disdaining her. She sat on a wooden school chair on the side of the platform. The air seemed filled with evil spirits climbing over the walls.

"Your parents don't love you. They pretend to but they don't. Even when they do nice things for you, they think bad things about you," Mengele said to us all. Many of the children started crying, including Elise. I didn't cry because I already knew my parents didn't love me even though they loved Marlene. Marlene cried. She didn't think our father loved her.

Mengele kept his eyes fixed on us as he held out his arm to Mrs. Twartski. We all watched his hand and arm movements because he often controlled us with them. His slightest gesture, his fingers barely moving sent us commands. Mrs. Twartski handed Mengele a bowl with goldfish swimming in it. The goldfish looked young and alive. Mengele scooped out a goldfish that swooshed its body. He twisted off its head and plopped it back in the bowl. The children, especially the girls, let out a breathless sound that had many R's. We saw its pieces sink to the bottom. He scooped out another fish.

"That's what will happen to anyone you tell," he said to us. His face became all lips. His nose disappeared.

I vowed silently to myself that I would never tell anyone and I also vowed that I would tell. I would have liked to tell Mr. Jacobs, the nice man who lived across the waterfall, who prayed with his family and wore a shawl, but then he would be killed too.

"Some of you still want to tell. Some of you are natural betrayers," he said as he stepped off Mrs. Twartski's platform, walked to the third row shoving two children out of the way with his right shoe and grabbed a tiny hunched over girl wearing a clean ironed dress and whose hair was in braids. I curled further into a ball as he lifted me, my legs flapping in the air like a fish's tail when pulled out of water.

"Here's a girl who wants to tell. What should we do to it? Push her head under water and let her drown in the fishbowl?" I thought he would hang me upside down. I knew my head wouldn't fit in the fishbowl. I glimpsed Mrs. Twartski's upside-down face. She smiled. I could see she hated me. "Or should we twist her apart as if she was a slithering snake, or should we squeeze her?"

Mrs. Twartski mouthed to the children "squeeze." Mengele liked to squeeze children the way Grandpa Max liked to pinch them. During each programming session, he took a child at random and squeezed that child until he or she almost died. The child would cough and gag for a long time. He squeezed me like a mother bear squeezes her prey. My legs dangled and the air went out of my body. He scooped out the live goldfish, put it in my hand and said, "Squeeze it until it dies." It felt slippery, slimy and helpless, like me. I couldn't squeeze. I fainted. He shook me, put his hand over mine and made me pick up the goldfish flailing on the cement floor and squeeze it to death.

"This is what will happen to anyone who talks, especially the children who want to talk and to anyone they tell." I cried because I had saved myself and not the goldfish. The goldfish was my friend. Mrs. Twartski nodded approvingly.

"Now take communion and scram," Mengele said to all the children. Communion meant licking his penis. We had to put our tongue on the slit where the semen comes out. The boys also had to stroke it. He told them it was a privilege because they were male. Mrs. Twartski lined us up and then let us out one by one. When I got outside, I vomited.

Boys and girls all around vomited, then ran in different directions. Some went down to the building on Cobblestone Avenue, cut across the courtyard with the waterfall and exited on 67th Road. Some ran up the steps, through the balcony and into the lobby at 108th Street. Many ran out the side entrance, through the swinging gates to 68th Road. They ran past the windows of Mrs. Twartski's first floor apartment and my family's garden apartment on the other side. The parents of the younger children waited for them. Elise's mother waited. Children emerged without a self and the parents didn't seem to notice. The children took their parents' hands as if nothing had happened. Kindergarten didn't exist yet, but the parents took the children's hands as if they had just had a good morning playing and having juice and crackers in preschool.

I overheard my parents' conversations and learned that when Elise turned five, her mother had given her a doll for her birthday. Elise told her mother she couldn't have a baby because she was Jewish. Her mother questioned her, and Mengele's teachings cracked. Mrs. Twartski became a detective, and asked all the children one by one what happened in her own schoolroom or at the Programming Center. If we were too afraid to tell, she used the hand signals we had learned to access the information.

From all the children, she heard "All Jewish girls may never procreate" or "Jewish girls may not have babies." And "You have contaminated our sacred Deutsch language with your Yiddishkeit. For that, you will be punished," and "You are an ugly people. When I look at you, I want to regurgitate." But the one that sealed the deal was Mengele's programming the children to kill their mothers. Mrs. Twartski was a mother. The handlers and parents called meetings—some took place in our living room. The lawyers in the community all got together. They discussed how to break the contract, whether the parents had to reimburse any of the monies, whether they could be sued for breach of contract, and whether Mengele had any rights under the law. They expelled him from our community, and that's how a just-turned-five-year-old girl brought Mengele down in Pleasant Hills, New York, in 1951, and how the children learned that telling could be good.

When my family handed me over to Mengele, they withheld some of the information in the separate, highly secret, black book on me, especially my governmental functions and links. Mengele did the same thing. He created red, green, yellow, and blue books on me. Mengele left these programs in me that my family handlers didn't know about and that were supposed to go off at staggered ages.

All during the 1950s and perhaps later, Mengele and his associates also created hidden personalities in me and other programmed children. These concealed personalities were designed to come to life and perform functions such as kidnapping, setting bombs in banks, stealing from banks, assassinating designated people, and in general causing chaos in the United States. He left behind other Nazis who attempted to follow up on the programs he had created, and Nazi programming probably continues to this day. There may not have been sufficient follow-through for the personalities Mengele created to perform their functions when they were adults.

Note

1. An excerpt has been published in Miller, A. (2014). *Becoming Yourself: Overcoming Mind Control and Ritual Abuse*. London: Karnac.

THREE

The foundational destruction

I am in a small plane flying from Baltimore to Toronto. The plane flies over streams of cars moving south and north on a highway, perhaps Route I-95. *So that's what we look like all lined up in a row.*

I hover above my life and look down. Pieces of it fly together. I spread a golden carpet. "Come to me," I tell my many inside parts, personalities, what clinicians in the field call "alters" but what is really my splintered brain cut and spilled like a diamond. "Come to me and speak, at last."

The clouds hide the earth. Barricades keep me from all my memories, from people inside me. I sharpen myself. I must pierce through. The clouds make a gentle clearing. I would have given my life to save the sacrificed children, but they are dead and I am alive. I must do what I can.

In awareness resides responsibility.

To divide a mind so that it doesn't know itself or its parts, programmers have to start young, at birth or before, in the womb.

The womb, 1943

We swallowed together, hummed together, and moved our bowels together. She was quite calm when she slept, and I used to stay awake and absorb the peacefulness. For moments she

53

enjoyed me. She would put her hands on the outside of where I was, spread out her fingers and move them up and down and around to the sides. I don't think she would have done that had she not loved and wanted me. She must have loved me some.

We were in a chair in a strange dark room with presences that encircled us. Suddenly lightning cut an outside wall and ripped through us. I became frozen and my mother went away. No trace of her anywhere. Gone. I was alone, trembling, shivering. Mother and I had been in the same vicinity until the shock. She came back eventually but I didn't want any part of her. How could I ever trust her? And sure enough, that lightning-earthquake happened probably thirteen times.

Decades later, in my forties, I learned that the handlers gave her electroshock with the purpose of separating us.

I floated in the most soothing chamber in the world with perfect temperature, enclosed, wrapped up in life. Then it leaked out, all that perfectly warm water. It leaked out, then poured out, and I was rushed along, hurried along before I was ready, without comfort and uncomfortable. I felt the walls on the sides and top pushing me out hard. Shiny steel cold things caught hold of my head and pulled me out without my agreement. The air felt cold on my neck, shoulders and waist. The rest of my body was still warm. The second half became slippery and fast. My mother screamed almost as loud as her scream during the shocks and breathed even harder. She didn't like my father. She didn't like her father. She said they should never have let their wives have second children. She was the firstborn.

Strange hands did all sorts of things to me. Other hands wrapped me in a cuddle blanket. The tighter the wrap, the happier I became. But I missed her smell and longed to see her even though I still felt angry at her for hurting and leaving me alone. My heart beat faster and faster and went outside my body, like a helicopter.

54

Then I was near her again. I knew her lavender, gardenia smell inside and outside. I felt her eyes. The eyes are what connect the inside and the outside. Something was wrong. She went far away again. She turned away. She was saying no. Something was the matter with me. Why else would she go away? She liked me better inside than outside. And even inside she had left me.

Birth ritual, May 1943

I was born during an outdoor ritual at Bear Mountain, New York. Right after I emerged, a fluffy white thing, maybe a bird or cloud, floated over me and pulled me up into the air. We went higher and floated above all the people. I felt my mother lying on the blanket with a ring in her left nipple. She lay so still and pale, I was sure she had died and I felt sorry for my mother who didn't move and who had never touched me or known me. I would have wanted a mother. The fluff rose and me with it and we went to the tallest pine trees. It nestled me in a branch and the large hooting bird didn't seem to mind and the smaller birds got a little excited but then calmed down. I felt my tiny body lying on the stone altar pale and still and felt sorry for whoever remained in that frail body. Its loneliness reached the high tree branches because the birds and I felt overcome with sorrow. A whole world of sorrow squeezed into the little heart and some of the birds had to fly away. The tree top swayed gently in the night wind and sometimes I feared falling off but I was glad not to be on earth. I also felt shame for having abandoned those below. I thought about returning and was sure I could get back but I didn't want to. I felt a stab of selfishness but I couldn't bear the pain of my sorrow and loneliness and now I was also sure my mother had died and I had to stay away. She lay so still. Even up here, the heart pain swallowed me alive. I was caught in the middle of two extremes. The Presence wanted me to return. It urged me, gently shoving me like a mother bird wanting her young to fly. But I was just born and too young to have wings.

As part of the consecration ceremony, my grandfather had stabbed my left nipple with the surgical needle. He paced around my body, agitated. His hands waved and he shouted at people. They rushed to my body from different directions and screamed orders to others. They called out "104.5 degrees". Someone rushed over with a bag and a man pushed something into the limp arm. The body coughed or cried, I couldn't tell which. My father picked up the body and walked it to his car as my Aunt Mimi followed, holding the bag, and my sister walked behind them.

If I went away, I would never see the frail limp body again and I would never know who I became. I would live as a mist in the trees and the birds would never accept me as one of their own. The birds looked down on the people and I could tell the birds thought of humans as bad animals. I quickly rode the white fluff down and returned to my shell just as my father closed the door to the car. My body flamed hot, especially my left side around my nipple, an armor of scalding pain. I heard the body groan.

As I write this at two in the morning in the bed-and-breakfast I stay in during my third therapy week-long intensive, I hear animal fights outside my bedroom window, squeals, grunts and fluttering sounds. A cat may have caught a helpless bird. Now it is quiet again.

My body rested in the back seat and Aunt Mimi held the IV bag as its medicine poured into me. I was not sure I should have returned to this body that couldn't contain the searing physical pain. Worse than that, though, was the line that sharply cut my heart. All around me grew a thick blackness and I felt in too much worry and fear to be able to cry. But then I did cry and made breathing sounds even though I also held my breath.

As we drove away, I felt a deeper cut of sorrow in my heart. I had hardly even smelled her from the outside. I'd had a mother inside and now I didn't have a mother outside, and this new world seemed too large to be in without a mother to guide me. This pain became too immense and the IV medicine could not touch this worse pain. I wondered whether one of the snakes had entered my body and wrapped itself around my heart and squeezed it. Snakes and spiders had walked over the stone altar they had placed me on as soon as I was born.

Even though I remained so far away from my mother, I felt her stirring and rising. I felt them putting her on a stretcher and holding the stretcher high in the air and parading my mother, who had just risen from the dead, high in the sky. The moonlight shimmered on her white body and on the ring in her left nipple to signify she belonged to them and was only an object of use. I didn't know whether I would ever see her again but I felt her alive in the world and alive in me and that gave me hope. I had a new determination to live rise in me despite this cutting pain that sliced through my heart and the throb of pain on my left side. Aunt Mimi held me on her lap and my sister stroked my legs. In the future, when they didn't force her to be mean, my sister would be nice.

It is five in the morning in the bed-and-breakfast and fear starts in my heart that I can't connect to anything. I get out the tapping machine searching for an answer. A small bilateral tapping machine sends faint electrical pulse sensations from side to side and helps unfreeze my brain. It can cut through the mind-control barricades and bring forward unknown, forbidden memories. I feel and then notice my upper chest turning bright red as the rash travels up my neck and face. And my left breast hurts.

They carried me into the apartment and put me in the crib with the IV. Much later, people came in, my relatives, my mother, and also the doctor. I had a rash over my body and the doctor said I had an allergic reaction to the medicine. He said it was not uncommon for newborns. He pulled the IV out of my arm and said my body would have to fight the infection on its own. The rash stung and burned and the left side of my chest had sharp pains.

I know tears streamed down my face then but I cannot cry now. I cannot cry.

People surrounded my crib, relatives and the doctor, but my mother was in another room, resting or sleeping and crying. They said she didn't want a dark skinned baby. I hadn't known that I had dark skin. My grandmother was trying to comfort me by shaking the crib. None of this meant much to me but then a huge finger from above touched me and to everyone's surprise, I lived. The finger gave me a good feeling, peaceful, comforting.

Familiar voices filled the room. "She has ten fingers and toes." "She's a good weight." "If you didn't want a dark child, why did you marry a dark man?" "You can't give your baby away." "She is your baby. She came out of you." "She has a chin. It will show more as she grows." "You'll feel better in a day or two." "You just need to eat something." "Why can't you be like the other mothers?" Someone sneezed and my mother screamed, "You're making germs." Then she said, "She looks like the doorman's baby."

I pulled deep into my cuddle blanket and tried to wrap my arms around me but they went wild. I tried to pull my knees up as they had been but the blanket was too tight. My heart was pouring out, but I went underneath it. I hid there from my mother. I crouched underneath my heart until I needed her milk.

How do I remember all this about being born and before? I don't know for sure but it is possible that the fetus-me and infant-me picked up my mother's attitudes and also the environment. Parts of my brain recorded the sounds and voices, which older personalities in my mind are translating as I put these memories together. All that I write is part of my adult journey of recapturing what has happened. I describe infant reality in adult language because the infants and adults in me are telling this story together. Traumatic memory is more chiseled than ordinary memory. Traumatic memory doesn't wash away, and dissociated traumatic memory, or memory that isn't remembered at first, contains the boldest lines and the sharpest details.

The first splits, 1943

In the apartment in Pleasant Hills, I lay in a large crib so I must have been between three and six months old because I was out of my bassinette. I knew my parents, my sister, and my handler. My relatives and handler gathered around my crib with purpose. Other shadowy presences were there, including the master programmer, Wiezenslowski. We were all in the larger bedroom my sister and I shared. Well-ironed white organdy curtains covered the two windows. Beams that I worried would fall on me protruded from the ceiling. We had two single maple beds and Mother, with her artistic eye, had hung Victorian prints of ladies in crinoline flared skirts. The narrow kitchen was pink and green, the living room bleak and gray. The air was also gray. My parents made the dining room overlooking the waterfall into their cramped bedroom. The basement or garden apartment was large enough for children but the adults lived constrained, one on top of another, with little privacy or solitude.

In this family I was born into, children had to be controlled. I am not talking about behaving-well-controlled. Children had to become marionettes of countless pieces strung together tightly, each string wrapped around someone's finger and pulled fiercely. Inside the pieces in my head, I had always heard babies sucking. Babies inside my brain pushed to come out. Sucking to hold onto life.

Little hands emerge stretching out, calling me now. I cannot turn my back and abandon them. No, I will travel into their countries of fear and exhaustion. I will believe what they bravely tell me even if my life as I know it will turn to wax, and the people in my world will melt and disappear. I can find the people inside me who have never known life. I can retrieve my forgotten, abandoned selves.

For over sixty years, I remembered nothing about my reversed, false Kabbalah foundation. Then one day recently, I awoke early in the morning and saw in my mind a shiny black material going over my tiny body in my familiar crib and Mrs. Twartski's tough hands. My infant-self was fascinated by the different colors within the black that undulated in the air, and the memory of this programming unfurled like the satin material.

Mrs. Twartski was a short, stout immigrant from somewhere in Poland, perhaps Galicia, where one grandfather was born, or Belarus, where one grandmother was born, but not from Budapest, where the other side of the family was born. She lived in a ground floor apartment across the courtyard. Each morning, she leaned out of her kitchen window that was close to the grass and said good morning to my mother. Each evening, she leaned out and asked my mother how her day went. They may have talked in between too. Her husband was a shadowy thin man who usually wore a business suit and conservative tie.

Mrs. Twartski started the mind-control programming when I was being nursed by my mother. She pulled me off Mother's nipple repeatedly until I went into a rage. When I was back in the crib, Mrs. Twartski held a bottle for me and then had Aunt Mimi pull it away. She also took off my warm pajamas and left me in the crib cold and naked and without comfort. Mrs. Twartski gave me a cuddly toy. I liked the way it felt. It was not as good as a mother but it was better than nothing. Aunt Mimi pulled it away. I tried to hold on but she was much stronger. "Give me that toy," she said over and over. I became angrier and angrier. Wiezenslowski came in. "The jacks will be her card," he said. He laid down four and said, "The blacks, for killing, the reds, for sex." He tried to seal my fate. He channeled my anger into distinct internal personalities whom he could access whenever he wanted.

Later, I was still in my crib and hadn't had a bottle for a long time. Adults were doing things to my body with instruments. Alison said they were probably taking my blood pressure and heart rate. Mrs. Twartski was always there. Wiezenslowski was there sometimes. Then they used my mother. She fed my sister Marlene conspicuously as I with hunger pangs watched from the crib. I went into despair.

"She was supposed to get angry. Never mind, we can use this," Mrs. Twartski said and showed me a card with a picture of a beautiful angel in blue.

"This angel helps you with your sorrow." She pointed to my tears and wiped the left side of my face with her pudgy fingers. "Follow the angel always." Then she turned to the adults and said, "We just established the basis of suicide programming. We already have enough anger to make her a killer."

The "killer" training was mind-killing or psychic killing. They tricked me into believing that I could kill with my mind.

Mrs. Twartski came into our pale blue bedroom. I waited in my crib near the two windows overlooking the courtyard and waterfall. I wasn't wearing a diaper. It was night and the birds were quiet.

Mrs. Twartski picked me up. Her hands were strong, determined, and blistered. They were the hands of a laborer. I was naked and my legs dangled. I liked the feel of my blanket but she left it in the crib. She handed me to my Uncle Richard. He was like a giant so I was high up in the air. My legs were free and moving. Uncle Richard just held me there. His hands were not chapped and rough, but they were mean hands that didn't seem to like babies. Nothing happened. I just dangled in space. The air was quiet and still. It was dark in the room and outside the window.

Mrs. Twartski grasped my left foot. I felt her fingernails. She twisted it the way years later my sister and schoolmates would

61

give my wrists "Indian burns". Something snapped, perhaps her fingers. I heard the word "good". The "good" came from my trainer, the woman who had taken over my life, the woman to whom my parents had to turn me over. They had no choice. They kept me but gave me away. They must have also been trained from birth.

I heard a sharp sound cutting the air, a blade slicing the invisible. My chest heaved and my tiny caterpillar legs curled underneath me. Once I began crying, I couldn't stop, the way later, when anger poked out, it wouldn't stop. I cried until I lost my breath and then cried breathlessly and in chokes. A piece of me popped away. Now there were two of me, the crying-gasping-for-air baby and this other baby, parallel to me but not me.

"Cynthia," Mrs. Twartski said. "Walk by her. I'm putting her back in the crib. Walk by her without making eye contact, without looking at her. Keep walking by her, back and forth without one bit of eye contact until I say stop."

Mother walked by. She was wearing one of her pretty cotton dresses with flowers. She always looked beautiful. Her hair was still black. When she turned thirty, her hair would start to gray but not yet. Later she became a redhead, which brought out the greenness of her hazel eyes. Mother walked by and she didn't look at me and didn't care that I was in my crib screaming and I couldn't catch my breath and there was another part of me dangling in the air and that dangling part wouldn't come back. She didn't care because I was no good. If she didn't love me, no one would love me. She walked by me with her pretty flowers on her dress and her black hair. She walked by as if I were Father's Camel cigarette butt tossed to the ground. I gasped harder. Mrs. Twartski—my only mother now—picked me up and tapped with her fat, squat hand on my back. I began to calm down and let some air float into me. That other part of me would not come back, the perpetually crying, floating part that they named "Jane".

"The infant is too delicate. We need a stronger child. I won't use Jane," Mrs. Twartski said. I felt a cold hush in the room. From the moment I came out into this lighted world, I felt a silence that meant that people thought I was not adequate. It was the way I looked. Now it was also my crying. They didn't like my crying. The more they didn't like it, the more I couldn't stop.

I smelled harsh cigarette smoke. It burned my swollen eyes and insides around my heart. It filled the gray air. All the windows and Venetian blinds were closed. They wanted no one looking in.

Uncle Richard wore a long hooded black robe. So did Mrs. Twartski, Uncle Sidney, and my father, who smoked constantly. Decades later, I would realize this was a religious ceremony. Uncle Richard took me out of the crib and dangled me again. Mrs. Twartski grasped my left leg, which swung loosely in the air. She pulled my loose skin as if I were a chicken. She pulled it and pulled it. I tried to be tough and fight her but I couldn't stay in myself and flew away from myself again. This time I flew further away from my body.

"There she is. Seal it. I can keep this one," Mrs. Twartski said. "Her name is Pam."

When she said "Seal it," Uncle Richard shot something strong through my body that I later in life recognized as electricity. The flash of it ripped through me, shredding me. It cemented the part of me that went away. She had split a part of me away. She had taken a part of me for herself. A numbness settled over me.

Electroshock is like searing raw meat in hot oil before you simmer or bake it.

It causes pain without leaving marks.

Mrs. Twartski laid me back in the crib. I shivered and peed down my legs. As soon as I cried, she said, "Cynthia, walk past her again. Don't look at her. You slowed down a little last time. No lingering or feeling. This is surgery. We don't feel. You do

63

this right or we will kill her on the spot. It's so easy to kill a baby. They suffocate in less than three minutes. If you don't behave, we will kill your other one too. The whole family is so damn sensitive. I don't have these problems with my other clients."

I saw that my mother who had started out tough was breaking down like the Jane part of me. Mother was crying. My mother with her beautiful flowers and graceful gait walked by without looking at me, but I felt her heart breaking for me. I felt her wanting to scoop me out of the crib and hold me even though she didn't like my skin and didn't think I was pretty. Mother didn't look but she slowed down by my crib. She even touched the rail when she walked by. Her hand looked graceful, like a white swan.

Uncle Sidney, who had been quiet until now, leaped forward and punched my mother in the jaw. She screamed, and everyone, even Father, told her to shut up, that the neighbors might hear. Mrs. Twartski made a big movement with her arms and Uncles Sidney and Richard pushed Mother onto a desk's wooden chair, tied her delicate hands and legs, and gagged her. My father did nothing to stop them. Uncle Sidney and my father had big round bellies. They turned the chair so that her back was to me. She still made wild sounds through the gag.

"Another misstep, Cynthia, and we will kill Marlene."

Mrs. Twartski waved a color in front of my face. It was a bold, bright green. She hung a pocket of the same rich color on the side of my crib. She and Uncle Sidney flashed two cards before me. When I was older, I recognized the pictures on the cards as birds flying, one getting caught in eaves. The birds were also on the green pocket hanging on the railing of my crib. Mrs. Twartski put on a black apron over her robe with a shape covering her breasts. Around the shape was the color green. I had never seen the shape before. The shape had a line going down and a line on the top going across. The top line pointed to the windows. When I was older, I recognized this shape on Mrs. Twartski's apron as a Khaf in the Hebrew alphabet.

All the time my father smoked Camel cigarettes. So did Uncle Sidney.

To separate each new infant Mrs. Twartski or one of my uncles performed a different kind of torture: twisting, burning, pulling, squashing, suffocating, sticking needles in me, or spinning me, then sealing each split with electroshock. Uncle Sidney put something cold and smooth in my ear. It made a high pitched screeching sound like an animal dying. I couldn't bear it. Every split left a gulf between me and my part. The splits came faster and faster. I had no more outrage or resistance. I was broken into pieces of me. I was a full adult before I went back to share the infants' pain. I am the infants.

Mrs. Twartski showed each new infant she detached from the core of me a color, a card, and a symbol. Each of these separated infants was a root from which an entire tree of parts with a particular purpose would grow.

Perhaps Mother's tiny bit of empathy allowed the programming to dissolve gradually. Her feeling for this withdrawn, afraid, bred-for-a-purpose infant, however slight the feeling—perhaps it was only a blip in the otherwise seamless structure, a kink in the otherwise carefully constructed world—allowed freedom to creep in.

"We will need a queen, you know. You will be our next queen only because of your bloodline though you would never know it from who your mother is." Mrs. Twartski pinched my neck until I gasped and could no longer breathe, put the sound prong in my left ear, and caught the split.

"The prophets said Cynthia's second child will reign, not the first, not the third, just the second. It is ordained."

Electroshock is like a virulent force of nature that saws through the body, its unstoppable pain leaving one thwarted, paralyzed. When a deliberate electroshock occurs, everything—all development, awareness, feelings of humanity—stops. A part of the mind is stunned and arrested in that moment and isn't aware of anything but itself.

The irregular shapes were like a rainbow, as I scattered over my crib in the air—I could almost reach out and touch the different me's looking down at my body. Like stars watching on a dark night, almost touchable but not touchable—my body and selves were parallel and not the same.

"Now the last one. We now dedicate her to Lucifer, our Lord and Master." They all started humming something excited. Their robes swayed sideways as if they were dancing. One by one they took off their black robes. First Father, then Uncle Richard, Sidney, then strangers I didn't know yet. People returned from the other room but not my mother. My mother was no longer my mother. It left a hole in me that never stopped yearning. Even when I will be old and dying, I will have this sadness.

Mrs. Twartski twisted my head off away from my body while I still lay in the crib. As she twisted, when I came to the point of wanting to die, she showed me the picture of the beautiful smiling angel in light blue and a second card with a picture of a beautiful sunset in pinks, golds, and reds.

"This angel will make everything all right for you. Follow him." The angel had a halo around him as if he were straight out of heaven from God. I would learn that this heaven was not the heaven of the regular world. In that world, people get to heaven by doing good things or by the grace and forgiveness of God. In this world my family belongs to, people get to "heaven" by doing bad things. The worse people were, the more they were valued here.

Mrs. Twartski gave some signal and one by one the people laid their robes over me. As the black fluttered, I saw silver, white, and purple in it. I didn't have enough smoky air to breathe. My sheet was black, my covers were black. The robes lay sticky and heavy on top of me. They smelled of men's sweat. Mrs. Twartski counted to thirteen. She reached under all the robes and put her fingers on my throat.

"Take the robes off her. She is still alive. An angel inter-vened. She will be our next queen. It's ordained," Mrs. Twartski declared.

My body betrayed me too. I did not suffocate.

"Hail to the queen."

"Hail to the infant queen."

"Hail to the witch of witches."

"Our ancestors are proud."

"Hail to our lines of witches."

"You will make us proud." Mrs. Twartski stretched out her five fingers, then one finger, and said, "Cursed be any man who disturbs what is set."

This memory has crawled out of me slowly but deliberately over days. After each memory sequence finishes, I feel exhil-arated for a few hours, then exhausted and blurry for days. Even as I recover, my inside organizers are pulling up the parts who hold the next batch of dissociated memories. Once this process breaks free, it unleashes. It is a difficult form of labor.

Thirteen of me lay disconsolate in the crib. The part who was too delicate and thrown away, "Jane," hovered by the side.

Mother closed the windows especially quietly. It must have been the middle of the night. I followed her seamless moves with my eyes. She left again and came back with Marlene.

"I don't want to go to sleep. I want to stay with the grown-ups," Marlene said, and cried.

Mother put her in her big-child bed and tucked her in. I heard a kiss. Then she came to my crib, her head hanging down.

"Don't touch her," Mrs. Twartski said from the doorway. "No holding or touching for forty-eight hours." Mother turned her back and walked away. I saw her glance back at Marlene sleeping in her bed.

Mrs. Twartski came to my crib and put a white blanket next to me. She picked me up—I didn't like being close to her face—and put me on top of the white blanket. She pressed both her crusty thumbs into my ribs. The touch hurt. All thirteen of my parts pulled away from her. This would be one of the last times all parts of me were in unison. The infant blanket felt good, as if I were held. I pulled away from Mrs. Twartski and sank into the safe blanket. She wrapped it tightly around me and pulled out my left arm so that my mouth could reach my thumb. I sucked furiously. All thirteen parts at this moment wanted the same thing. I rooted my mouth over my thumb and sucked until the world with all these people left and only the vacuum between my mouth and thumb existed, as I drifted away in infant sleep. I could comfort myself. I could find comfort in soft material and my own body. I did not need people.

The pictures spun in my head. I saw the yellow rose and the death card together, a skeleton riding on a horse. A circle of dancing children and parents coupled with a landscape frozen with ice translated into "Only here will I have a family and friends, nowhere else in the world." A card of a naked hand-cuffed girl with rats told me I would be a sexual slave. All the colors and letters and pictures crashed down on my mind. The joker, hanged man, ace of spades, quarter moon with stars, seagulls flying over an ocean, and candle holder spun around me laughing. I was so filled with electricity that I became an electricity baby.

Flashlight demons

Primarily religious, these criminal groups believe in demonic entities and the supreme beings of Satan and Lucifer. They also believe in their enemies, God and Jesus and the masses of good angels.

Although they believe that these entities are invisible, they make representations of them for children. This kind of pro-gramming starts in infancy and continues throughout early childhood. Children's gullible young minds are caught in the snare of preposterous beliefs.

The infant lies in its crib. The room is dark. The programmers give the child a small bottle of water laced with psychedelics. It tastes bitter but the child is hungry, dehydrated and drinks it. Shadows of huge "birds" (at first called "birdies") cover the walls. The birds fly around the room, go through and into the terrified infant. The infant hears hooting sounds, smells something like tar burning. Suddenly an excruciating electroshock comes out of nowhere. The relative who secretly administered it says "The demons did that to you. They bit you. If you love them, they will stop." The infant looks up and sees a red eye as large as the room. The relatives say "Satan's eye is always watching you."

The child doesn't know that flashlights and cameras, tinted lenses and colored paper over flashlights, hand puppets and large puppets on poles and handles formed these illusions. The programmers reinforce this core training recurrently and consider it necessary for the creation of paralyzed, mindless automatons. When the children grow up and when the adults in them figure out what happened, the adult parts will have to coax their child parts to release their frozen terror and cognitive distortions.

During a therapy session, Alison showed me how a flashlight could make shapes that would trick a child to believe in demons invading the crib. I had no idea that children in me lived in this arrested, fabricated terror.[1]

Note

1. The late Stella Katz gives a detailed explanation of how programmers create the illusion of resident demons in children under five in A. Miller (2012). *Healing the Unimaginable: Treating Ritual Abuse and Mind Control* (pp. 107–108). London: Karnac.

FOUR

The difference

Security programming

When I was almost two years old and lying in my crib, every person I knew put a needle in my gums. My sister put it in hard. Some of the grownups put it in roughly, others gently. A boy I hadn't met yet who lived in the same building pretended to put the needle in. He whispered to me to cry, and we fooled the adults. I thought we even fooled Satan whose eye shone above my crib all night and who watched everything I did. My father projected the eye onto the ceiling. His projector made shadows on the wall to terrify me.

In my conscious mind and ordinary life as an adult, I remembered nothing of this boy Daniel, the most important person in my life. But he touched and taught every insider. Insiders are parts or personalities in the brain living underneath the front person and hidden from normal life. They do the bidding of the cult trainers and usually do not know about the front person. The front person is the part of the mind assigned the task of living in normal life. The front person doesn't know there are insiders.

In the late 1980s, I am in bed in my 108th Street Manhattan apartment and writing in my journal. My hand starts drawing. It draws the silhouette of a tall, lean, curvy boy. I add a

71

mass of dark curls and deep, haunting dark eyes. I dress him in well-fitting black pants, a cracked leather belt, skimpy shoes, and a V-neck machine-made sweater. Under the picture, I write "Daniel David Baker". Then I sob. My front person doesn't know what is going on. My insiders have begun to talk. It is as if Daniel has come back from the dead to guide me.

They put needles in my gums to teach me that I was not allowed to tell anyone about Satan or what we do. I would feel dental pain if I even thought of straying. Every bit of my programming addressed security. Joseph, another of my handlers, gave me a little voodoo doll and told me to put a needle in its chest, on the left side. The doll represented me. He shocked my heart with electricity and told me to feel those pains if I ever got close to remembering and telling. After a while, he didn't use the needles and electricity and just told me to feel the pain. I had to watch a metronome going back and forth hypnotizing me as my uncles and father chanted, "Don't tell, don't know." All through my recovery until I consciously remembered this training, I had dental and chest pains as I approached new memories.

Dedicated and marked

I watched as my grandfather made the bed furthest away from me into a ritual arena. My sister slept in the other bed, closer to my crib. She was seven and I was three. He placed a thick white towel over the pulled-tight white sheet. He took two shiny silver swords with fancy handles and placed them on the sides of the towel and polished the rubies and emeralds on the handles with his handkerchief from his pocket. He patted everything down and measured with his eye, like a dressmaker. He glanced at me but didn't smile, left and flicked off the light by the doorway. I lay in the dark, trying to reach the mobile with my wiggling legs and looking at this world through the bars on my crib.

The neighborhood was shrouded in darkness. There were different kinds of black, the blacks of restfulness, sleep, death, evil. Across the courtyard, light surrounded Mr. Jacobs' apartment, a rocking peaceful shimmer of gold. The rest of the neighborhood had particles of evil forming a solemn and lugubrious aura.

My grandmother entered furtively, glancing quickly behind her. She took something out of her dress pocket and rubbed it on the towel with her squat, strong hands. She wore rubber gloves, the kind Mother and Mrs. Mathies cleaned in.

My mother stood in the doorway holding a bottle for me. She also looked as if she had been rushing. My grandmother looked up from her rubbing and said sharply, "Cynthia, go away for a while." My mother, always obedient to her mother, turned around and went away with my bottle. I felt angry and swallowed hard out of thirst.

Grandma lifted the ceremonial sword closest to me and put something on its tip with the same rag that she then tucked back in her pocket. She placed the sword in its exact spot, straightened it a bit more, peeled off her gloves, and rushed out, switching off the overhead light.

Hours later, after I'd had my bottle and slept some more, the ritual began for my second dedication. My grandfather lifted me from my crib. He wore a purple robe and looked to me like a girl. His hands felt dry and rough, though his nails were always perfectly manicured. He placed me on the towel on the bed prepared for the ritual. It burned my skin and I cried, but he and everyone else continued as if nothing had happened. I felt my back turn red and crinkly. Grandpa Max and Uncle Harry, also wearing a purple robe, each held a sword with a jeweled handle. Only men were present but Mrs. Twartski stood in the doorway.

They held the swords with tips touching and forming a V over my baby body. They touched the tips together, then moved them to the left side, right side, and center again, all while chanting "Hail Satan, hail Satan, hail to the master of the universe, hail to our guardian Lucifer who foresees all events in his dominion." Then it all started again. "Hail Satan …" with the curtains billowing and their voices rising to a pitch of frenzy, each hail more impassioned than the last. They seemed to rise off the floor, and sweat poured from their faces. With the tip of his sword, Grandpa made a slit on my stomach and chanted, "Bless this womb that it may provide an heir for Lucifer's kingdom." That's when the angels took me above the waterfall, and I felt what happened in other people's apartments, and the goodness that came out of Mr. Jacobs' apartment. We stayed there for a long time in a peaceful, delicate mood. When I was in the sky far away from this bed, I felt something higher that was pure and good, and I reached to get there. But that golden, inviting space said, "Go back," and I was falling, tumbling. I heard the chanting and clanging and was enraged.

When I somehow returned to my body, a doctor was there with my parents and grandparents. They called my grandfather by his nickname that I had not heard before: Wily Max. My grandfather was not wearing any one of his masks. Just as I returned, the doctor told my relatives that I would be all right. I felt a leftover peacefulness from my excursion and also a sorrow all mixed together.

"Wily-Willy-Wily-Max, you've still got a granddaughter," everyone cheered. But the doctors said I had a fever of 104 degrees. The doctors gave me medicine, and put ice on my feet because they considered the fever more dangerous than the rash all over my body.

I had this memory in May 2013. I hadn't known that my grandfather was the infamous international traveling programmer who ruined many people's minds. I thought he was just an unlikable grandparent who pinched. It is a hard adjustment. As a child, I remembered this well-known master programmer traveling around, programming me; and as an adult, I heard of other survivors who had a similar experience. Then I had a memory in which this Wiezenslowski, who is the same person as Willy Max and Wily Max, peeled off one of his masks, and a second one underneath the first, and there was my grandfather. I wonder whether Hitler had granddaughters and whether they and I could form a support group.

"The kingdom will proceed, hail Lucifer, hail Lucifer, hail Lucifer …"

The clanging ritual swords formed a roof over me. A rash appeared all over my body. It formed almost straight lines the length of my body, wrapping around my feet.

"It's a bad omen," Mrs. Twartski said.

My father came in, "We'll say she has the chicken pox, that she caught it from Marlene who had a very mild case." When my mother came in, she saw the rash and screamed. She pulled Marlene away by the arm and would not let her near me.

Now it is 2013 and I am in an airplane flying to Alison Miller. The plane is crowded and cramped. I find a vacant seat next to a young couple with a baby boy. I guess the other passengers don't want to sit next to a baby.

Grandpa called everyone into the big bedroom where I lay with my rash that went right to the bone. It felt as if the rash ate up my body. Grandma sat on the edge of the mattress where they performed the ritual. Mrs. Twartski tapped with her fingers in sequence on the wood desk. I lay back in my crib looking through the bars. Grandpa tried to find out what had happened to me. He was adamant. Mrs. Twartski tapped louder and faster and also shook her crossed-over top leg faster and faster. He asked my grandmother, his wife, whether she had done this, meaning caused my rash. She answered "No," and resented the question. He asked my mother, and she shook her head furiously. He asked her whether she knew what had happened or whether she had seen anyone alone with me, perhaps when she went to give me the pre-ritual bottle. Grandma's eyes latched on Mother, and Mother continued to shake her head. Grandpa said, "I am getting nowhere and this is a grave offence and a serious investigation." Mrs. Twartski stopped tapping and shaking. She stood up and hooked her arm under Mother's and walked her down the hall outside the bedroom. Mrs. Twartski was going to do something to my mother but I didn't know what. Mother appeared docile. Grandma frowned deeply and looked as if she wasn't there anymore. Grandpa walked over to my crib, looked me over, and made a disgusted sound in his mouth.

Around April 2013, a month before my next therapy intensive, a rash starts on my right foot around my big toe. After a week or two, it spreads to my chin and neck. I have straight lines of rash over my body and go to my holistic doctor.

The doctor isn't sure what kind of rash I have. The rash isn't poison ivy, shingles, a fungus, or from gluten. It is a body memory of this dedication ritual. The mind is that strong.

In the airplane, flying over the states, the rash on my hip sends out shoots. It becomes a blossoming flower.

They tied Grandma to a chair in her own living room, gagged, and Grandpa whipped her. He said everyone there had to take a turn; Father, Aunt Mimi, eventually me. He held his hands over mine and we whipped her around her calves. He said to her, "We'll mark up your skin the way you marked up hers." Mother received a punishment in their small bedroom for not snitching on her mother.

That night, they wrapped me in a white blanket, put me in the stroller and walked me to the ritual site in Old Pleasant Hills, off Enterprise Avenue, one and a half miles away. It was after midnight and the only people on the streets were families also hurrying to the site. Children sat in strollers and parents carried babies. Older children walked behind their parents. Everyone rushed quietly. When we got to the ritual site, my mother picked me up out of the stroller and carried me in. The crowds chanted, "Hail to the queen's mother, hail to the mother of the queen." The crowds wore black robes and swayed like waves in the ocean. Even when my mother picked me up and carried me to the raised platform and everyone cheered and chanted—even then, she did not seem proud of me, just proud of the attention she received.

The mother and father sitting next to me on the plane are absorbed in their baby. They watch their baby's finger movements and beam every time he moves or gurgles or burps.

At the ritual in the courtyard near the train station, Grandpa took me from Mother's stiff, bony arms, removed the cuddle blanket, and held me high up. Doctors in the congregation spotted my rash and rushed over in their black hooded robes.

"It's poison ivy."

"Or poison oak."

"Or poison sumac."

One of the doctors put calamine lotion on me.

"It's a pity," another doctor said. "It's such an important festival."

The rash hurt more and more, turned butterfly colors and spread.

"Poor little butterfly," someone said.

"It's an omen," Mrs. Twartski repeated.

"She should go to the hospital."

"We can't take her to the hospital."

My grandfather insisted he could see lines he had made underneath the rash. He needed a prophetic sign.

Rituals adhered to tight schedules. As part of my consecration as the mother of the future heir, Grandpa put me on the altar with snakes and bugs that hurt my skin more. The sacrifice always signaled the beginning of the festivities. To signify the importance of this ritual, there were two victims slaughtered simultaneously. The two killings had to take place at exactly the same moment. If anyone were too fast or too slow, they would have had to sacrifice other people until the executioners got it right. The tall man, who must have been the executioner, held his hand over my tiny hand. We held the sword at the first altar and my grandfather was at the parallel one. On one altar lay a drugged or dead six-year-old boy and a baby was on the other. I didn't want to kill those people. I wanted to be the one who died. The executioner plunged the weapon into the dead or sleeping child's body and Grandpa Max killed the baby. Through his masks, his underface turned into a tiger's as his beads of sweat turned red and purple. I can see now that these were lighting and film effects, but I thought it was real then. The sacrificial blood the tall man poured over my body stung my rash. They made us all drink the blood. Everyone cheered, then began a frenzy of dancing and chanting. I looked at my hands; they seemed like strangers. No one yet had told me that killing was wrong, but something in my soul recoiled and my heart had another pain right down its center. My wrists felt exhausted from the inside out. My hands wanted to fall off. Rage could have split me open.

I vomited. I didn't want the boy and baby killed, but other people were in a high religious state that built as the tall man lifted me and turned slowly to the left, holding my ribs too tightly. The air was cold. I felt alone even though a man held me up and I saw the tops of many robed heads. I tried to make friends with the stars checkering the midnight sky. I wanted to touch the stars. A longing almost ripped my body open. A sadness swallowed me. I cried. My father, who was near the platform, frowned and looked worried. He had told me not to cry. "Little queens grow into big queens. Little queens are princesses and princesses don't cry."

The tall man kept rotating me as the black river of robes chanted. When he put me down, doctors ran up to me with their stethoscopes, IVs, artificial respiration breathing tubes, oxygen masks, and something like Demerol, which made everything look as if I were floating above water. Seven more people split from me and hung out in the black sky above the branches away from my body. I came back to my body filled with iciness. They were not letting me die.

A machine pressed on my chest. Over my face, a hand held something down which got my lungs to work. I pushed as hard as I could against his arm. I felt myself shrinking in.

All these ritualized procedures are ordained and performed in a certain sequence at an exact time according to ancient rules. After the doctors worked on me, and I revived, my grandfather attached a ring to my pierced left nipple and said, "If she lives or if she dies, I dedicate her to Satan and consecrate her to Lucifer. If she dies, her bones will return to Lucifer and be made into ash." As the ring went into my skin and I bled, I wanted to kill him but I passed out again, and the doctors started all over. The same doctors who cheered the sacrifices tried to save my life once more. They whipped their heads around with authority as if they were in a hospital and said my grandfather would have to leave. Grandpa Max shouted, "I will not leave my own ritual site." My father and uncles took him away screaming.

After I was revived, Mrs. Twartski began the mind control. My brain recorded Mrs. Twartski's words, and when I recalled the memory, I finally knew what she meant. "You had the chicken pox. You caught it from your sister. If you ever remember this ritual, your hands and feet will be chopped off." A little later, my father returned with the car to take me home.

The doctor said my nipple was infected and he set up an IV with a bag on a stand by my crib. My parents strapped my arms down so that I couldn't scratch. My grandfather stood by my crib sobbing into his well-ironed handkerchief. The infection spread and everyone expected me to die. A big white bird flew through the window and perched on the railing of my crib, like a stork. I thought it had come to take me away the way it had brought me. It lifted me by the diaper and we went up into the blue sky. My grandfather folded the joints of his fingers and examined his nails.

Everyone felt sorry for me for having chicken pox during such an important ritual in 1946.

As soon as I recovered, my grandfather began the preparation for my use as a government servant.

Butterflies for monarchs

Children had to emulate butterflies. We didn't dance in costumes doing little routines in ballet shoes on elementary schools' stages. We were strung up in the air like the murdered prison guard in the movie *Silence of the Lambs*. It took three men to hoist up one child. One man held the child who was being attached to a ceiling hook, and two other men attached the child's wrists and ankles to ropes and clamps on either side. They had to fasten the child's arms simultaneously, because a limb could be dislocated if one side was done before the other. This positioning happened to many children, teenagers, and even young women. I saw them in politicians' hidden chambers. Perhaps these male criminals identified with the kingly aspects of the monarch butterfly, dominant in the butterfly skies, whose drenched coloring is breathtaking and majestic.

This secret, deep training took place in my grandparents' second bedroom, his unofficial office. In this second bedroom, where non-relatives were not permitted, my grandfather often did not disguise himself with the masks and personalities he presented to the criminal cult world. He was just his sadistic self, mean and raw. He liked to work in contained, private environments, but sometimes he demonstrated to his sons-in-law. And he needed their help getting me strung up. To start, he held me over his lap and gave me an injection in the same spot he always used, the left side of the lumbar spine. "You tilt the needle up and head for the bone. It doesn't matter how much they scream. It's supposed to hurt," he said to my uncles.

"Are you a butterfly?" he asked me.

"No." Even though I was starved and physically weakened, I answered, "I'm a little girl." Often as the body weakens, the spirit gets stronger. But when the body passes out, the spirit can't do much. My answer earned me more electroshock, spinning, and then being strung up by him and two uncles. All that might have happened anyway. Being in the air, even when held up by a hook and ropes, increases dizziness and disorientation. My uncles told me I had to flutter my wings, but I couldn't because the straps were taut. Before I was strung up, I had to balance on one foot and wave my arms as if they were wings flapping in the air. It was a little dance, sometimes fun.

For the first timed training session when I was three years old in 1946, shortly before Daniel entered my life, I hung for two minutes. My grandfather always timed it with his stopwatch. He built my suspension gradually to sixty minutes, then ninety, then 120. He needed to create endurance for when the "monarchs" of the world would want to use me. While I was suspended, he stretched my two orifices with rods of gradually increasing widths. My grandfather wanted his specimens to be perfectly pleasing.

I was very sore. So were my muscles and bones. I often had rashes, infections, and dislocated joints; but worst of all, I felt like a rag to dirty and throw away. I felt that that was the reason I was born, to be used up. If I was being prepared for "monarchs," then this was too big to fight. How do you even fight your parents? My grandfather gave my father cash on his way out, and he said to one of my uncles that soon his daughter would have this same training, meaning he'd get cash too. Powerful people must have been paying my grandfather, and he would give the legal fathers a cut of it.

After my grandfather spun the drugged young me, and finished with his other tortures of a head vise and putting me in a freezing compartment, he said to these shivering parts with head pain, "Spin, little butterfly, spin over there. You are on a long string, a pole flying hither and there. Dangle little butterfly. You are no longer a girl. Forget about having curls. You are an insect, pure and simple, made for man's use. Listen to the wives, but do as the man says. Always listen to your Grandma,

81

but it's only I who gives orders. Forget about your father. But the rulers, our monarchs, those are men. You do what they say. Bring honor to your family. Perform your duties. It won't hurt. You are prepared. Everything is stretched. You are a perfect specimen stretched under glass, pinned in the air. Now fly, little butterfly, and do my bidding for the sake of your family." He created thirty-six butterflies in me. At the political offices, silent girls of various ages who were the butterflies had to stay in a cage until the wives of the politicians called us out.

All of this is coming out in writing. These parts can't speak. I'm writing from my journals. Our butterfly wings flap against the wires of the cage. We're all in the same big cage.

In his second bedroom, my grandfather had an open book of photographs of butterflies, and he wanted my body painted like one. He instructed my artistic Aunt Mimi where to paint. With poster and finger paint, she drew thick black lines and put red, green, pink, blue, or yellow inside, according to his instructions. He especially liked orange, the color for government privilege. He left my backside and legs unpainted. Grandpa was delighted with this innovation. "I should have done this long ago. I should have done this to all you girls." To me, Grandpa said, "I should have done this to your mother." Then he talked to himself even though we were still there. "What a unique idea, what an invaluable idea. I'll be a millionaire." His eyes were visionary but framed in sadism, insanity, and greed. Before I went home, my grandmother had to scrub the paint off me in the bathtub, as she muttered, "Another one of his crazy ideas." Paint bled onto the porcelain of the tub, which she also had to scrub. The paint clumped on human skin, and pieces fell off.

The wife of one of the monarchs was appalled when a clump landed on her dress. She then would have no part in painted girls, whose painted-on-naked-skin costumes might get dye or chunks of paint on the staff's or her designer clothes.

Half a century later, video sex-symbol stars entertain dressed in butterfly wings painted with the new technologies and deliver secret messages to new generations of victims.

The difference

I do not believe that I ever would have known there was such a thing as love on earth, that people could be kind, that there was a divine presence that lived through people—never would I have known had it not been for a tall, thin boy with dark curly hair whom I first met when he pretended to put a needle in my gum and who became my friend when I was three years old, at the moment before my heart would have barricaded itself off.

He moved gracefully like a dancer or swimmer. He had pale white skin with an under-layer of rose, brown eyes with long lashes, and cherry-like lips. He was born into the same distorted world as I, but he somehow knew what love and compassion were, and he gave them to me. His mother was kind.

He knocked on our front door.

"My name is Daniel David Baker and I've come to play with Wendy."

I looked at him through the bars in my crib, which was placed in the living room next to the planter that was also a room divider. It divided the foyer that was also our dining room from the living room. Usually, my crib was in the big bedroom that my sister slept in. His eyes looked sad, filled with sorrow. I didn't know why he was calling on me.

"I've come to play with Wendy," he said again. "They sent me because my sister just died." He was tall, narrow, and had a bouncy walk. My heart leapt out of my body. Perhaps there was a safe person in the world. He smiled at my mother and looked at me sideways. His eyes were like a velvet path. A new me was suddenly growing within. This glance was the one that changed my life. I went from being one of my family to being an outsider.

"Who sent you?" my mother asked.

"The masters," the new boy answered. They bowed their heads a little, and the new boy entered our apartment that most people would have wanted to escape.

"She's three years old and often a bad girl," my mother said.

"I'll be careful with her," he answered.

"Come here, Wendy," he said as he lifted me out of the crib. He smelled like the outdoors and leaves on the trees. His skin was very soft and didn't have hair on it. He wasn't an adult yet but he wasn't a child either. His cheeks were smooth, his hands gentle. My body snuggled into his shirt. He carried me walking back and forth in the gray living room. His body didn't jerk or move sharply. My body melted into his bones and flesh. It was the first time I had ever wanted to be held.

"It's okay, Wendy. I will take care of you," he said.

Maybe he found me before it was too late. Maybe he would let me taste this thing that I didn't have but that I seemed to know about, even have a memory of. I felt my heart shed the plaster and brick walls that I had constructed. Windows opened, spring air entered, wild flowers in blues and greens sprouted inside me. I felt for the first time like a person with arms and legs and a stomach that didn't hurt and a face that could spread out. My body was feeling and singing and not just aching tight. I started crying.

"It's okay, Wendy. Cry if you want."

The tall boy who came with trust even though he was sent— it was impossible but I felt safe with him even though I didn't know the word yet or have the concept. I wrapped my dangling legs around his thin waist. When my father and grandfather carried me, I pushed away. Mother never carried me.

The tall boy carried me to the wing chair closer to the kitchen hallway. It had a washed-out blue corduroy cover over the chartreuse silk. Everything in the apartment was colorless except the chartreuse which Mother covered so it wouldn't get dirty. He sat down slowly, holding my back and backside. He pushed his back into the soft chair, leaned back, and let my front fall against him.

"Don't be afraid any more, Wendy. I'll take care of you," he said.

His chest got large when he breathed in and hollow when he breathed out. I made my breath the same as his. I breathed faster than he did, so I held my breath at the top and the bottom waiting for him. I wondered whether this was what people called heaven, where it was peaceful and calm. I took a finger from my right hand and put it in the middle of one of his curls on his head. I circled it to the right and then the left. His hair felt like silk and the softest cotton. I took a curl and made a moustache on my lip. We both laughed. It felt delicious underneath my nose. My breath naturally slowed to match his and I didn't have to hold it anymore.

"You're a good girl, Wendy Sue, and I love you," he sang.

Mother paced around the apartment. She watched me as if she were threading a needle. The fire in her smoldered within but did not lash out to burn. A barrier of angels or something kept her from charging in and ruining this too for me. I leaned my right ear onto the center of his heart. I heard his heartbeat, pulse, and breath all at once. My ear sucked in life and hope. I was not alone in a whirlwind. I matched my breath to his, he matched his breath to mine.

I moved my left hand up past the little buttons on his white shirt and reached my thumb into my mouth. I sucked hard while matching my breath to his and feeling his heart beat life into mine. I rode on his breath as if it were God's. It was. For me.

Cool air swam through the walls of the living room windows like love. Swans outside in the waterfall screeched, the sparrows chirped. I sucked away fear and torture. In this nest, my brain began to be silent. I drooled on his shirt.

Now as an adult, trying to sleep or in a crisis, my mind returns to the wing chair; I put my ear on his heart, I feel the up and down of his breath. I surround the scene with pointy pine trees. I sleep. I smile. All else stays away from me. But thinking of him still makes frozen me immediately cry.

Daniel, the tall boy, visited me every day. One day he walked me out our front door, down the basement hall and into the elevator that was in front of the garbage room with the fiery furnace and next to the laundry room. He took my hand, which fit into his palm the way my breath matched his. He pressed the button for three. We got out of the elevator, made a sharp right turn, and rang his doorbell. His mother answered. She had the straightest back, her hair was pulled tight into a bun, and she wore plain, drab clothes. When she smiled, her eyes disappeared into her face. When she looked at me, her face got wet. Daniel took me into his parents' bedroom.

On the dresser in their bedroom, large compared to the other rooms in their apartment, was a small photograph of a little girl, maybe four or almost five. She looked like a nice little girl with dark thick curls, white, white skin, puffy cheeks, and big, round, startled, soft eyes. I couldn't tell the color because the photo was black and white. I would have liked this girl for a friend. She wore a white starched dress, pale ribbons that were probably pink, patent leather shoes, and white anklets with lace. Or the socks may have been pink to match the ribbons. Her eyes were soft. They drew you in through tunnels to different worlds. Worlds of love for her mother and brother, and fear of her father, monsters, demons, life. She wanted to hug her mother and dig her soft head into her chest. She wanted to cling to her brother and fold her body over him. Her patent leather shoes wanted to run and dance and fly. In this family, each child had the mother's good heart. She wanted to go to public school and learn, and then grow up and take the E train to Manhattan where she would work as a secretary. She would have lunch with the other secretaries, who would confide in her. She wouldn't marry a man like her father. She would have children like herself and her brother. She would have added a sweet pea smell to the earth had she lived. Maria, this Maria, this innocent with cheeks like plums, and eyes like blackberries, and lips like slices of peaches. Luscious girl. Miracle.

The word in the neighborhood was that she had died from a virus. Daniel told me they had killed her during a ritual when she turned six years old. His mother cried because I reminded her of her little lost girl. I must have reminded Daniel of her too. *Maybe they don't love me for myself,* I thought. *Maybe they are just lonely for a little girl. Maybe they love me because they have a hole in them.*

All summer, Daniel still came to my apartment every day and my mother let me sit on his lap in the armchair and suck my thumb. In the fall, when his school started again, I watched the clock and when the little hand was on the three and the big hand on the ten, I slipped out of the house with my shoes on, went out the main side door, turned right and walked to the corner and stood under the ancient maple tree whose branches bowed down like a willow's and whose samaras spiraled down to the cracked sidewalk. I stayed there, never crossing the street, eyes fixed like a terrier's on the corner down one block and across the street. I was on the corner of 108th Street and Sixty-Eighth Road. I looked to the corner of Sixty-Seventh Road and 108th Street and at five minutes after three, he was there wearing his jacket, carrying his school books, surrounded by boys his own age. When he reached the corner, his eyes looked for me. Our eyes were like sailboats floating toward each other, cementing together, locked. He left his school friends and walked toward my corner. Each day he said, "Did your mother see you leave the house?"

"No," I said.

"I'll walk you home," and we walked side by side down the sloping half block, through the side door into the hallway and then the door to my apartment that I had left unlocked. My mother knew I was out but pretended I had never left.

"Hello, Daniel. How about a snack?" she said. In my family, everyone got offered food. Mother took things away from me, everything I wanted, but she was letting me have Daniel. Why? She let me have what would be most valuable and irreplaceable.

Daniel and I sat at the kitchen table or on the love-seat in the foyer eating Dugan's wholewheat muffins with raisins and drinking Walker Gordon milk. Walker Gordon non-homogenized milk had disgusting clumps of cream floating in it but with Daniel everything tasted delicious. I've searched for those wholewheat muffins but never found them again, anywhere. The company must be out of business. I can still taste them. For years as an adult, I ate muffins for almost every meal and never knew consciously why I found them so comforting. Now that I have conscious memory, when I bite into a muffin, I cry.

Daniel sat on the loveseat doing homework and I watched him. I watched him swallow and frown and think. His Adam's apple protruded and then was flat when he swallowed. His writing had heavy curves and he stabbed the paper with his pencils. Then we would sit on the wing chair with our hearts beating, breathing together, and I sucked my thumb.

Without this interlude, I would have been like my twisted family and not remember what happened or what I did or who I was. My brain would have stayed sealed into isolated and barricaded sections.

Our job was to get rid of the body parts. After the rituals, the butchers cut up the sacrifices into small pieces so that children could manage picking them up and throwing them away. It was always the children who scattered them around the neighborhood. At the ritual site, the men cut the bodies up and wrapped them in towels so the blood wouldn't seep out. They moved them to a storage bin in the concealed rooms off the furnace and laundry rooms. Daniel kept his Schwinn bicycle in his apartment on the third floor. He rode down with it in the elevator. My father and I were waiting when the doors opened. My father handed him the body parts that needed to be disposed of. Daniel put them in a basket on his bicycle. Then he and I walked the bicycle up the steep ramp to the sidewalk. Daniel was an expert bicycle rider and had strong arms too. And I was an excellent lookout even at 3 a.m. when we did this task. Sometimes we were out at 2 a.m. if it looked like it would rain early in the morning. He lifted me between him and the handlebars and we were off crossing 108th Street and heading toward the woods. No one was on the street. No buses, cars, pedestrians, police. Just us and the body parts that hadn't yet started to smell. I leaned my head onto Daniel's heart. My ear felt the throb of his heart beating fast. I didn't care what we did. I was safe with him. He would never hurt me. I would do anything for him.

He put the small parts like hands, feet, eyes, and tongues in the trash cans along 108th Street, Cobblestone and Enterprise Avenues. We stayed away from Paradise Boulevard because sometimes there was middle-of-the night traffic on that big road. The larger body parts we put in the woods where other people had dug holes. Later other children would fill the holes with dirt. The children's battalion had to do this chore because no one would suspect children of burying people or their body parts. I didn't care what we did as long as I could rest my head with my ear pressed onto his heart. But he cared. He cried when he pedaled. Tears wet his shirt. He said if we didn't do it, something worse would happen and they would kill me. He said he didn't care if they killed him but he didn't want them to kill me. The choice was always between two evils.

Daniel was so graceful and curvy; he looked a little like a girl. The men used to line up to put their penises in his rectum. I saw it at rituals and he spoke about it.

"He's the sweetest with the softest," the men said, even my uncles and father. It made him want to die. It didn't just happen every now and then. It was another of his chores. I could keep living because of him, but I wasn't enough for him to keep living. Maybe if the real sister were still alive, that would have been enough for him. But she wasn't, and I wasn't enough.

We lived like this for one year, me walking unnoticed to the corner, my eyes latching onto his, our having milk and wholewheat muffins, wholewheat because my mother cared about nutrition and health, and my breathing with him while I sucked my thumb on the wing chair in the living room. I had a year to heal from the early ravages of not having love. Then he was turning thirteen, the year boys like Daniel were sacrificed. We knew it was coming. Everyone talked about it. It must have been December 1947.

All during that year, his mother did not knit him a sweater. She was a seamstress and made all the clothes for her family, even her husband's. Daniel's slacks always fit perfectly. She kept a dummy and a sewing machine in the corner of her dining room. She often had a tape measure hanging around her neck. Baskets of wool were everywhere in the apartment. A glass jar held a mass of knitting needles, their heads and numbers pointing up proudly.

"The children who are the most loved are put on the altar first," Mrs. Baker said. "I should not have dressed Maria so well. I will stop knitting him sweaters. I will not put home baked bread and desserts in his lunch bag. I will not touch him in public. Maybe we can fool them and they'll let him live longer," she said out loud but to herself in her narrow kitchen, while she baked oatmeal cookies with Irish oatmeal. His father scowled.

"We need the money soon," he said. Mrs. Baker looked at him with hatred. They were poor. They had hardly any furniture and only had a radio. Mr. Baker went to work but didn't get paid much. At night, he drank from bottles with red liquid. She babysat to bring in a little money and pushed a baby carriage up and down Sixty-Eighth Road. Mother said everyone should have posture like Mrs. Baker's. She always looked proud and plain. That's how the breeders of sacrifices looked. Breeders are girls and women who give birth to babies, usually for sacrifice, though sometimes for positions of power within the cult. The babies are sacrificed either right away or later in childhood. You'd think the children to be sacrificed would be mean and angry but they weren't. They were sweet, kind, feeling. For weeks, Daniel had been preparing me. When I sat on his lap sucking my thumb, when he walked me home from school, when we walked down the basement hallway to take out the garbage for my mother.

Walking home from school, he said, "Wendy, you know my turn is coming." When I sat on his lap, "Wendy, don't cry. You know it is coming. It's why I was born. They say it is an honor and for the good of the community. They sacrificed my sister when she was six. Boys are usually thirteen. I will be thirteen soon. I will be leaving you, Wendy, but I will always be with you, always looking out for you. You are my sister. It is my turn now."

The last night I saw Daniel, he wore a V-neck medium gray sweater that was not hand knit. We were in the basement hall that led to the laundry room. It was after dinner but not ritual time. Rituals start after midnight. I ran my hands up his sweater and along its long sleeves. I could feel the life in his body underneath the sleeves' machine-made stitches.

"Run away, hide," I pleaded.

"It doesn't pay, Wendy. They'll find me and punish you," he said.

"I don't care. I stole money from my father's wallet."

"Put it back, Wendy. Don't get in trouble. We can't fight them."

"Yes we can," I insisted. "Run and hide."

"I can't fight them. They're too big for me."

"I'll fight them."

"You're too little. Wendy, you know the swans outside in the waterfall, how white and pure they are. Grow up to be pure like the swans. Don't be like the rest of the people," he said.

"You're the only good person in the world, Daniel." I couldn't bear the thought of Daniel just disappearing, like the petals that fall off the glorious tulips that give beauty to the universe. "I will memorize what happens and tell the world about this ring of rackets. They will know who you are and your name. They will know you as the best person who ever lived. I will write and make your life everlasting."

"That's a very good idea, but don't bring too much trouble on yourself, Wendy. Just be pure and good, like the swans gliding outside. Grow up to be pure like the swans."

"Take me with you. Don't leave me here alone."

"No, Wendy. You have work to do, I don't," he said. Then he turned around and walked down the dark basement hallway. Halfway down the hall, Daniel turned around and said, "I'll always be with you, Wendy. I love you."

He turned around again and walked. I was crying too hard and my knees were failing so I could only mouth the words back to him. Tears came from my whole body. Then he walked down that grimy hall, rays of light surrounding him in the damp blackness. He pressed the button for the elevator. It was slow in coming. It was probably on the fifth or sixth floor. The doors opened, and he stepped into the jaws of the elevator, his slender, graceful silhouette moving away from me, bravely going toward his death at thirteen years old. He turned around in the elevator, raised his right arm and opened his right hand as if he were holding my hand, then waved to me as he had waved to me for a year after school. Our eyes locked and his soft mouth formed the words, "I love you." The elevator door closed with its familiar creak and moan but I could still see him. I saw him walk down the hall to his mother in their corner apartment. His mother would be at the table sobbing. His father would be pacing back and forth with his hands in his pockets, jingling change. His mother would offer him nutritious food, an Irish stew, and even though he would want to please her, he would not be able to eat. He would lie on his bed unable to sleep on his last night on earth. All during the night, our eyes remained locked though separated by three floors and many walls.

I went back into my parents' apartment. My mother was in the foyer. I walked past her. I lay on my bed, stomach down. I did not take my shoes off, even though it wasn't allowed. I did not have the energy to follow her rules. In bed, I formed the words "Daniel David Baker" over and over. I said those words all night every night for a long time. Sometimes I still do. I became old in those moments, when I was four.

My parents came into my bedroom. They must have given me a drug because my body became rigid. They turned me over and sat me up in my bed. My legs and arms were stiff. My father spoon-fed me Campbell's tomato soup. I could eat some of that. My mother wanted me to eat a banana but I couldn't. Then she wanted me to eat American cheese but I couldn't.

When it was time, my father carried me down the basement hallway where last I saw Daniel. I felt as if I could still touch him there. My father carried me into the back rooms, down a shaft into the second lower level under the basement. People were already there. They stood me up naked. My body would not fold or bend. They smeared me with dog or human shit mixed with mud, poured blood over me, put a cape on me. It was ice blue with white fur on the edges. They tied Daniel up. He looked more gaunt than usual and seemed almost unconscious. He must have been drugged. Uncle Sidney held the scepter with my hand over it and his over mine, while my mother masturbated me. I don't think I was being spun, but everything went round and round and I collapsed or fainted as they chanted, led by Uncle Richard: "Hail to the new queen, hail to the new queen of Pleasant Hills, hail to the new queen of the Feast of the Beast, hail to our princess forevermore."

93

And then my life was over.

Young healthy blood rushed out. They cut up his body into parts. Daniel was no more. They told me they had to kill him because I loved him.

"Anyone you love will be killed," the masters said to me again and again. "Anyone you love …"

I thought I had killed the only good person in the world by loving him. The masters and my mother made me believe everything was my fault. Mrs. Baker said her children were born to be killed and that it wasn't my fault. *Maybe if I hadn't sucked my thumb so much*, I thought. Mr. Baker filled their apartment with furniture and a record player. He carried around a stack of cash in his trouser pocket. Now I understood why Mother had let Daniel be my friend, why they had let me taste love.

He and I have gone through life together, dead and alive, merging worlds where we leave scents, one following the other, always.

They cooked his cut-up body in a large black pot. The pieces swam around like goldfish.

The neighborhood learned that a boy had died from leukemia. His teacher and classmates were very unhappy. I couldn't let Daniel go, so in my mind I decided that I had twelve Daniels in my life. I told everyone I had a dozen brothers but I pronounced dozen "muzen." Some people understood what I meant. My mother loved my telling people because a few said to her "But you look so young."

A few days later, I retraced his steps on the bicycle ramp in the building, then stepped onto 68th Road. My heart burst out of my mouth and I collapsed on the sidewalk. A neighbor saw me and called an ambulance. I lifted my arm, the one they used to hold the scepter, against the plastic in the oxygen tent in the hospital and my finger outlined over and over the letters DDB.

Only recently have doctors noted that there are two kinds of heart attacks, mechanical and emotional ones that mimic the physical ones.[1] I had an emotional one that didn't leave

94

physical scars. After they killed Daniel, I could no longer eat. I needed to be with him. My uncles stepped in to get me to eat. They held a gun to my head right there at the left temple and pulled back the lever so that I heard the click. They said "Eat." A bowl of spaghetti, a food I used to like, was in front of me even though we were all seated in the living room. I couldn't, wouldn't. "If you don't, we will kill you." I still wouldn't. They sat Marlene on the piano bench and held the gun to the middle of her forehead. "If you don't pick up some of the spaghetti and eat, we will have to kill Marlene," my uncles said. We could hear Mother groan in the kitchen.

UNCLE SIDNEY: "And it will be your fault."
UNCLE RICHARD: "You will be killing your sister."

They didn't let my father talk much any more because he said unnecessary things that confused the programming. Mother always complained of his premature ejaculations. He had premature ejaculations in everything.

I didn't much like my sister and often hated her. I did think that if she weren't around, maybe Mother would love me, but I didn't want her to die, not because of me or anyone. I, or parts in me who were still able to eat, picked up the spaghetti with our fingers. Once I started, it tasted good with the tomato sauce. Uncle Richard called to Mother in the kitchen, "She's eating." Uncle Sidney put the gun away. "Because you ate, we don't have to kill Marlene. Say thank you to your sister, Marlene," Uncle Richard said. Marlene said, "I'm not thanking her. We wouldn't have had to go through this scare if she would just eat in the first place." I was angry at Marlene for not thanking me. They didn't punish her. As an adult, Marlene had a blatant lack of empathy. They must have programmed empathy out of her. That night, in our bedroom, Marlene twisted my arm—more than an Indian burn twist, more like a near-break twist. She said if I told, she would kill me.

At the next ritual I told Uncle Richard what Marlene had done. The reaction, led by my mother, was that I should have eaten and Marlene was right. That night in our bedroom, Marlene twisted my arm harder. She, like everyone, had been taught to be as vicious as possible. The adults were really only unrestrained children doing harm.

Before I was four years old, I had developed a pleasure principle of life. If I could look forward to something, then I could be wrapped up in that delight all day. I could look forward to walking outside when the flowers were out, noticing new cracks in the sidewalk, which made delightful patterns and designs. Any time I was not in physical pain, I rejoiced. Before Daniel died, every moment was rich because I either was with him or felt him with me, or was looking forward to seeing him and smelling him and feeling his breath and his eyelashes. After he died, I could still talk to him and hope to catch a glimpse of Mrs. Baker. I might be able to pet a soft dog or friendly cat. The air had changing hues and was not polluted in the 1940s. Each day, I looked for another color, one I hadn't seen before. Perhaps all the color coding Mrs. Twartski did when I was a newborn made me sensitive to the glories of color. And any day I could have vanilla ice cream or a Mallomar cookie would be a good day.

I enjoyed thinking. When I was almost seven years old, I watched a television show in which the host asked people from all stages of life what was the best part of life. People gave answers like getting a first job, buying a first house, marrying for the first time, having a first child. One person said having sex for the first time. From their wing chair seats, my parents gave similarly silly answers. I knew right away that the best part of life was all the parts, depending on what you made of it. The last person interviewed was eighty-nine years old. The camera showed her stooped over, wrinkled, barely able to walk. She said the same thing as me. I realized then that out of my suffering, some wisdom had grown. *I will use this wisdom to outsmart them and survive*, I thought, *because Daniel wants me to.*

There were at least monthly rituals, if not weekly. They continued deep within the basement levels of the apartment building, on its roof, in hidden ritual sites. Many took place at Bear Mountain. Worship of Satan or Lucifer, sacrifices, orgies, and cannibalism were mainstays. The events of these rituals were scripted, carefully planned and organized. Sometimes, however, domestic scenes went wild. Once they gave people permission to harm others, they never knew what would happen.

Note

1. Wittstein, I. S., Thiemann, D. R., Lima, J. A., Baughman, K. L., Schulman, S. P., Gerstenblith, G., Wu, K. C., Rade, J. J., Bivalacqua, T. J., & Champion, H. C. (2005). Neurohumoral features of myocardial stunning due to sudden emotional stress. *The New England Journal of Medicine, 6*: 539–548.

FIVE

Scripted scenes

When I was an infant, Mrs. Twartski separated one piece of my mind to be the person who walked the pathways. She put the child-me on a baby scale, tied me down, put a support under my bobbing neck, and spun the scale. With each new rotation, Mrs. Twartski said, "You will do whatever you're told." Spinning, I passed my families' faces and representations of wild animals, monsters, and devils. I spun until all the faces became one and my family's faces melted into the animal-devil ones. This dizzy infant surrounded by people who didn't rescue her grew into the child who walked the inside and outside pathways in the bitter blackness.

Over sixty years later, the pathways still shiver in my mind. The leaders of my false-Kabbalah-based cult indoctrinated small children by having them walk a dirt path alone, usually in a secluded forest. The path was like an exploding tunnel. I felt alone despite Daniel's telling me he would always be with me, and my being surrounded by people. I never had a family and no longer had a friend, yet at times something insulated me. The pathway earth was filled with electricity, the kind the world made naturally. The earth breathed the way Daniel had breathed. I felt his breath through my feet. The forest with its trees reaching the black sky and breathing soil was not criminal, only people were. The earth molded to my feet. Typical pathway messages were, "You may never escape us," and "You belong to us", or "This is your destiny." "What is learned in the pathways is applied to life," they taught. By "life" they meant normal life, what all people lead. And I was deliberately given "normal life" experiences that echoed or foretold what the pathways taught.

The foundational pathways, reverse Kabbalah training, 1945–1952

My father lifted me gingerly from my white crib and carried me over his shoulder to the car parked outside the side door. I lay on the back seat in my blanket sucking my thumb hard. My sister sat in the front seat between my parents. My mother and sister wore sneakers instead of their usual dressy shoes. My father wore his everyday leather shoes. He drove slowly and carefully. He wasn't speaking and didn't call any other driver an ignoramus as he often did. It was as if he were trying to be invisible. When we reached a highway the car went faster. Behind us was a car with my grandmother and grandfather, another with Aunt Eileen and Uncle Sidney, and another with Aunt Mimi and Uncle Richard. My cousins had not been born yet.

In the middle of the night, we arrived at Bear Mountain, where bears lived. My father had a hand-drawn map that I could see from the back seat, and he searched for a certain section that had been prepared for us. He had one hand on the steering wheel and one hand holding the map to his side. He went up and down and back and forth along the dark dirt roads with the relatives following his car until he found it. People high up in the trees flashed lights that led him to where he needed to park. Other cars were hidden in the bushes. The ritual had to be on this night because a particular ranger was on duty then. I had heard my parents say that he got this job to protect us but he had really wanted to live in the Midwest where it is quieter than in New York. Rangers like solitude.

Before they took me out of the car, someone put a cloth over my nose. Now that I was drugged, the world seemed to fold in on itself. The dirt was soft and moist. The trees had survived storms. People sprayed insect repellants on their skins. Others with flashlights looked for snakes.

Darkness hid our people stationed among high wires in the tall branches of the trees. Stars dotted the dense sky. The set-up crew made catcalls to one another.

I could just manage walking on the gray carpet in our living room. Uncle Richard in a hooded robe told me to walk along the rocky dirt path where wild animals lived. When I lost my balance and began to crawl, voices behind the trees said, "Bad, bad, get up, get up." Eerie sounds rang in the dark, and there was no one to love me. I wanted to be home, inside. I didn't want to be eaten by a bear and I didn't like the hooting and howling. I didn't know where my father was, the only person who might give me a little protection. At the end of each path was a symbol on a tarot card and a Hebrew letter printed on sheer material that waved in the wind. People's cheering pushed me forward until I finished the walk.

The most intense loneliness I have known has been on these pathways. Even people cheering and chanting at me could not make a dent in the feeling of being hopelessly alone.

After I had already walked several pathways, Wiezenslowski (who was Grandpa Max, though I didn't know it yet) and Mrs. Twartski worked on me in a programming room underneath the Pleasant Hills apartment building.

WIEZENSLOWSKI: "A person is no stronger than her weakest part. Bring out the split we didn't use because it was too weak."

101

MRS. TWARTSKI: "Humpty Dumpty sat on a wall, Humpty Dumpty had a great fall. All the king's horses and all the king's men couldn't put Humpty Dumpty back together again. Come out Baby Jane."

Grandpa Max pressed his thumb between Baby Jane's eyes.

"You will be our pathways' queen. You can cry but you must finish. It is your destiny. Your mother wants Marlene to be our queen but we will not permit that. It is your destiny according to the prophecy. But you must complete the prophecy." Then he said to Mrs. Twartski: "We'll test her on the next pathway."

I had to wear a crown, which kept falling off. Baby Jane cried but finished. I had known they put the snakes on the ground. But I also knew they wouldn't go through all this trouble training me if they were going to have a snake bite me to death. The snakes were hapless beings like me. I thought it would be good to have these non-lethal creatures as my friends. I liked snakes better than I liked people.

Another pathway with candles along its edges happened soon afterward. I had to go through two doors with my crown on. I was too faint to walk. I crawled as crowds chanted, "This is your destiny. Praise to Lucifer our Savior, Lucifer our guardian. We give you the next queen. Hail to the King Lucifer, hail to the god almighty. Hail to his son Satan, hail to the trinity." The crowd's cheering was seductive and I was caught in grandiosity for the moment. Grandpa Max rubbed his semen over me. Now I could be queen, though I had no idea what that meant. My father talked about how the bloodline came from this grandpa, my mother's father, and this grandpa was always rubbing his semen on me at the end as an anointment. Then Joseph and Grandpa led the procession to the altar. Uncle Sidney lifted me up beside the altar. Joseph held my hand over a sword and stabbed as the chanting roared. I went so far away from my body that I'm not sure I ever fully came back.

It was my first killing. Blood spurted. The body was so soft. The sword went in as if the baby were cottage cheese. They had little cups that they passed around and everyone drank blood. I felt as if I had entered a new world, and that everyone hated me. I didn't trust anyone and thought that no one trusted me. My mother and sister called me murderer, but when they used that word, I didn't yet know what it meant.

When we got home and I was back in my crib, the bumper guard spun around. I was sure I was going to be killed at any moment. When my father put me in the crib, he said he was proud of me. Mrs. Twartski had said she was proud of me. I was a murderer.

I witnessed my cousins walking the pathways at Bear Mountain and I became one of the people in the bushes jumping out and scaring them. I should have been relieved to be on the other side of it, but that first split in me took over, the delicate Baby Jane, and I cried. My father put me in the car so I didn't see the whole miserable walk, ending in the customary sexual assault. The trainings had the same themes: You won't escape. You belong here.

Grandmother's noodles and the monster, 1946

The family was at Grandmother's lavish table filled with homemade-from-scratch foods. My grandfather placed me in a booster seat with my back to the kitchen. A thick phone book was under my seat so that I was higher up. My father sat at one end, my grandfather nearer the kitchen, Marlene and Mother by the window. Everyone seemed especially happy, and I watched with interested caution. Even happy moments could turn in a second in my family.

My grandmother never sat down to eat. In her apron with the big butterfly bow, she went back and forth in her kitchen stirring, opening and closing doors, dishing out. Grandpa had just finished his plate of hot food. I was two years old.

103

GRANDFATHER: "Rosie, don't you have to do something? Get something?"

GRANDMOTHER: "Just a minute, Max, I'm in the middle of something."

GRANDFATHER: "First things first."

GRANDMOTHER: "I can't do everything at once."

MOTHER: "The strudel's delicious."

Father wanted a third piece.

My grandmother, in animated spirits, left the dining area for a moment and returned from the bathroom holding one of Grandpa's single-edged razors. Holding up the blade, she said, "I'm going to make noodles, but first I have to cut the dough in half," and rushed to my booster seat. She still had her floral apron on. She made a line down the center, a deep cut in my scalp. "I'm making a half and half cookie. This half is bad, this half is good." Grandma cut lines horizontally then vertically on my scalp just as if she were making her broad noodles from scratch on her worn wooden board that she brought over on the boat from Belarus. My scalp stung, and blood dripped onto the towel on my shoulders. My grandfather and father sat as if nothing had happened. My mother and sister stood up and clung to each other as if they, rather than me, needed comforting. I hadn't spilled or thrown anything, said "No", or thought anything bad. My torso fell forward onto the table. One arm was outstretched and the other descended in slow motion on top of it. Hopelessness sealed me in this sorrowful position as I watched the kitchen walls crash into me.

My grandfather came over to my scalp, pressed on the squares on the left side one by one, and said, "You, and you, and you belong to me forever and ever. Whatever I tell you, you will have to do. I'm going to give you each a letter and a number, and when I call you by those, you will have to do it."

On the other side of my head, he used the squares to put in functions so that it appeared as if I behaved well, such as

"You will smile when people talk to you," "You will say 'thank you'," and "You will curtsey". The distractors and reporters are also in the "good" part of the head.

That night, we did another pathway. As usual, I had to walk down the dirt pathway alone. It was cold and rocky but I was able to balance a bit better now that I was over two years old. They brought me a hand mirror. I looked in the mirror and saw that I had no hair, because my grandmother had cut up my scalp. They all chanted: "Monster, Monster, decrepit you, Monster, Monster, no one would choose you, Monster, Monster, into the fire with you." They said I was born a monster, would always be a monster, and that they were going to sell me because I was no good. I thought, *but monsters have a lot of hair.* I felt ugly and it was a world where prettiness was everything. I was no good and would be sold to bad people because I was bad. I wanted to die. I didn't have a place on earth.

Angel of mercy, 1946–1947

In the middle of the line my grandmother had carved that separated the bad and good parts of my brain (both parts mind controlled to belong to evil)—right there in the middle, my grandfather placed a representation of the Angel of Mercy. This angel was to lead me into suicide. The angel was slinky, squished, but it could grow enormous.

My grandfather, grandmother, and Mrs. Twartski tied me on a hard chair in my grandparents' second bedroom. The lights grew dim as Mrs. Twartski fed me teaspoons of a brown syrup, and my grandmother injected my scalp. My grandfather showed me a picture the size of a tarot card of this beautiful Angel of Mercy dressed in a pale blue robe. As I looked at the picture, my grandfather talked to the angel. "Your assignment is to follow this child all over. I'm placing you in her mind, right in the middle where Rosie made the cut. And you will be perched and nestled there until she dies, Angel of Mercy ..." All the fight in me was gone, and I had sharp pains in my eye. Alison said it was from the syrup, and that they probably get this effect with pills or injections in modern day programming sessions.

Grandpa started his projector. He put the picture of the angel in front of it. The projector made the image of the angel go from small to huge on the wall. Grandpa said, "If the bad side and good side of your head talk to each other or weave together, then you and the Angel of Mercy will be one." The angel travelled up to the ceiling, around me, over me, finally landing in the center of the wall. He projected an image of me onto the one of the Angel.

Mrs. Twartski kept giving me teaspoons of brown syrup, and Grandpa said, "You have people who do very bad things, and people who do very good things. And the two will never meet, and never know about each other. The bad side is very bad and nobody should know about the bad side, or they will never like you and never accept you as part of the world."

Normal and pathway life

During these early years, there were also moments of peace, rare like spring days in January and snow in April. We four were strolling. My father and mother were arm in arm. The apartment was clean but Mother was not exhausted. Marlene and I were in the row behind. Marlene did not have to be Mother's confidante or I, Father's wife. We wore mother and daughter outfits that Mother had designed and Father wore a tie made out of the same green and white checkered material. The family walked over the cherry blossom petals spilled on the sidewalk. The hills and breeze were comforting and exciting. Lilac bushes created a cocoon. Marlene and I held hands, swung arms, and giggled until we were sore. The parents looked over their shoulders and smiled from their inside. My mother smiled at me as well as her, and my father smiled at Marlene as well as me. They were glad we were theirs. The earth, sky, air radiated warmth, fragrance. Tulips, red and yellow, tall and proud sprouted. We smelled them until we became intoxicated. Each pansy had a dreamy face and eyes, a soft soul. We crossed the street. Father bought two chocolate coated and two toasted coconut ice cream bars from the Good Humor truck singing our song. I could have eaten ten of these. The cold sweetness slid down to my hunger.

"We had our moments," Mother said to me right before she died. We had moments.

My family's ancient cult had been training children on pathways and combining scripted, known life with secret rituals for many centuries. The mind controllers anchored the pathways teaching in scripted scenes of family life that family members played like actors. The only person who didn't have a memorized role was the child victim. The scripted scene staged a family conflict and an assault on the child's self-esteem. Then the pathway training threatened the child into submission and rendered the child loyal to the criminal group. The leaders made a point of not sharing this information with Mengele.

The pathways training took up a small percentage of my life. I had one or two pathway treks per year, and perhaps one or two programming sessions a month. The programming not to stand out or succeed in everyday life continued, and affected all areas of my regular life. Most of my life was spent in "normalcy," going to school, with my mother shopping for clothes and food, going to Manhattan three times a week for ballet, speech, and art lessons, plus having weekly piano lessons in my home until Mr. Brown fired me for not practicing. How could I practice when I wasn't allowed to succeed in the normal world? I had to look bored and lazy during ballet lessons because the Russian master teachers came to Mr. Yanvinsky's studio and spotted me. I was double jointed and had high extensions. In normal life, our theater-mother couldn't be stopped from being ambitious artistically for her daughters. Mother, who had talent, must have been madly frustrated.

Pathways trainings resonated all my life. The experiences captured some of my soul. What they didn't capture, they scratched. I remembered few normal life setups for pathways until I began to delve into my inner world in the early 1980s, shortly after my mother died.

Four hundred dollars, 1949

When I was in my twenties, living in Pittsburgh, I put my toddler in the stroller and walked him to the Arts & Crafts Center, which had an exhibit of Marcarelli's paintings. This artist cut or ripped unprimed canvas into strips and pasted the raw lengths on other canvas. When I saw his work, I froze.

Strips of canvas. More strips of canvas. Strips of uneven widths. Pleasant Hills. Gray living room. My mother's portrait in oils. With these spurts of narrative, a living room scene charged out from my stunned mind.

For three days and three nights before it happened, she lay motionless in her bed like the center sardine in a can. Then, as I watched from the hall doorway, she emerged ponderously, a sleepwalker. In the portrait, she wore her diamond ring, pearl choker, and a blue satin gown. Only its scooped bodice showed. She smiled with perfect teeth. She appeared American enough to be a first lady but looked too alive. In the oil painting with an ornate gold frame, Mother had thick, dark, wavy hair; the painter made a big deal about how white her skin was. She looked proud of her beauty and like she wanted sex. The perfect blue tint of her enormous ring glowed.

The knife. I don't know whether she had the knife in her bedroom the whole time or whether she had detoured into the kitchen. It had a black handle. I watched from the door-way. Strips of canvas, flying curlicues attached to the wall. They looked cheerful, like my doll's hair, the flickering of sunlight dancing on the wall. Her nose that she would later have fixed and that we weren't allowed to touch gone, her high forehead, creamy breasts. Only her hand with the ring remained intact.

More memory dragged across my brain. My sister and I were in bed. I was in a deep sleep the way I slept as a child when I did not have one of my frequent migraines. My sister shook me. It must have been the middle of the night or at least around midnight.

"Wendy, get up," my sister said. She took my hand and led me to the doorway in the hall that contained the long sliding door closet. Marlene, who was much taller than I, stood in front of me near the foyer. We all wore pajamas except for Father who just wore boxer shorts. My father was already in the foyer; my mother in front of her recently hung portrait held two kitchen knives, one in each hand. Mother's eyes were fixed and wild. Whoever was out in her was not one of Mother's usual parts. Bambi, our miniature Doberman, must have been hiding.

"Watch," Marlene said. My father smiled slightly. I yawned since I was still asleep on my feet, but noticed my father nod to my mother who was holding knives. My father told Marlene to go back to her bed, but I stayed glued in the doorway.

My mother screamed and started slashing her portrait. The strips flew away from the canvas backing and curled at the bottom. They looked like a blossoming flower in papier mache. Mother screamed as she shredded. "I'm not happy, I'm not happy," she sang to the knife sounds. Pulp left my heart. She glanced at me. "It's your fault. Why is she standing there always in the way? Why can't she be good like Marlene?" Marlene colored much better than I, chose better colors, and stayed within the lines of our coloring books. But I didn't want to be like her. She was a show-off.

And then Mother threw the knife at me. I ducked and the knife went into the material-covered sliding closet door behind me. With her other hand, she threw the knife at Bambi, who was under a side table. He was whimpering and bleeding by

109

the side table in the living room near the planter room divider. Bambi had a knife in his stomach. Blood spread like my fear. I rushed back into my bedroom and dove under my bed. My heart felt like skin rubbed raw.

Decades later, when I asked my father about it, all he said was that the portrait had cost four hundred dollars.

My sister was safe in bed. I was under my bed and Mother poked the knife trying to reach me. I kept sliding away from her. My father's hand pulled the knife away. He was barely stronger than she at that moment. Finally, my father shouted "Cynthia, Cynthia," which stopped her, and he was able to pull her out of the bedroom. My mother must have been trained as a witch to have had such excellent aim.

The penultimate part of the memory that I associated was my sister waking me up and leading me to the doorway. The last piece that I brought into the memory was my smiling father watching my mother slash. My mother should really have been on the stage. The handlers didn't create a personality in me to watch this scene unfold. They took whoever spontaneously came forward. My controller called that same person out to do the pathway walk that night.

It was hard for me to accept this memory and that my parents would act in such a drama. In the 80s, when my first memories shoved out and before I had the memory of my mother's slashing, when I was creating and exhibiting visual art in New York City, I reproduced the hallway wallpaper, put a knife in it and a representation of a small child huddled on the floor. The knife had just missed.

I wondered what had happened to Bambi's body. My father said he wrapped him in a towel and carried him out. I wondered whether he threw him down the fiery furnace. He wouldn't have taken him to a vet. I had never felt close to Bambi, but I hated to see him violently killed and was aware it should have been me, according to my mother's intent or at least the script.

That night, there was a pathway at Bear Mountain. Its goal, like that of the other pathways, was to terrify me and make me feel that within the criminal cult group was the only place I would be safe. Mrs. Twartski said, "We want to talk to the person who saw her mother throw the knife," and that part of me emerged from pools of terror. Towards the pathway's end, the ground was covered with the same strips of canvas that my mother had slashed with her knives. On the altar was Bambi with the knife still in his stomach. A chorus of people chanted, "You killed him." The other half chanted, "It should have been you. It was meant to be you." All together, they sang "You are always in the way," and "Marlene is better than you." Wiezenslowski held up my arm—the left one—with a sword in it.

Contradicting themselves, at the end of the pathway, people chanted "Queen Philomena, Queen Philomena" over and over. "Here you are wanted, here you are something, here you will rule for ever more."

Pressing his thumb on the back of my neck, Grandpa Max said, "Only here will you be accepted, with us. All else is ashes and shreds." He held up the tarot card pictures of the skeleton riding a donkey and the queen on the throne holding the scepter and globe.

Someone in a devil suit danced around, opened its mouth wide and put my head in the mask's mouth, then raped me. "You will never escape us. You belong only to us. You belong to Lucifer." There were more pictures of a field of daisies, a mountaintop and a hanged man upside down, then the letter ayin.

The morning I remembered this part of the pathway, I awoke in hollow fear with the image of Bambi on the altar and the strips of canvas on the ground.

During the pathway, Baby Jane fainted and stronger parts stepped forward. Grandpa Max was probably wrong, how strong one is does not depend on one's weakest parts.

Later I remembered another scene from the day after the pathway: My parents had a big party. Noisy people filled the whole gray apartment. Cheeses and crackers were everywhere, and my grandmother had brought platters of interesting concoctions that grown-ups like. My mother cooked little cocktail franks, which I liked but wasn't allowed to eat until after the company arrived. My father sliced salamis paperthin. Everyone drank hard liquor. On the carpet where there had been Bambi's blood was a patch scrubbed almost white, which served as his memorial monument.

Even though I was the only child in this crowd and I hardly knew anyone at the party, the party was ostensibly to celebrate my sixth birthday. My sister was present, but she was so mature that she didn't like playing with me anymore. Some people brought me presents. One woman gave me a red and white checked blouse. My mother thought both red and white were becoming with my dark skin. I was sure I had said thank you. I don't remember the other presents. What was not traumatic washed away. Trauma sticks through a lifetime.

Around midnight, when everyone had left, Mother came into my bedroom. I had a walk-in closet in my bedroom and I stood in front of it. She hit me over and over with the red and white checkered blouse. It resembled the waves at Jones Beach undulating, rising, and falling. "You didn't say thank you," she screamed. "I did, I did too," I answered.

Then she said, "You killed Bambi." The rotating axis of the apartment froze. My father shouted "Cynthia!" and pulled her away. My parents disappeared into the remains of my birthday party.

The next day, the Council was in the living room sitting on the two curved half sofas and wing chairs. The apartment was clean and neat again. My parents or father must have stayed awake cleaning. I was not invited but my sister and I eavesdropped. Grandpa Max wearing his Wiezenslowski mask, Joseph, Mrs. Twartski, and my parents attended.

"Cynthia, I had to fly here from the west coast, which was very inconvenient. You have broken a cardinal rule. You are not allowed to refer to a pathway event in your other life. The pathways are holy, secret events. Yours is a grave offence," Grandpa said. I could feel the others nod their heads. Mother was in trouble. And I hadn't killed Bambi, she had!

"We will have to do double programming on Wendy to prevent consciousness. That will cost in time and money." *What about me?* I thought. That meant more drugs, electricity and spinning for me—torture.

"We have a family in Salt Lake City that is willing to take her or you in. We could say you have an illness, which is true, and need convalescence. If anything like this happens again, one of you will go and it will probably be you. That means you would not be with Marlene. Marlene would stay here under Morris' care. In the meantime, Morris will take you to Dr. Brown tomorrow. You will remain on sedatives. Morris, you must make sure she takes them every day. Cynthia, you have crossed a serious line. We never refer to a pathway in mundane life. No one in our community will speak to you for ten days." Then the front door closed, and Marlene and I believed everyone had left.

Mother screamed wildly at Father. "You told them, how could you! You're trying to get rid of me." Then the pounding that we recognized as Mother's fists on Dad's chest began. Marlene and I went to our room and sat on the floor between the beds with a blanket over our heads.

In the 1980s, I watched the movie *Bambi* with one of my bad boyfriends. After Bambi's mother was shot, I began to cry uncontrollably. One of those long New York City lines that went around the block was in front of the theater when we exited. A woman in the line saw me sobbing and asked what movie I had just seen. I ignored her, but the boyfriend gratuitously answered *Bambi*. The gawking busybody repeated *Bambi* in disbelief, turned to the person behind her and said, "She saw *Bambi*." This information traveled quickly down the

113

line. My suffering became comedy. I had as yet no memory of the tragedy with Bambi.

The ermine collar, 1952

Marlene kept doing her English homework, but I left our side bedroom window from where I could see the waterfall, swans and geese and rushed out to greet Father at the front door. Daddy sniffed and his neck and nose stretched almost to the ceiling. I could tell he was relieved to smell food cooking. If meat were cooking, he wouldn't be angry and then there wouldn't be fights. Mother was in the kitchen broiling a sirloin steak, warming up peas from a can, and baking potatoes in a potato baker on top of the stove.

He hung up his overcoat and hat in the hall closet and said, "Get your mother. I have a surprise …. Cynthia," he called. I wondered why he told me to get her if he was going to call her himself. He unwrapped a package from the furrier and took out a sleek white fur collar. Its smoothed out white hair all over reminded me of Slinky, the cat on our block.

"It looks alive," I said. The fur collar was the gift for Marlene becoming a grownup. They had been talking about it all week. She was thirteen but already had birthday presents that took her up to her twentieth year. Anything to keep Mother from going deeper into one of her moods. My special things were hand-me-downs.

"It is stunning. Oh, I love it, Morris," Mother said. "It will look beautiful on Marlene. Perfect for a girl becoming a woman."

Mother cooked in her apron over her housedress. She was slim and petite with dyed red hair and amber eyes that shifted colors with her feelings. Mostly Mother was sad. She was around thirty-five now, and Dad was older. She was unhappy about getting older because she thought that looks were everything.

114

Marlene came out of the bedroom slowly, wearing an ironed paisley dress and black polished shoes. Her long brown hair was braided and pinned in a pile to the top of her head. Mother spent a lot of time on Marlene's hair. My sister had rosy cheeks, what my mother called a "Greek nose" and a sculptured chin. She reminded me of Queen Elizabeth.

Mother took the ermine collar, put it around Marlene's neck, and joined the hook and eye together. No one watched me watching.

"Ouch, it's hurting me. It's pressing on my throat," my sister screamed.

"Oh, no, Morris, it's too tight for her. You brought too small a collar home," Mother said. She was angry. "How could you do that?"

"Well, try it on Wendy. It should fit her," he answered. I knew that oily tone in Daddy's voice. He used it when he was trying to trick someone. Mother handed the white collar back to Daddy and looked away. He hooked it around my neck.

My heart was pounding as I imagined myself a Hollywood star in a fur coat or one of the glamorous women in Mother's magazines.

"There, it fits her fine," Daddy said.

"It does look good. It's becoming with her round face and it gives her a lighter look," Mother said.

That compliment may have been the first I ever had from Mother. I could always read disappointment in her eyes. Once, after I had had my own ordinary-life child, I tested her. I asked "With you so beautiful and Daddy so handsome, shouldn't you have had a prettier daughter?" She smiled at me as if someone finally understood her. I wanted to rip her dyed red hair out then.

I rushed to the mirror in the hall closet with my collar on, sucked in my cheeks, lifted and pushed forward my right hip and shoulder. Daddy looked happy and Mother smiled a little.

If I could be prettier, then Mommy could be happier. And maybe even love me.

I had thought my father was relieved to have done something nice for me. He knew Mother ignored me.

"That's a size four. I'll bring you a size seven tomorrow, Marlene," he said. My older sister's soft brown eyes narrowed into steel. Her self-satisfied expression changed into cold hatred and envy.

"You promised. You promised me the ermine collar for my thirteenth birthday," my sister pleaded. "I will not wear the same thing as a nine year old. I'm not a child. I have to have better things than she has, not the same. I'm older. Mine has to be special. I'm thirteen. If she wears one, mine won't be special."

Marlene was holding herself back from hitting me in the face. And I wanted to lunge forward and put deep scratches on her cheeks and leave scars.

"You're acting ridiculous, Marlene. Her having the same collar doesn't take anything away from you. I'll bring you the right size tomorrow," Father said.

"You promised me," Marlene screamed, as she left the room and slammed our bedroom door. Daddy let out a breath that said he was the only reasonable and just person in the house.

"I can see her point, Morris. It's humiliating to wear the same thing as your younger sister, and we did promise her," Mother said.

The wind roared outside. The water was restless. The ducks swam zigzag, the swans in circles. My chest swelled.

I will hate Mother and Marlene forever, I said to myself silently and meant it. I felt myself sliding out of my body, going to the window, and watching the waterfall. The bushes sprouted red and yellow berries. Rust and orange leaves floated down the falls. My father's voice startled me back into myself.

"I'll bring an ermine collar in a larger size tomorrow. I'll bring a different kind of collar in a size four for Wendy," he said.

Mother's angry mouth smiled. Marlene's smug look came back on her face, and her chin went up again. I returned to my station at the smaller of the two bedroom windows and looked out into the courtyard. I stared at the swans shrieking and the ducks moving their wings. One swan was particularly loud. It was getting dark. The birds made large shadows on the water. The wind was blowing. The swans circled. The ducks rested on the shore. The moon was out. Then my chest filled again with hatred as Mother called us in for dinner.

It must have taken consistent planning to script regular life so that it backed up cult programming. We all drove to Bear Mountain in the middle of the night after Father brought home the ermine collar. Mother and Marlene got out of the front seat and Father said to Mother, "I'll get her. Go ahead." They went into the woods. "Listen to me," Father said. "Don't go with the man, don't listen to what anybody says, and you can fight back if you want."

I was angry about the ermine collar and angry that I had to do another pathway barefoot and in my pajamas, even though I was nine years old. The pathway training was supposed to be just for small children.

Lookouts and temporary lights were in the trees; members hid in the bushes. As I walked down the path, a tall, thick black robed figure came towards me and said, "Follow me into death." I said "No" and the people in the bushes cheered. I had passed the first test. I thought these pathways were getting more and more concrete. "If you follow me, you can have this," he said. I kept walking straight ahead, about a quarter to a half mile. It was chilly on the mountaintop. My mother came onto the pathway. I was surprised to see her. She said, "If you follow him, I'll love you more than I love Marlene." I spit in her face and thought this pathway was getting to be fun. My mother would love me more the day I became a blond with blue eyes or maybe a boy. My father came toward me from the front. "Wendy, I just lost all my money in the fur market. If you follow

117

that figure, I'll get my money back." I walked around him feeling guilty. I knew they were playing and testing me, but I felt sorry for my father because he had gambled away all his money and all the family's money that he invested for everyone, and that had ruined Mother's popularity in the family. My father had saved my life many times. I walked through a screen and there was a card. Someone shone a flash-light on a picture of the beautiful angel in blue with wings and a crown and another Hebrew letter, I think this one was lamed, then an ugly picture of a skull and crossbones. Mrs. Twartski came forward holding a mirror. "Follow the angel and you can be pretty." The girl who had tried to kill my mother spat in her face and attempted to kick her. I had overcome these temptations, because of my father's advice.

The next night I had no memory of the pathway temptations. Dad brought home a sleek white ermine collar in a size seven for Marlene, and a round brown mink collar for me. Marlene put on the ermine collar, which made her look like a princess. She wore it for three days straight and then forgot about it. Everyone said the mink collar was beautiful, but I didn't want it. "I don't like the brown," I said. "I don't want to wear the brown one."

My fingertips and nails ached. Sometimes even my toenails felt the rage. I so wanted to scratch my sister and parents. I went back to my bedroom and looked out the window. The water was frozen, thick and green. Cracks were around the edges. The ice looked like a giant jigsaw puzzle.

I remembered the ermine collar scene but never knew it was scripted and a setup for a pathway. I realized that only last year.

In the 1980s, when I was in New York City, I choreographed a dance about a tall hooded and robed figure tempting a little girl. The death-robed figure strolled on the stage. Someone in the wings unrolled satin material onto the stage. An anorexic dancer wearing a child's blue flannel pajamas with a white ruffle across the chest moved on the satin material that resembled a pathway. I found the actor for the part of the tall robed figure on the street. He looked like my ex-husband. He turned out to be a theater student and accepted the role. The tall dark figure tried luring her into death several times and she resisted. When I choreographed this piece, I had no conscious memory of the pathway temptations.

SIX

Breeder

The Rosenbergs, 1951

My father brought home one of the first televisions that he got probably from one of his clients or perhaps he stole it. A stranger and my father carried the bulky console in past the heavy front door, down the long hall where my parents each had a large closet, and through the foyer that we used as a dining room. The man wearing a cap and my father turned the corner and with difficulty put the television between the two curved sofas, where a small table had been, and opposite two winged chairs centered against the wall, where my parents usually sat. My sister and I sat on the gray-carpeted floor. My mother liked pale gray. The carpet and walls were seamless, hushed. The emotions, fights, stinging voices, aromas of food added the color to the living room. Our family's ordinary life was monotonous, with eruptions interrupting the numbness of childhood, the intensity of boredom.

The television screen was bare, not covered by doors. It stood about three and a half feet high and about two feet wide. When it entered our tiny apartment, the world came in too. We watched television shows in which families listened to one another and didn't pretend that what happened didn't happen. People were not objects for use.

My father reached into his pocket and flicked bills. He caressed each one as if he were in love with money, then slipped the mystery man a pile. The stranger left and my father plugged in the television, raised the antenna, and started fiddling with knobs on its back. First there were dots on the screen, then horizontal, then diagonal lines. It reminded me of people rushing along the streets of the city. An urgent-sounding male voice was coming through the helter-skelter designs. My mother, sister, and I shouted "now" as soon as the picture came into focus. Faces, bodies, scenes emerged from green-tinted, black and white patterns. It was like a radio with live pictures, like having the Atlantis movie theater in the living room. Sometimes Father didn't stop turning the knobs just as we shouted "now" and we lost the picture. Then he would reverse the motion and the people would come back into view. It was magic.

On the front, the TV case said "Hoffman". I thought at first that the name referred to my family or perhaps my Uncle Arnold who was an inventor. I asked my father whether we had the TV engraved with our name, but he said it was a coincidence and that Hoffman was the name of the company that made it.

Television created a happy time for my family. Every Saturday night, we watched *Your Show of Shows*. Imogene Coca was just like my mother, crazy and funny, and Sid Caesar was like my father, baffled and obstinate. We laughed as a family. Suddenly, my parents' personalities weren't just peculiar. They were universal. Stars had the same idiosyncrasies, and they were famous for them. My parents took on a Hollywood sheen. And nothing bad happened while we watched *Your Show of Shows*.

A while later, when the family was hypnotized in front of the television, maybe during the evening news or maybe there was a special news show, an outline of a face popped out. The accused spy, Ethel Rosenberg, came into view. She was in a

122

drawing of a courtroom on television. I had seen photos of her in the newspapers. Now there were newsreels on the evening news. She wore a dress that my mother said flattered her. Her face was like a risen moon, pale white but also material, physical. She also looked like a housewife: a moon-housewife. The television cameras panned on a photograph of the judge, a thin man in a black cloak, a gavel in his hand. The announcer said his name was Judge Irving R. Kaufman. He frowned. His mouth went way down and his ears flared out and looked like they were about to fly away. He was looking down his nose at everyone. I would not have wanted him to resolve an argument between my sister and me. The screen went back to Ethel's face. Her eyes were like little bungalows and behind the eyes, I could see her soul flittering down into her body and coming up occasionally for air. Her eyebrows rose in defiance. She could have been one of our gang when we were called into dinner and didn't want to stop playing outside. On March 6, 1951, she was thirty-seven, about the same age as my parents. The television left the courtroom and showed an interview with her that they had done months before. She appeared in what looked like an east side tenement apartment then, held a butcher's knife and chopped a raw chicken into parts that she would cook for her husband, Julius, and their two sons, Michael who was almost exactly my age, eight, and his three-year-old brother, Robert. That's very young to be away from your home and parents. The walls behind Ethel were streaked with grease. Why didn't she clean her kitchen before letting the television cameras in? Mother went wild with cleaning before company came. I wondered who advised her. She seemed disorganized, like Mother.

One night, after dinner, we watched again and the television announcer said the lawyer pounded her with questions, the way my father cross-examined me when I had done something wrong and not admitted it, which I did often, sometimes for spite. My father questioned well, trying to get you to admit.

This Judge Kaufman asked about the atomic bomb. The judge asked Ethel if she was a Communist. And about typing. He wanted to know if she typed for her brother. Mother said her brother betrayed her. He saved himself by sacrificing her. I looked at my sister with suspicion. She would do that too.

Another night they talked about a Jello box cut in a curved line. I couldn't believe grown people were talking about Jello boxes on TV in a courtroom. My mother and I had just gone to Foodland grocery store on Paradise Boulevard. They had a promotion on Jello. If you bought twenty boxes, you got a paper house you could put together. I loved to put things together. I thought my mother would never buy so many boxes all at once, even though we ate several boxes each week. But she did. She bought twenty boxes of orange and strawberry. Every now and then, my mother wanted to give me everything. It didn't happen often but when it did, the skies opened and stars fell on me. I thought, "Now she loves me" and I felt mellow and peaceful. I supposed other children felt this way. Soon, however, she beat me again just for being around. The television talked about fitting pieces of the box top together. Why would grownups fit a box top together? The mean lawyer asked Julius about a box of raspberry Jello and an atomic bomb. I didn't know what an atomic bomb was. Perhaps it was like a rifle. I asked my sister, who was twelve. "You drop it and it wipes out the whole world, all of us too," she said, "in one fell swoop. Russia wants to do that to us." I believed my sister because in school, we had to squeeze ourselves under our desks to practice hiding in case the Russians attacked. We had to curl ourselves up really tight so the Russians didn't kill us right there in our school and blow us all to smithereens. But when you curled yourself into a ball, your shoes touched your dress and smudged it. Mother didn't like having to wash my dress again. The television announcer kept using the word "espionage". I didn't know what that word meant but it sounded as if someone had to use the bathroom. I wanted to ask what "adjourned" meant but both my parents were too absorbed to be interrupted.

They showed more pictures and drawings of Julius and kept using the word Communism. Maybe that meant a neighborhood all together having a party. Julius kept saying, "I refuse to answer on the grounds it might incriminate me". "Incriminate" sounds like "criminal". Maybe they were criminals. Maybe I was a criminal. My mother said if they wouldn't answer, they were guilty. Father said everyone was Jewish, the judge, lawyers, accused. He said the world had them in a hole that was like a pit bull fight with a gentile jury watching.

They showed pictures of Ethel's eyes wandering. Mother said she was searching for Julius. Ethel did not answer. A wall between her and the world existed, but she yearned for her husband. Mother said she was a woman in love. Photographs in the newspapers showed Julius kissing Ethel in an endless kiss; they fused into each other. Julius kissed Ethel the way Mother always wanted to be kissed. Mother seemed jealous of Ethel even though Ethel was going to be electrocuted. Electrocuted, that means having electricity run through your veins and kill you. I knew all about electricity but it hadn't killed me yet. But it had ruined DeeDee's mind. And Mother's mind. And Marlene's nipples. I didn't remember any of that while watching television with my family. I wouldn't remember until the turn of the century. In the photograph, Julius and Ethel grasped onto each other as if they were the only ones in the world. Mother sighed. Father was disgusted.

"Did you receive gifts from the Soviet Union?" a lawyer asked.

Julius' face was huge on the screen, the natural green of his complexion mixing with the television's hue—he looked sick, there but not there. It was as if he were focused on a faraway mountain, maybe an ancient mountain. His ears listened to the inside of the earth. His spirit danced in the clouds. He was not in the courtroom. He was not being tried. In his listening eyes, distant and fragile, I saw myself. I felt close to him. He was not listening to the courtroom drone. He was listening to angels. I didn't listen to my family's fights. I went far away, like Julius. And both of us looked delicate and hopeless.

My family had just finished dinner. My mother cooked pot roast that night and we had mashed potatoes that she placed under the broiler to form a crust. We wolfed the meal down. I wondered what prison food tasted like. Did they serve just bread and water? Did they give them something more because the world watched?

Julius answered questions. He sounded smart. He didn't elaborate. Ethel liked to talk more than he did. I knew what film meant. I didn't know the micro part. My father stirred in his wingback chair covered with the pale blue corduroy cover. My father's body moved. His arms and legs jerked. His stomach bloated out. Sounds came from his moist mouth. He dribbled and stood up. He stood up for hatred. My mother responded too. Julius again said, "I refuse to answer on the grounds it might incriminate me". My mother jumped out of her chair. Her chin jutted out. Her bottom teeth showed. This was the mother-face that scared me. Something bad would happen when she made that face. Saliva came through her teeth. Whom did she hate so? Europe? My father? Her parents? Her friend Edith, who had a better marriage? The 1930s when she should have gone to college? Me? Her voice formed a knife, silver, serrated, with an invisible handle. It could go anywhere and stab anything. My parents poked in the air at the screen. My father poked at the air trying to hurt Julius. I thought he liked to help criminals. They thought Julius and Ethel were real people in their living room and they were poking and hurting them. It was like a ping-pong game between the TV and my parents on the covered wing chairs. Everything seemed life and death. Words and energies bounced from my parents' shouts to the lawyers' words to my parents' gesticulations to Judge Kaufman's gavel to my parents' curses to the

Rosenbergs' eyes. Our gray muted living room turned into a courtroom.

"They should be killed. They should be shot. The electric chair is too good for them."

My mother answered, "How could they do this to us? The Jews haven't had enough trouble? The world doesn't hate us enough already?"

"Traitor," my father screamed. Spit curled around his lips.

"Jew hater," my mother said, her arms waving like a wild ballerina in the air. World War II had ended less than a decade ago. It was still dangerous to be Jewish.

"Commie," my father snarled out. It sounded like the nail in the coffin. "Come-me." Did it mean "come here?" My parents' voices slit the air stretched taut in our apartment. I covered my ears with my fists. My nails dug into my palms. I pressed my knuckles inside my ears. I had to keep out their voices but still I heard, "Commies, traitors". Then I heard my thoughts. *If you go against the family. Traitor, spy, betrayer.* My head crashed in, a tower crumbling. Tiny bones couldn't hold. Spinning, reeling. The gray became continuous, three dimensional walls and floors of gray. The walls of my mind, the walls of the living room collapsed on top of me and my family, because of me. *If you go against your family.*

Back on the screen, Ethel started to dissolve. It started in her waist folding, her shoulders falling forward, her head to one side. Ethel Rosenberg was having a breakdown. She couldn't stop crying. She couldn't go on. Her lawyer asked for an intermission. The judge allowed her to see Julius for a short visit. She needed to see her husband and they let her. Just for five minutes. It was private. She was like the exhausted Olympic runner who caught a glimpse of his girlfriend on the sidelines and ran faster. Now she could go on. She could fight. Her melting was from my parents' hisses. They were killing Ethel. Mother suddenly understood Ethel. She understood dependency on people. She saw herself as a woman who would do

127

anything for love and sex, including sacrifice her children. She softened. She stopped lynching Ethel Rosenberg for the rest of the night. My father remained disgusted with all this female goo. Women slowed everything down. But my mother had begun to forgive Ethel.

The television went to commercial, and my mother served chocolate cake with strawberries and whipped cream between the layers of the cake. She had whipped the cream herself and added vanilla. She had baked the cake herself and used buttermilk. We ate in front of the blank television. My parents had two slices each. Then Ethel was back, as defiant and physical as ever. Mother nodded. She said to herself, "Ethel needed that". Mother didn't feel close to Father. She had always wanted a communion in marriage like Julius and Ethel had. Once when we were visiting Aunt Ruth at her farm in Florida, Mother and I took a walk and saw a banana stalk unravel into bloom right in front of us. "Why not me?" Mother said out loud. I felt her hunger for love. But Father only liked children. He came to life around a child, any child, and Mother became jealous.

The judge said, "Ladies and gentlemen, you will be asked to return Monday morning at ten thirty. In the meantime, I want to wish you all a very happy Easter and a pleasant weekend." I wondered whether the court killed people on Easter the way the Satanists did. My parents grunted but didn't answer. They talked to each other and forgot my sister and me.

"They won't snitch," my father said.

"They are protecting others," my mother said. They looked at the Rosenbergs as if they were fools but underneath I could see they respected them. Deep inside my parents' dead eyes, something glowed. The Rosenbergs didn't tattle.

Later in April, with spring vacation from school over, Julius' face appeared large on the nineteen-inch screen. His eyes, watery and prophetic, strong and fragile, had a tribal look. No one cared what he said. They hated him and wanted him

128

dead. My parents hissed. My sister, in her own world, was not watching. She liked to make up stories and write them down, so she didn't see what really happened. I saw Julius. I saw myself. I didn't know the word yet or even had a hint of its concept, but when I saw the still photos of Julius' face, I knew that I was a "revolutionary" and that a revolutionary would sacrifice everything for a belief and a purpose that he thought was right. Julius was thirty-three when arrested, like Jesus, and he sacrificed a wife and children for his protest beliefs. I was a child in the third grade knowing I would betray my family and tell. The TV announcer said Julius grew up in lower-east-side, tenement-immigrant poverty, and I was growing up with a family that hated. I didn't know whether these conditions made Julius and me who we were or whether we would be like that anyway. This was long ago, but I knew something then in my child's mind. I knew that like him, I would do some-thing that was not allowed. I would break rules. I would tell my family's story even if they killed me for it.

When they sentenced him to death, I became inconsolable. I could not look at what happened, I could not face the pain. I became like my sister ignoring the world. As I crumbled, and as he died, I realized he looked like Daniel.

Green fruit

When I was ten and a half in 1954, Grandpa Max said to Mrs. Twartski in front of me, "I want to bring her to frui-tion soon and I need more pounds on her." I thought he was going to give me fruits to eat, though I was confused because I knew fruits didn't have many calories. I loved peaches and cantaloupe and could eat any number of green grapes as I sat with my family under a beach umbrella at Jones Beach every summer in ordinary life. My father took me into the endless ocean. I floated on my back and he hooked his feet under my arms and also floated. The waves caressed, but I felt as if I could drown. I could sink into the waves and rest on the wet sand floor. We floated out to deep water that I could not stand in. I had to trust that my father would keep me afloat, but that trust was impossible. My mother and sister sat linked together under a striped beach umbrella rented mostly to keep my skin from getting any darker. While I swayed on the unpredictable waves of Jones Beach, while the waves flung themselves high and low and I felt entrapped and also banished from my mother and sister—something descended from the skies. The force was stronger than the piercing sunlight and turbulent wind, calmer than the blues, greens, and salty smells; a force reached down and held me as if I were a nurtured fish in a pond. Though heavy and huge, it coated me gently. The air seemed to smile like Mr. Jacobs' face. The clouds emitted love that felt like Daniel's presence. The precarious Atlantic Ocean did not feel unsafe. I felt like I was on dry land, in an enclosed watery garden, secure and with the fragrance of ripe peonies and roses. For a moment, I did not feel enslaved. The intense sun framed my eyes causing me to see rainbows of translucent color. Even when the waves peaked and spilled over my face, and the inside of my nostrils and eyes stung, I still felt a solid, indestructible presence rain on me. I was alone in this liquid garden but filled with a presence that was goodness. I don't know whether it covered all of Jones Beach or the universe or whether it was trying to make me less distraught, but it was there even while I was drowning in waves of hopeless loneliness. As my father turned his feet at a sharp angle, stood up, and yanked me out of the ocean by the arm, even then I carried this protected paradise into any abysses he and my other handlers had planned.

Grandpa had no intention of waiting until my body menstruated in its own time. He started injections to bring it on by eleven. He must have been working for the Mafia group then because the Illuminati hadn't wanted to start impregnating me until I was thirteen.

In ordinary life, I was sitting on the toilet in our long, narrow Pleasant Hills bathroom with a floor of miniature black and white ceramic tiles. I was eleven and menstrual blood poured out of me. I must have made a sound because my sister rushed into the bathroom. We were not allowed to lock the door. I wanted to die, foreseeing what lay ahead. Crisp blood flew out of me as if I had been cut in half. Life would become a tidal wave that pulled me into the sea with sharks, then washed me to shore with family. If no one would help a child escape, who would rescue a bleeding girl? Previously, life was set with my parts in place, now life would be executed. My father came in, attracted by the commotion. I said, "What are you, a sex maniac!" My mother had retired to her bedroom.

I began to feel sexual feelings for the first time. I was finishing sixth grade and starting junior high school.

For my eleventh birthday, before they sent me away, my mother bought me many gifts including a leather jacket with knit sleeves that I had admired in Klein's discount department store for months. She filled the two curved sofas in the living room with a panoply of beautiful clothing either from love or guilt. My sister didn't even seem jealous. My mother also baked a masterpiece for my eleventh birthday, a gorgeous, round, four-layer chocolate cake. She baked the batter in two round nine-inch pans, then sliced each layer in half and put hand-whipped cream in between them. She wrote Happy Birthday in pink whipped cream, and around the border put pink decorations like rosebuds, and added giant fresh strawberries. As if that weren't enough, she then said, "I want to take you shopping and have you point your finger and I will buy you whatever you point to." Perhaps that's when I realized how transitory and meaningless material possessions are.

In normal life, my father practiced American law. In later years, he was on a White House committee and was a law partner with a congressperson's father. But deep within him, he believed in ancient Roman law. Like the church leaders who think pedophilia is a not a crime, my father felt entitled to use his daughters' and other children's vaginas and rectums. He preferred younger children and impregnated me by accident. I had remembered this pregnancy when I worked through my incest memories in the 1980s. As I worked more deeply into my mind control and ritual abuse memories in 2012, a body memory brought this phase of my life roaring back. I felt nauseated and almost vomited. Then I realized the eleven-year-old child my father impregnated had suffered from morning sickness. My vomit had informed my mother and grandmother that I was pregnant. Since my father raped me repeatedly, they deduced it was from him. This was right before the Mafia group started impregnating me deliberately at Brothel 8.

My mother and grandmother rushed me to the family doctor and Dr. Brown gave me an abortion, which I hadn't wanted. I thought it would be nice to have a baby. I loved my Tiny Tears doll. I knew nothing of the societal implications of having an incest baby—to me it was like having a doll.

I was well aware that my father kept me alive, but perhaps my mother would not have hated me so much if he hadn't kept raping me. Or perhaps she would have anyway because she was programmed to hate me. My father, when confronted, said, "She's so cute and adorable," blaming me for being raped weekly, sometimes nightly. After the abortion, it was quieter in the apartment. My father was trying to make it up to my mother. I found myself in multiple double binds: I didn't want to be raped and I was raped; I had sudden sexual feelings and I felt confused and guilty; I didn't want the abortion and was forced to have the abortion; I was blamed for the whole thing; there was no way out. Mostly I wanted to rip my skin off.

Driving to the brothel, 1954

This inside girl never hid. I always remembered her. She never told me her whole story but she told me the beginning. Or perhaps that's the only piece of the event she held. Then other parts inside of me finished the history she had begun.

They put me between them in the front seat of the light blue Packard and later the green Pontiac. I held my body in so that no part of me touched either one of them. I wore my brown coat and brown hat with a feather that curled around into a question mark-type shape. The brown hat covered my whole head and the feather wrapped around my left ear. My brown coat went below my knees and matched my hat. This coat was my dress coat, not the storm coat I wore to school. Underneath, I had a simple dress, a starched white blouse, a sweater, and good, new, white underwear and a training bra. I was shiny and polished like my shoes. Mother had arranged my hair in curls along my forehead. I had had to sleep with the bobby pins holding them in place the night before. This was how mother dressed me when she took me to the brothel. Anyone would think I was the most cared-for child in the world. My mother looked out the window of the front seat through the polka dots on her hat's French veil. Her gray suede gloves matched her pumps with fat heels. She wore a mink stole with mink heads dangling down the sides that collided with her belt. I wondered how many dead minks those dangling heads represented. It must not have been the dead of winter or she would have been wearing her mink coat. My father had on a stylish hat. I was almost eleven and a half. The girls in the car, my inside girls, didn't know about the past experiences in the brothel. It was all new to them. The older girls who had been at the brothel earlier shivered deeper inside me. But even they didn't know what was coming. I should've been at Oldtown Junior High School. They thought, *They are driving me to the brothel. Soon my parents will leave me at the brothel.*

How this girl with the hat never got sunken into the forgotten is unknown, but I thank her for never disappearing. To stay connected to the person who lives ordinary life is a feat. Tons of electricity and torture discourage communication. I hadn't remembered where she was going. Just that she was in the front seat flanked by my parents and shaking, wearing that hat. Sometimes my heart hurt so much that I could feel its outline pierce through my torso. Big bold strokes outlined its shape. The center of my tongue was dry. The back of my throat had a chute that went past my tailbone.

My left leg started shaking violently. My father ignored me as he drove recklessly. My teeth rattled and smashed. "Stop that shaking," my mother snapped. Her bottom teeth jutted forward and her bottom lip dropped. The minks' heads bobbed. "Stop it." I tried to hold my body still but my left leg jerked wildly.

"Stop that shaking!" My father drove on.

At the entrance to the brothel, Father handed me over. Mother stayed in the car. No one saw her mink stole or her coordinated outfit. The thin male greeter gave me a shift, slippers, and a number, and tagged my arrival clothes, the same way as when I was younger. Another man who always looked down and was probably from the same country as the first took me to an empty room with a bleak single bed on a cold, uneven floor. The window was fogged over and the wall streaked with dirt. Rusty pipes made sleep apnea sounds. *This place is putrid.* I wanted to go home, even though I had no home.

The visit

I looked down at my chest all the time and prayed that it would not grow. I inspected to make sure it was flat. Several years later, my breasts did start to change but they grew wide rather than out. The relief I felt that I still didn't have breasts was as huge as the town I lived in. The girls in the brothel did not want to be pregnant, and they knew that the brothel keepers impregnated the older girls. The older girls were salmon swimming upstream. Once they deposited their babies, they died unless their parents came for them. Even girls in regular life were hyper-conscious of their breasts forming. What distinguished us was who wore an undershirt, a training bra, or a real bra. And who had a boyfriend, the most exotic accomplishment.

My parents visited me at Brothel 8 in the Bronx weekly, on Wednesdays or Sundays during visiting hours, which were from two in the afternoon until six in the evening for the younger girls and three to five for the older ones. My mother brought me chopped liver and other foods I liked, like Mallomars. Mother broke off tiny pieces and put them between my lips. My eyes were sunken. I was often chained to the bed when they visited. Mother sobbed. Father looked down and around. They seemed to feel bad, but the fact was they had sold me into this slavery. My father always left with fifty and hundred dollar bills and a few thousand dollar bills thrown in; I saw the stack with a rubber band tied around it. I imagine that they thought they didn't have a way out of this, and that they might as well take the money.

During one visit, my mother wore a new, elaborate pearl choker.

"That's a pretty necklace, Mom," I said.

"Your father bought it for me for our anniversary," she said.

With my money, I thought.

I wonder, when my parents visited me, did they know? Were they conscious or so programmed that they didn't know what they had done? My father flicked off a fifty dollar bill, handed it to a man wearing a pale green medical shirt and said "Make sure no one beats her up." If my parents had stopped visiting me, the men would have killed me the moment I got sick. Sometimes the men sold the abandoned girls to foreign men. The parents had already got the money. They didn't want the girls any more. And just looking at the girls probably made them feel guilty. My parents were better than that. It's hard to believe my parents were better than anyone in the world.

The harvest, 1954–1959

Pamphlets were scattered all over the downstairs of the faded warehouse:

> See your sperm spread over the world.
> Have offspring on every continent.
> Be a real man.
> Give your sperm to one of our girls.
> Grow babies in lots of our gals.

I had overheard the managers telling the nurses, "The eggs have to be fertilized—we can't afford a bad batch, we'll lose our customers." Nurses on the floor drew our blood after we had a series of rapes. My left arm and leg were tied to a bed, this time with metal bracelets and chains like the African slaves wore. My life consisted of rapes, attempts at impregnation, hormone shots, vomiting, and having my insides scooped out. It felt like diarrhea and cramps when they scooped out my eggs to ship them to places around the world. "You have to keep stimulating her. I want constant orgasms. We need an uptake for the sperm," a nurse in the brothel said. The stimulation was painful.

The air outside was clean, the sky a dreamy blue. Sometimes birds chirped a sharp and harmonious sound. The women had left the window open a crack because they were too hot. The employed women always kept photographs of their children, especially the babies. These women who had the hardship of leaving their home country for another, who struggled with the language—these women loved to make circus-like bows and put them on their children. I realize now the bows were a code saying, "don't tell or you will be killed". My grandmother also

136

made butterfly bows. I would not mind leaving this country for another, but I thought every country had these brothels and parents who were forced to sell their children and think of themselves as farmers and their children as their crop.

The air was warm and playful. I longed for a glass of orange juice—Mother squeezed oranges for us and left the pulp in—and to go out and play, perhaps ride my bicycle, later go to the drugstore for a vanilla egg cream. When I moved, the metal cut my skin. The men liked to see blood on the girls. The more wounds and scratches the better. *Maybe Mother will bring me orange juice when she visits on Sunday*, I thought. I had tried to infuse ordinary life with as much pleasure as possible. The key to not going crazy or killing yourself was to find some enjoyment somewhere, somehow, possibly. Daniel had wanted me to go on living. Therefore I had to find a way. But here at the brothel, all I could come up with was that my mother might bring me freshly squeezed orange juice on Sunday. My throat was sore. It would taste good.

I also thought of my eggs going to all these countries. Some would create babies I would never see or care for. Would they grow up to be slaves like me who would die soon or be bought by a middle class or rich family that wouldn't know about me lying here in chains? If they thought about it, they might know, but why should they bother thinking about it? They just wanted a baby, any baby.

It was springtime. I was on spring vacation from seventh grade. Maybe one more week and they would send me home and back to school. I would be home for my birthday. Where I lived, the hills were soft and caressing, like a lullaby. The woman sitting on a chair here in the corner sighed and wiped her forehead. She wanted to be home also.

I prayed that my babies would find a good home, not here but perhaps in a small country where parents didn't sell their children. Maybe when my children were eighteen or thirty, they would look for me and find me. But how would they know who I was? There would be no records. Maybe my children would never be. That would be the best. I prayed for that, that my children would never be.

The woman, Trixie, came over with a rag and swatted my cheeks.

"No cry. No allow."

I wondered what they were doing at home now. Mother and Marlene would be getting up late since school was out. They would have breakfast, probably pot cheese and corn rye bread, slowly dress and then take the F train downtown to Klein's. Mother would buy Marlene nice clothes. Mother might buy me a welcome home outfit. I wondered whether Marlene had ever been sent to Brothel 8. Sometimes she disappeared and I didn't know where she had gone. In September, she'd be going away to college. Then I'd be all alone with my parents. Mother would have stopped Marlene from going to the brothel if she could, but she might not have been able to. Me she just handed over. But she would never have chosen to do that without the masters making her.

My heart got caught in a hard knot. I was trying to coax the fluid in it to move around. The air outside smelled clean. It was funny how it didn't show the pollution outside or inside. I felt a wave come over me. It was light and careful and touched me gingerly. I felt a peacefulness.

"No cry. No allow," Trixie said.

I didn't know whether the peace was coming from inside me or perhaps from God outside in the sunshine or maybe from the spirit of Daniel. My nerves were always tumbling around my body, crashing into poles inside me, making dizzying circles. Crash, crash, jump. My mother was driven crazy and these nerves would drive anyone crazy.

I think they charged $500 per vial, or maybe it was fifty dollars? The men who delivered sperm were mostly businessmen, politicians—sometimes a truck driver. The men were rough and came into the girls' small rooms one after the other.

138

Some just laid their entire over-two hundred pounds on you, didn't move, just sank into you, all their weight crushing your child bones, and let their semen dribble around you. They fell asleep and the guards had to be called to get them off. A matron in each room watched that we weren't killed. Each room did not have its own set of guards, and there were nights when more girls were having emergencies than there were guards. That's when a girl or even two were killed. They carried the dead girls out in the darkness in large bags. We envied those girls.

There was a time limit and the matron timed it. "Cigars outside. Rest it in ashtray," the concierge said. "All men are like this, not just these. They want women, girls chained."

For exercise, we walked only within the building and up and down the steps while a male nurse held a gun to our ribs. For air, I stuck my head out the window for an hour each night. The matron always watched so I couldn't jump.

Some men were there because they wanted to propagate children all over the world, the way Florida exports citrus fruits and California mangoes.

A cleanup team was supposed to wash the girls off, and bring them a bedpan and water, but often the cleanup crew skipped people because they were lazy. We showered and washed our hair after every ten clients, and we were supposed to wash our parts after every client. The clients, who included a rare woman, didn't notice how sticky and dirty our bodies were. When men wanted to ejaculate, all they cared about was their own sperm. And when they wanted to beat and whip, the dirtier you were the better. It justified their need to make you bad.

Physicians came to the Brothel 8 every ten to eleven days, sometimes every fourteen days, if it was a holiday. They spoke with accents. I don't know whether they were really doctors. They wore street clothes and carried a little black bag. They had a stethoscope, took our temperature orally, pressed on our stomachs, examined us for bugs and venereal disease, and determined whether we were pregnant. We were tied up during the examinations. They didn't treat us as human beings. To them, we were also just bodies that could bring in money. One time I was sent home early because one of the pseudo-doctors had done a bad procedure and I hemorrhaged. They couldn't use me for a while.

Mrs. Twartski was sometimes there, checking to see that none of my programs broke down so that my parts would cooperate, not fight and, when released from the brothel, remember nothing. Some of us, however, did remember. She or another programmer would press on both my temples together and a stream of these inner slave-girls would come out. Each girl had to take care of five men, then another girl would take over. All these girls were parts who were inside me, who were me. The temple squeeze also told me to hold still and be silent. Even during the five deliveries, I had to bite on a stick between my teeth and be quiet.

When my parents visited, we talked about nothing but it was better to have them near me than being alone. They stayed for fifteen or twenty minutes, less time than it took to drive to the brothel. Then they got up to leave, walked out together and didn't glance back at me. They were robots walking away. They didn't know what they were doing. The masters had control of their minds, souls, and wallets. When they got home, they would think I was at a recreational camp. They may never have had a moment of truth. I had no one in the world.

In my mind, I flung myself from side to side against the walls. After they left, still in my mind, I flew to the side bathroom with a skylight, out the window and perched on its window ledge with the free pigeons, or I jumped to my death. If I jumped, maybe an honest person would find me splattered on the sidewalk and the workings of Brothel 8 would be known. No, honest people didn't hang out around this neighborhood.

I would just be dead but I was ready. I could have stayed alive for my children but I will never know who they are.

The girls who were kept in the brothel were separated and weren't allowed to become friends. My body and mind were like locomotives racing across country, never stopping at stations, never slowing down at intersections. In sleep and awake, I rushed, sped, flying off tracks. Anguish ate up my pounds. I found no comfort except in the memory of Daniel. I saw his curls, eyes, felt his still smooth but becoming-a-man skin—some nights, I thought I felt his weightless ghost body covering my writhing-in-pain body and then the smell. Within the dusty, leaking warehouse, I would suddenly smell daffodils and wildflowers. A perfume filled my nostrils and sinuses even as my ears listened to other girls' whimpering, and the occasional horn honking outside.

"Eat or we will break your jaw." A guard socked it. After that, I had some sort of contraption around my jaw. They fed me with only a straw. I couldn't open my mouth. They gave me milk shakes.

When I tried to sleep, I spun. The attendants held my arm and walked me to the bathroom or I would have fallen. I started spitting up saliva and retching. The attendant called the doctor.

"She's got to eat something."

They hooked me onto an IV. Another time, a crew rushed in after the attendant pressed the bell. They came with an IV, blood pressure cuff, and oxygen mask. That same bell rang all through the floors. They never sent us to the hospital.

I used to outline the Pleasant Hills apartment floor plan over and over again in my mind endlessly. I imagined walking from where my parents double locked the front door for the night, past the square gray foyer that we used as a dining room into the hall, past the elongated bathroom with scrubbed tiles, past our room where my sister had the bed closer to the windows with starched organdy curtains. I ran my eyes along the bumps and crags of the walls, came to the deep blue crevice of the corner and rested in its arms. I looked at the Victorian prints of ladies in hoop skirts and samplers stitched by children who lived one hundred years ago, went into the kitchen that mother had painted yellow and green, past the long windows of the living room, and back to the double locked front door for the night. I noticed that I didn't include my parents' bedroom in my mental outline. I wondered whether the girls who stitched the sampler had to go to a brothel.

"If you eat, we'll let you keep the baby."

We girls rarely saw one another except in the one large bathroom. We were all chained in our separate rooms. But we felt one another. We communicated in our minds and supported one another. I tried especially hard to contact my cousin Rhonda.

A hand has reached out to me in the twenty-first century. It has five fingers with nails and is covered with mud. How brave of it to reach for air even in this polluted world. I lick the mud off covering the self-importance, the deceptive specialness, I lick in between the fingers and pull and tug on the slippery skin. I will not let go. At last, I have found another one of my selves.

Breeder, 1954–1959

In the brothel, men in white coats had conversations in a foreign language that I somehow understood. In the hallway men said, "We have a big order. They want live newborns. We have an especially big order for half Jewish, half Asian newborns." They calculated numbers. It would cost them less to keep me here chained to the bed during the pregnancies than for me just to produce fertilized eggs.

They found Asian men on the street who weren't the brothel's usual clients but were workers in the neighborhood, or men they imported from Canal Street in lower Manhattan. The Asian men were rounded up about twenty-five at a time. The managers of the brothel wanted to make sure I and the other Jewish girls got pregnant. These men were violent. They were there only for use of their sperm and the guards often stationed themselves by the beds with their guns drawn. After the clients attempted to impregnate me, they were handed money.

But when the brothel was closed down for the morning, the guards would put down their guns, loosen their shirts, and start unzipping their flies. One of the matrons would storm into the room and shout, "These girls are not for your use." The guards would slink away because they needed their jobs. Most of me was out the window.

Now that they are remembering, the girls on the ledge talked to the girls left in the bed:

GIRLS IN BED: "Why did you leave me?"
GIRLS ON LEDGE: "We couldn't take it."
BED: "You left me alone. You shouldn't have left me. You were selfish like Marlene, only caring about yourself."
LEDGE: "That hurt."
BED: "It's true, you were cruel."
LEDGE: "We're sorry. We were not as strong as you."
BED: "Ha."
LEDGE: "Why didn't you leave too?"
BED: "Someone had to stay and protect. Everyone can't leave."
LEDGE: "Why not?"
BED: "Then the body would be completely abandoned and unprotected."

A short stocky man with an eager but mean face in a tweed suit, tie, and hat and a taller blond woman who had a page

143

boy cut and sprayed hair, a fur coat in winter, a trench coat in the fall and spring, or a summer suit, walked the halls, peering in rooms, holding briefcases and clipboards—looking over the mothers, while planning on taking the babies. The matrons called them "angels of death". Holding a clipboard and a box of chocolates, the blond woman entered my room when the clients finished with me. She had a tag on her jacket that read Rebecca P. Smith.

"We're from the Wyoming Family Aid Agency, and we're here to help girls like you. We specialize in placing beautiful babies from unwed mothers. We want to get these babies far away from the East Coast, into the clean mountainous air. Don't you want your baby to be raised in clean air and not here in a Bronx ghetto? Don't you want that for your baby as a mother? Your sister gave us all her babies. She wanted a better life for them. Don't you want to be like your sister? We have so many couples who tried for so long to have a baby and would give anything to raise your babies."

Knowing she was lying, I said, "Maybe they should lie here—then they'd get pregnant."

"They are very sad and you could make them happy. The Wyoming Family Aid Society specializes in earnest adoptions, meaning adoptions where the birth mother doesn't renege. We are longstanding partners with the Nebraska Aid Society that believes in mother and baby happiness. All little pregnant girls like chocolate candies," the blond woman said as she shoved the box towards me. The attendants pricked up their ears, knowing I would give them the chocolates as soon as the vulture left. Sometimes they ate the chocolates on the spot, other times they brought the box home to their families.

After the adoption woman and her partner left, a sole Asian worker with kind eyes came in. He looked tired as if he had just come from work and had been rounded up. He wore a white shirt and loosened tie. Maybe he was a waiter or *maître d'* of a restaurant. He looked at me and his body curved backwards

144

into an opened parenthesis, his fingers stretched wide and he stood frozen in the doorway to my room. Beads of sweat appeared on his face and his eyeballs bulged and receded. His white button down shirt became wet under his arms. His shocked face reminded me of who I was. My handlers had told me this happened to all girls and that I was special to have so many men who would pay for me, that what I was doing here was what life was about. But the man's face shocked me back to the truth. The skinny man with kind eyes looked at me chained to the bed, crying, struggling, and he turned on his toe to leave as he said "No, too little girl."

"You have to or you'll be killed," I called to him. He answered, "No little girl, no tied up," and left.

"If you don't, they'll kill you," I screamed. I'm not sure he was able to hear me because he spun around and ran. The guards wrestled with him. I heard noise and shouting. The men in the hall followed him. And then the silenced shot in the alley. The inside girls in the bed felt guilty even though they had warned him. *If we weren't crying, maybe he would still be alive*, they thought to themselves. The guards may have killed the one good person in the neighborhood because he knew what was going on inside and they didn't have anything over him. The basis of this kind of criminal security is co-opting. That's why they have the children of these groups kill so young.

In a fairly wild state, my father came to Brothel 8 on his own one afternoon, not during visiting hours. I don't know how he got in. He probably bribed the guards with cash. My father sat on a hard chair near my bed sobbing into his white handkerchief that Mother had ironed for him. He didn't say anything, just sobbed next to me. Two of the male attendants who patrolled the halls with hand guns came in, held a gun to his temple and told him to leave. He reached into his deep pocket. Twenties were on top. He peeled off two twenties, gave each man a bill and sobbed, "Don't hurt her," and left without turning back around.

My first baby was born on May 17, 1954. The attendant-doctor held her up in the air, mucus and blood coating her perfect body. Beautiful toes. Then he quickly carried her out of the birth room leaving me on the table, my arms extended, longing to hold and sniff her. I never saw her again. My second child was born on February 23, 1955, a stillborn, they said. The people at the brothel whipped me for it but I'm not sure the infant boy was really dead. When a baby leaves a mother, even an overly young mother, it's as if a meteorite hits a farmland and leaves a crater, and the land will grow no more crops. When a baby leaves a child–mother, it may be even worse. I searched for a nice person in the world, anywhere. Daniel was always there with me, as a ghost always protecting me from the environment, grief, and sadistic workers. In between deliveries, I went home to Pleasant Hills. Sometimes my sister was home from college, with a sophisticated air of the outside world that intrigued me.

This year, I contacted agencies that specialize in trafficking cases and might have access to black market files, but none so far handles "cold cases". I imagine they have enough trouble investigating current cases. I put ads in newspapers with the dates of my children's births, but so far I've had no responses.

SEVEN

The right choice

Feast of the beast, 1955

The most important moment of my life started a cascade of punishments that would continue my whole life.

During this festival, a third brothel baby grew inside me while death was all around outside, in the same spot where the ceremonies took place every twenty-seven years,[1] in Prince Edward Island, Canada.

Until now, the executioner's hand or one of my handlers' hands had been over mine. It embarrassed the cult leaders that a designated queen of a county had not killed with her own hands. Even eight-year-old children in this cult had already sacrificed for their god. I thought that perhaps they wouldn't send me back to the brothel if I cooperated, but I didn't think they would let me keep my baby.

Killing with your own hands is how you become an adult in this subterranean world. I was walked to the altar at the stroke of midnight surrounded by all the swaying participants chanting, "Daughter of King Saul ... royal bloodline ..." I and everyone else wore black hooded robes. Two flags on long, high-up poles, higher than the tall pine trees, waved in the cool air. One said *United Brothers of Israel*, the other, the name of my maternal bloodline.

Red strobe lighting flashed. The masters swayed before and behind me. This was the moment I was to step into my prophesied role of queen of this county, which had been the fourth county and was now the first, the one endowed with spiritual importance. This county is composed of the United States, Europe, Canada, and Greenland. Thirteen geographic areas called counties make up the satanic world. Grandpa Max held a sparkling crown in his open hands. Since before my birth, he had been working towards this goal. Everyone present was pushing me to kill with my own hands without assistance, which meant my acceptance of my prophesied position. Even my mother and sister wanted me to do it. The dull hum of chanting suspended for a moment. In my mind, I heard Daniel speak to me, "Be as pure as the swans," and saw Mr. Jacobs pray with his family in his apartment across the waterfall. His face and heart vibrated goodness and kindness to his children and the world. My spirit had become one of his children. When you are taken this deeply into the jaws of evil, you have to go one way or another.

The leaders had a drugged Caucasian male prepared to be sacrificed. He was probably thirty-three years old, according to tradition. He would be killed no matter what I did. I was only a pawn. If I killed, I could have an easier life on earth, with less torture, prostitution, and other illegal activities. These groups gave women two husbands: a poor choice of a husband for ordinary life, and a better matched husband for their cult life. My cult husband, Eli, was chanting and expecting me to join him and kill with my own hands. Rhonda was right behind me and watched, neutral. The executioner put the jeweled sword in my left hand. No one breathed. The air was like silk and the earth moist and mellow. The worst crimes take place in the most beautiful landscapes.

In my mind, Mr. Jacobs' hand went over mine, the hand that was over his boys' heads as he prayed in his tallit and as his emaciated wife fingered her rosary. Daniel breathed into me with the familiar breath that had nurtured me for nine years. Daniel, the swans, my parents' deeper unconscious, some place ancient in my bloodline, the strength from the bridge walk— something whispered to me. I would not do it. I passed the test. I failed the test. In this underworld, that is about as close to having free will as it gets.

The emblazoned sword lay on the ground as if bleeding. The chanting turned to a hiss. The strobe lighting ceased. After I dropped the sword, they chanted, "Fall on sword" and "Queen Philomena is a failure" as guards handcuffed me. The executioner stepped up to the altar, took Rhonda's hand, and killed the drugged adult sacrifice.

Grandpa Max wearing his Wiezenslowski mask, Joseph, and Mrs. Twartski whipped me in front of the participants. The other twelve counties performed successful 1955 Feasts of the Beast.

The last days at the brothel

After the feast, my father parked the car in the Bronx slum. My mother got out of the car, took my arm, and dragged me out to the brothel. She had probably been told that if I didn't return to the brothel, Marlene or I would be killed.

Run, run, I thought, but there was nowhere to run. Overflowing trashcans were on the dark corners. No one was around. Mother shoved me to Mrs. Twartski, who took me inside the heavy, squeaky door and pushed me up many flights of wooden wide steps. I looked frantically for an escape route. On the sixth floor, we went into a large dingy room with a cot, chair, and lamp that had a dirty lampshade. Pale green paint peeled off the walls. The filthy wooden floors rocked. It was like an oversized cell without a single comfortable or pleasant thing to look at. There was a hanger for my coat, a hook for my hat, and a dresser for my clothes.

My second daughter was rushed away from on December 14, 1955. From the glimpse that I got, I saw that she was delicate, serious, and Asian looking. I don't know what happened to my children. I felt more numb when the other children were born but not completely. I suffered severe chest pains and waited to die from a heart attack, but it was just grief playing with me. I had given these babies all the pent-up love I stored in myself. They were purity among foulness.

Parts of my mind have kept records of everything that happened to me. These parts or personalities were self-created, not affected by the concussions, and my programmers didn't know about them. I think this self-recording started in infancy. I imagine all survivors of these kinds of abuses have this recording mechanism in their brains.

On the last days at the brothel, the supervisor took the girls to the basement. "When you get in your father's car, you will dissolve in a million pieces and no piece will know of the other. Once you are home, you will remember nothing of your experience. You will be a silent child, a quiet child. If you say one word, this is what will happen to you." They showed us images of girls with black eyes and missing front teeth being thrown off a cliff, and crows and vultures eating them as they said, "If you ever tell even one little bit, the tiniest little bit, or give a hint, then this will happen to you." They also showed us pictures of mountain lions devouring children. Sometimes now I awake in a panic attack with these images. "This program starts when you hear the bell ring for the next girl to leave. Whenever you see a yellow bow or any kind of bow, you will remember to forget us here."

They checked us out by number. They returned our small valises and coats. We put on our street clothes, which we had arrived in. Sometimes the mothers brought different clothes from those we had arrived in to accommodate the season or growth. Psychically, I said goodbye to the girls. Trauma and abuse bind people for life. We all had the same experience. My father was waiting double-parked outside. Another man made sure my father was there.

"We don't want any trouble." Then he told me to leave.

The man rang a desk bell for the next crippled girl to check out. The walls of evil crashed in on my child's body like an avalanche. No possible escape. The world was an empty abyss, and I was filled with terror.

I got in the front seat and my father and I didn't say anything. By the time I arrived home, I didn't remember anything. It was as if I returned from a regular school day or summer camp. When I got home, my mother either went into her own bedroom and closed the door, or frantically paced the small apartment, or acted as if nothing had happened and put milk and cookies on the kitchen table, either Mallomars or her homemade butter dough cookies with ground walnuts on top.

A friend, 1955

Back in the twenty-first century, yesterday, I began to feel particularly bad about not having a real friend. No close friend with whom I could share everything. Then I remembered Sally and understood my current grief. She and I had been friends about this same time. An emotional explosion often precedes the narrative of my dissociated memories. I remembered being at Sally Kraus' home in Pleasant Hills. I used to walk to Sally's apartment building five blocks down from mine, towards Enterprise Avenue. We were together in the seventh grade and close for months, before Mengele reappeared.

An only child, Sally invited me to a sleepover at her apartment. We ate meat, mashed potatoes, and dessert at a small table with her parents. The mother commented that I had a sweet tooth and asked me questions about myself. There was almost no other talk. The parents were divorcing. Sally and I got along wonderfully. I had not had a friend for a long time. Given that we were both programmed with mind control, it's amazing that we were able to be spontaneous and play. Then suddenly it ended.

Mrs. Kraus, whose first name was Dorothy, was one of the better mothers because she knew enough to divorce, but still she couldn't protect. When the father, Marvin, picked Sally up off the bed, he said, "You're next" to me. He paced back and forth as he carried my friend around with his penis in her. Sally's mother called from another room, "Marvin, leave the girls alone, come out of there, or I'm coming in." Then she was at the door, knocking. I couldn't understand why she didn't just barge in. Mr. Kraus dropped Sally on her bed in the middle of the rape and left the room. Sally was crying and ashamed. "Now you know my secrets," she said to me. We clasped hands, her left hand with my right hand, and lay there heartbroken. She had thought he wouldn't do it if I were there. Without television, I don't know that we would have ever found out that there was another way to live. The fathers in *I Remember Mama, My Life with Father*, and later *The Brady Bunch* never raped their children, or at least the television never showed it.

With our fingers intertwined, love passed between us, stronger, deeper, more permanent than all the electrical shocks Mengele and the Satanists could muster with all their elaborate machines. Two friends knowing what each other's nights and families were like and loving each other because of it. I felt our souls touch and our hearts take in what we endured. That feeling of communion is still with me today.

Maybe Sally reported to her handler that she had a sister-like friend, or perhaps her parents did, or my mother might have told her own parents who told my handler, or it may have been my sister who told on me. Or one of the reporters in me may have told though no one inside me has confessed yet.

When Sally and I were holding hands, she still sobbing, we put our heads together with our temples touching and fell asleep like that, our heads like joined mind-controlled twins.

Almost every day, I walked the five long blocks on 108th Street under the cherry blossom trees from my apartment to

Sally's apartment building. I took the elevator to the eighth floor, turned left, walked down the hall, and knocked on her door. Her mother Dorothy opened the door about two inches and stuck her eye out. Her knee was between the door and the doorframe. She dressed in street clothes, not the housedress my mother wore inside. "Can Sally come out?" I asked, thinking that if she couldn't, I could come in and see her.

"Sally can't play with you," Dorothy said. I was too stunned to ask why not. She closed the door. I heard the double lock click in place. I began crying. I walked back the five blocks under the cherry blossoms trees sobbing, trying to understand what had happened. *I hadn't done anything wrong. Sally's father had done something wrong. I knew something about them I wasn't supposed to. Were Sally or I not allowed to have any friends?* I felt boxed in loneliness even as pink petals softly fell on me. This block was an Eden and a pastel loveliness caressed my sorrow. Without success, I called on Sally every day for about two weeks. My mother said not to, that either Sally was sick or her parents didn't want to let her out. I couldn't stop crying. My eyes stung without stopping.

In my normal, everyday life outside the cult, I had the problem of automatically transferring to any friend all the feelings I had for Sally. Most of those friends, of course, did not warrant such trust.

The last time I tried to call for Sally and was refused, while I was walking home with my eyes burning from sobbing, Mengele's big black car pulled up under the cherry blossom trees glistening in the sunlight. He hopped out and told me to get in. He called me Wendy and put chloroform over my nose. He and I were in the back seat as his driver and another man were in the front. I naively thought he would drive me home, but we went right to the programming quarters at Montauk Point, where Mrs. Twartski waited. My parents must have told Mengele where to find me. Now Mrs. Twartski and Mengele were friends and working together.

153

The assistants put me on a stretcher and wheeled me to the second floor. I was barefoot, naked, with electrodes on the soles of my feet, up the sides of my trembling legs, above my knees. They fastened on a helmet with inside spikes that especially hurt the soft spot of my head. I got quick shots of drugs in the right and left arms, and had to follow Mengele's watch moving back and forth hypnotically, with commands followed by brutal shots of electroshock. Mrs. Twarstski instructed, "You are not allowed to have any friends. Jewish girls have no friends. Any friend you have will be killed. You can't be friends with Sally Kraus, and she can't be friends with you."

Sally was a great loss for me, but now the possibility of not having any friend was an even greater loss.

MENGELE: "Any friend you make we will kill."
MRS. TWARTSKI: "I thought you learned that when we killed Daniel."
MENGELE: "We can see your every move. You cannot have friends. You are ours to do with what we like. No other people in your world. Only us."

But Sally and I had already tasted the nurturing love of a friend, which they couldn't erase.

Polio, 1955

In front life, Aunt Eileen in the Bronx had called my mother to say two children in my cousin Rhonda's elementary school had come down with polio. She wouldn't let Rhonda go to school and she was sterilizing all their dishes. At the same time, Aunt Mimi in Flushing called and told my mother she wouldn't let her daughters outside, not even the older one who was younger than me. No one in our school, Public School number three, had it yet. We still went to school, sat at our desks, learned fractions, and studied countries, this time Hawaii with its luxurious blue skies and sensuous fruits and dances. But I knew my mother worried. She never let us take bites from other people's sandwiches or licks of their ice cream cones. My parents watched Dr. Salk on television. They worshipped the man who was saving children's lives.

"Dr. Salk should have been in charge of the distribution himself," my mother screamed at the T.V. "Then the inoculations would be safe." She had heard stories of children getting polio from the vaccine. "I'm not giving the children the injections," she said to my father, who sat in his wing chair half dressed, dubious, placid. "If everyone else gets it, they won't have germs to catch," Mother argued. Father, who was a professional arguer, didn't agree or disagree and he didn't argue with Mother, even though he was a trial lawyer. *Was this a script for my punishment or how my mother really felt*, I wondered.

A few nights later, my father and sister were in the small room adjacent to the living room, which was our foyer and dining room. My father had his overcoat on. It was after dinner on a school night, already starting to get dark outside. My sister had her green mid-weight coat on. My father wore his fedora hat, which he also wore to his office in downtown Manhattan. Lovingly, as if she would never see her again, Mother straightened Marlene's collar. She was fifteen; I was twelve. My father and Marlene left and I didn't know where they had gone. My father never went out alone with my sister because Marlene belonged to my mother, not him. I belonged to him, not my mother. Yet I was left behind with my mother. Where was he taking Marlene? Why didn't I go? Was it a doctor's appointment? Was something wrong that they hadn't told me about? Mother didn't answer. They closed the heavy front door to our apartment. Mother did not double lock the door.

"They'll be back soon," Mother said nonchalantly and returned to the kitchen to finish washing the dishes. I went back to my bedroom, sat at my desk and finished my math homework.

It was soothing to do math problems and have everything turn out right. An unknown that had an answer that was either right or wrong. It was an alternate world to the unclear one I lived in. Maybe they were buying my sister something big but not me. Maybe it was so heavy that my father had to carry it. A secret. When my sister returned from this outing, she wouldn't say anything. She just hung up her coat and got ready for bed.

The next night, a Thursday, when he came home from work, Father flung the folded newspaper on the dining room table in the foyer. Mother hated when he didn't put it on the small side table but he never did. He liked to aggravate her. He sniffed deeply the dinner smells. Mother cooked meat for him. He went into the kitchen to find her.

I studied Norman Rockwell's drawings on the cover of the *Saturday Evening Post* but didn't usually read the newspaper. But this night, something led me to the folded over local paper on the dining room table. I opened it slowly. On the front page, in the right hand column, was a headline: "Polio vaccine given out at Public School number three from 5 to 8 P.M. yesterday." A photo of lines of children with their parents, both parents, was underneath. I looked at the photograph of many children, many parents. And there was my sister, her green coat a medium black in the picture, Father's Stetson hat a light grey. They stood towards the back of the line, the bigger figures in the photo on the table in Pleasant Hills. The small figures must have gone there before their dinners because they were first in line.

Mother called from the kitchen, "Wash up, get ready for bed." Why did they want Marlene to have an inoculation and not me? I couldn't figure it out but felt silent arrows piercing my skin, first my heart then my brain. I didn't have the word for it yet but it was forming into a feeling of betrayal. Did they want me to die? This part of me had not known of all the times they showed that they would willingly let me die.

One afternoon, I returned from Oldtown Jr. High School and found Mengele sitting on our curved living room sofa, his legs tightly crossed. When I saw his dark, dry hair, I felt as if the floor had disappeared and I was standing on a huge spring. Mother and Mengele seemed like giant bats flying around the apartment, bumping into each other. I pictured all the stars as dull black and me in the middle of their evil universe. I wanted to run away but my legs had stiffened and there was nowhere to disappear to. He was smoking his brown filtered cigarette, sipping ginger ale that Mother had brought him in her good tall glass with hand painted flowers on it. In the living room, my parents called Mengele Uncle Charlie.

"Hello again, Wendy," he said. His face folded in. His beady eyes seemed to dance with death. His large black shoes glowed with shine. I wondered whether he had slave-children shine them. His overcoat was open and his dark suit didn't have a single visible wrinkle. His skin still smelled of burnt and decaying bodies. His legs were stiff as if in a perpetual Nazi stance. His fingers were delicate like a woman's, though he used his nails to bite into people's flesh.

"I hear you're a big girl now, bleeding," he said. I glared at my mother. I never knew how my body would react, and I peed through my clothes in the foyer. Barely surprised, Mother told me to change my clothes and began scrubbing the grey carpet as Mengele kept talking to her and as I eavesdropped with my heart galloping around in circles. "I just want to borrow her for a few days," he said.

"I'll have to ask Morris about it," Mother answered.

"Let me have this child on the operating table while you think it over," he said. "I'll make it worth your while. I can start the experiment right here in your own building. No transportation necessary."

I felt there was something so wrong and bad about me that my parents would hand me over. When these feelings reached a peak and I could take it no longer, I splintered into hundreds of pieces and floated above myself, shivering and ashamed. I had so much anger that some made its way out of the pieces of me and into the air in front of me. My body became a Swiss cheese with deep holes sprouting rage. I said to my mother, "Why don't you send Marlene?"

"No, not Marlene. Your father will decide," Mother answered.

"She's just the kind of subject we want—someone who fights back," Mengele said. "She's got spunk." The air became sick with gaseous poisons.

My father must have given permission. We were underneath the apartment building in the second lower level, where the medical surgery took place. His surgery room with an operating table and IV drip was a square room off one of the tunnels. "Lie down on the table," he ordered. He had a tape measure and took measurements of my vertebrae, and the width of my thighs, forearms, wrists, ankles, toes.

For the experiments with polio, Mengele wanted to be called Dr. Menkel or Merk. He called this sub-basement room his "laboratory." He attached the IV drip into the vein in my right arm and said he was dripping the polio virus into it. He continued measuring me as the container of virus emptied. I filled with dread and fear and my body shook violently. *This was death*, I thought. I waited for death. When the container emptied, he unhooked me and it was over. My Aunt Gertrude and another person came into the "laboratory."

They dressed me, then pushed me up the shaft-like tube that ended up in one of the basement rooms on the ground floor, off the hallway. She knocked on our front door in code, one, three, two knocks. My father opened the door. Mother stood behind him. Their faces were emotionless masks, not a snicker or sneer.

"Don't let her eat or drink anything for forty-eight hours. He wants the virus to settle in," Aunt Gertrude said. *So my parents knew what Mengele was doing to me*, I thought. *Of course, they sold me to him*. I felt too weak and spent to think about killing them at that moment. Half of my top lip curled.

158

"She'll need something to drink sooner than that," my father said. "This isn't a concentration camp." *It's worse than that*, I thought, *because my own parents did this to me.*

"I'm just repeating what he said," Aunt Gertrude said and walked away in a huff. It seemed that Aunt Gertrude had become Mengele's assistant.

I didn't know whether they pretended to give me polio or whether the virus was real. I still don't know. I felt as if I had the flu with more severe pain than usual. I did have polio around these years, and my back and legs changed shape. I was most unhappy because I loved to run and dance and walk to Queens Boulevard to buy a loaf of rye bread. I ate half of it as I walked home. I didn't want to be a cripple. I preferred to be dead. And I preferred to kill them before I died. Until I started my recovery, I hadn't remembered about the polio though I knew about the curvature in my upper back, my skinny legs, and extreme sensitivity to physical pain, heat and cold.

In the middle of the night, my father brought me water. "I don't care what he says," my father said. I gulped the water.

Sometime later, after the inoculation period, Mengele reappeared in our apartment.

"We have to do a second round. I need more advanced equipment," he said. "I need to take her to the main offices."

"When will you bring her back?" my father asked.

"Tomorrow," Mengele answered.

"Take good care of her," my father said. I added my father to my list of people I would kill. My mother stayed in her bedroom. Marlene was not home. At that moment, my hatred rose stronger than my fear. I didn't feel anger. I became anger. My rage, like a locomotive, swept through my life. I enjoyed the fantasy of killing people. I vomited in the foyer, outside hall, and Mengele's limousine. I had to control my anxiety and depression or I would be ruined and they would win. My depression made me passive and hopelessly heavy. I figured out that if I could think of something pleasurable to look forward to every day, I could survive. A piece of chocolate, the smell of a flower, the breeze on my skin—all these could keep me alive. Montauk Point was always flooded with children. Maybe I would see someone I knew. That anticipation kept the octopus of depression off me, which allowed me to keep fighting. But the injections Mengele constantly gave me in my upper right arm blunted my ability.

I had to leave myself Hansel and Gretel breadcrumbs to get back to my mind and retrieve myself. I knew Mengele would starve me but when he had finished, I would eat again. That would be a pleasure. I would drink water. When I returned home, Mother would squeeze oranges. And she would cook Wheatina in the morning and make it lumpy, the way I liked it. My lips would be chapped and it would feel good to put Vaseline on them.

At Montauk Point, I became a demonstration model as Mengele lectured to a medium-sized audience of handlers, scientists, and specialists. He pointed to a diagram of the human body on a stand, while vials of his poison dripped into me as he kept me on stage in a hospital bed and sometimes a wheelchair.

"She's a good subject for polio," he taught. He pointed to a large screen filled with illustrations of body parts. In front of everyone, Mengele injected the top side of a tendon below my knee and fastened an IV drip on my arm. I don't know whether fake chemicals came out of the IV both times, or whether one was real, or perhaps both.

I returned from Montauk Point with braces on my legs. I felt determined not to be a cripple but hadn't realized what a huge disease I fought. I lay on my back and made cycling motions with my legs. The second my legs got tired, I stopped and slept. Then I started again. I did this all day and night despite the pain like swords going through me. I dragged myself to the toilet. Eventually, I got rid of the braces and walked.

Months passed, and I returned to school. I had no strength and could hardly lift my arms. The pain felt like a cluster of nails being hammered into my vertebrae. Every time I took a step, the ground fell away. I couldn't stop crying. I couldn't remember my name. I didn't know my address. Mengele sent his Nazi-trained assistants to re-assess me.

"She's frail," two of them decided.

Mengele telegraphed, "Close her down."

"You will remember nothing that we have put in this vault. You will never approach this vault. If you ever touch the door to this vault, you will be electrocuted. You will tell no one of this vault. You will speak to no one of your life. You have never heard of Mengele, Dr. Black, Dr. Schwartz, Dr. Green, Merkel, Merk, or Uncle Charlie. If you remember anything about your treatment under Dr. Mengele, you will explode on the spot."

Using drugs and electroshock, they sealed this storage unit. The inside girls Mengele worked on remained in the subterranean tunnels within these vaults. They stayed in the middle of a chronic nervous breakdown until I found and rescued them.

Ordinary life, 1956

When I was home from the brothel, and before I was sent to the monastery, I remembered nothing about my real life. I attended regular school and thought that the reason I didn't know anything was because of my stupidity and limitations. I looked for ways to win Mother's love. We were in Manhattan and she admired a gold bar brooch in a jeweler's window on West 47th Street. Later that week, when I was alone in the apartment after school, I made my way to Enterprise Avenue and took the subway downtown, bought the brooch for eight dollars, and gave it to her. My mother most likely did not remember that the child she had left at a brothel and sold to Mengele and whom she was about to send away again, that that child spent her life savings trying to please her. Mother wore the brooch often on her crisp white blouses.

In my parents' ordinary life, they loved avocados and hated to see anything go to waste, not thrive, or die. They bought a thin book on how to grow avocadoes from pits, and learned to place an avocado pit held up by three spaced toothpicks in a jar with water. When the pits sprouted roots, my father transplanted them into a clay pot with dirt, and my mother inspected the textured, bright leaves regularly. They delighted in the growth, and every sunny windowsill had these plants in various stages of development. But I went to waste, my life.

Note

1. The Passport Office struggled to cope because so many people were arriving for the ceremony:

   New York Times (1955). Passport Office strained by credit travel rush. June 11, p. 2.

   New York Times (1955). Travel boom overtaxes U.S. passport facilities. July 11, p. 25.

   New York Times (1982). The mighty dollar, the wilting traveler. June 16, p. 3.

   New York Times (1982). Passports are being delayed by a backlog of applications. June 20, p. 42.

   New York Times (1982). Passport crunch. September 12, p. 4.

EIGHT

The monastery

The Mafia got its grip on children with the sole purpose of making money. Its leaders were not interested in the spiritual dimension of depravity. But the Illuminati group imposed on the same children its archaic, twisted religious beliefs about extending the rule of their deity, Lucifer. One aspect of these beliefs was that there was a royal bloodline that would birth their rulers. A prophecy had told the Illuminati leaders that my second-born Illuminati child was supposed to rule over our county.

Mother of the heir, 1956

For these Illuminati pregnancies, I had to take up residence away from home. Before I was sent away, I had mind-control sessions to persuade me that I was going to la Madeleine church in Paris, that I was being honored, and that I owed it to Lucifer to obey. They programmed me to believe that I was flying Air France, but instead of driving to the airport, my father switched me to another personality and drove me to a church or monastery in a middle-class section of New York. That's where I would live, with Father Anthony, who dressed like a Vatican priest, and the Brothers. Not until I put this memory together did I realize I had never left New York.

My father parked his car and walked me to the front entrance. I carried my own suitcase. An expensive, engraved sign by the arched wooden door read "La Maison aux Jeunes Filles Perdus". I was thirteen years old and had already learned some French in Junior High School. My handlers hadn't thought to program me not to learn in a foreign language, and I absorbed its grammar quickly. My brain experienced unimpeded learning. It felt like cold, salty ocean air. At the church's front door, I immediately spotted the mistake in noun agreement, that "perdus" was missing the "e" and should have been spelled "perdues". The sign meant "lost young girls" and the "e" was needed for feminine agreement. I thought this clumsy mistake should not have happened in France.

Brother Gregory answered the door. He wore a long brown cloak with braided cords and decorations around his neck, appeared chubby and had a forbidding, musty smell to him. A West Highland terrier rushed down the steps and flew to the door. Pow Wow sniffed my feet and never left my side for the rest of his life, except for the times when they sent me home. I would not have survived without this spunky dog.

One of the robed brothers walked me past the entrance to the large kitchen, up the side stairway and to my attic room. My father did not follow, but Pow Wow did. My father did not say goodbye and I didn't say goodbye to him; I just followed the pretend-friar in the robe. My sterile room had a cot with a white enamel head and footboard, a wooden dresser, sink, closet, table, and chair. Its windows were barred. Pow Wow jumped on the bed, and I was able to take in a bit of air and even exhale partway. The furnishings were minimal but much less grim than in the brothel rooms. Father Anthony brought in a bowl of water for Pow Wow, which I thought was a kind gesture. He must have figured out that Pow Wow had become attached to me. All the friars seemed fond of quirky Pow Wow. I sat on the bed relieved not to see pamphlets scattered on the floors and the sharp mumbling of auctions as background noise. It appeared quiet and clean, but I held my head in my hands.

Later that night, a man and a woman entered and told me to undress. Before I left home, Mother had scrubbed me like a bathroom and had given me starched and ironed clothes to wear. I laid my clothes neatly on the cot. Mother yelled if I ever left my clothes crumpled and scattered.

"She's too thin," the woman said. She was solid, stocky with dyed blond hair pulled back in a bun. She looked like an actor playing the part of a villain in a movie. I had noticed that overweight women always hated my skinniness. The thin, white-haired man with a puffy face and eyes wore a hospital coat. "It doesn't matter," he said. Apparently he was a doctor. "We'll inseminate her tomorrow." He poked around my naked body. The woman, whose name was Bertha, came back with a bowl of rice pudding with raisins and a blob of whipped cream on top. I put on my pajamas, bedroom slippers, and bathrobe, sat on the hard chair by the table, ate the bowl of rice pudding and fell right into a heavy sleep—they must have put drugs in it. A round clock on top of the dresser said it was about ten minutes after five in the morning when the team woke me up and examined my body again. "She has shingles," the doctor said. He went away and came back with pills. He said he had never seen shingles on someone so young, and he couldn't impregnate me until the shingles had run its course, which took about ten days. He said the delay would not affect their schedule. I had no idea what schedule they were on. They discussed whether to send me home or keep me at the monastery. I wanted to go home despite loyal Pow Wow at my feet. They decided to keep me there. I remained a prisoner in this room for ten days with nothing to do, and the burn and sting of shingles around my waist. I missed my mother and sister, even though I had no mother or sister.

Bertha used the time to give me mind-control sessions. "You are at the Madeleine church in Paris, France. You are a queen;

everyone loves you. You are special and important. Your babies will rule the world. You will rule the world through witchcraft," she said as she showed me pictures of Paris, the parks around the church, my room in the church, and Pow Wow. I only went out when she took me with her to test the new mind control. I had to believe I spoke French and ate French food. She took me to the deli, and I had a salami sandwich with mustard and chips with ketchup.

"You are eating a crêpe and croissant," she said. "Whenever you hear English, you will think you are hearing French." When I had a bagel, I had to think brioche. The neighborhood seemed somewhat clean and family-oriented, but not stylish like Paris.

Too soon, the doctor said I could be impregnated. My body didn't explode from anguish as it had when the shingles appeared. First I fasted for three days and was only allowed to drink water. A technician shaved my whole body—scalp, eyebrows, arms, legs, pubic area. I can still hear the sound of the electric razor. In the basement tunnel, they started the preparation rituals, calling on Satan, demons, and in particular Lucifer to open my young womb. Cult artists drew black and red ink occult designs over my naked hairless body—lots of swirls and spirals, upside-down crosses, broken Swastikas—then poured blood, semen, and urine over me, while the chorus chanted prayers and invocations, and incense burned constantly. I felt nauseated, and doubly naked without hair. Black candles flickered. The popular 1968 movie *Rosemary's Baby* captures a bit of the atmosphere of ritual preparations, drugs, devil worship, cannibalism, sacrifices, double binds, and enforced pregnancies, as well as co-opted outsiders.

The church's basement held operating rooms. The doctor used my assigned cult husband's sperm that they had flown in from Israel. He started the artificial insemination, and the Brothers punctured tiny holes around my vagina. "We are conducting spirits into your womb that will accompany and

166

influence the fetus," they said. They claimed test tubes contained my ancestors' spirits and showed me a whole wall of them. The Brothers believed wholeheartedly in the demon and spirit world.

"Tilt the foot of the bed upward. Raise her legs. The sperm has to stay in."

"Keep stimulating her. We need her womb to pulsate."

"Now lower her legs. Let her rest."

"She's cramping. Give her an injection." They gave me morphine.

The workers wore masks, like oxygen masks, while they operated on me. "Clean her up. Put her to bed. Keep her in bed for two weeks. All meals in bed. She can get up to go the bathroom. Every few days, she can walk around the balcony. No bending or lifting. Clean up the dog shit. It creates germs." The last part reminded me of my mother and grandmother, caring about a speck of dust when the whole picture was filthy. My grandmother only let us have machine-made ice cream cones that "no human hands had touched" because she was afraid of our catching germs from strangers.

Puppy mill bitches are made to breed over and over until either they can no longer produce good litters or they die. The doctor took his gloves and hospital coat off, picked up his black bag and left. They determined I was pregnant through urine and saliva tests, and when it grew back, smelling my scalp and pubic hair.

After a few weeks, the Brothers in gray or brown hooded robes let me go downstairs to the kitchen, where I met Rosalita, the Italian cook. She was a pleasant, almost wholesome-looking woman in her forties who liked to mother people and had been an outsider. She always wore her apron, was buxom and comforting. Her smile filled her whole face. Her hands were soft and warm. She stroked my head and rubbed my belly. My young skin was tight and hurt. Rosalita had taken this job because she needed money. She was one of the immigrants they employed and made dependent on them. She would not have known of all the criminal activities going on, but she would have sensed them. Once the Brothers get you in their grip, it's almost impossible to get out even if you weren't born into it. If someone like Rosalita ever talked, the Brothers would have killed her or had her deported.

The Brothers insisted I only eat human flesh. My body screamed for raw fruits and vegetables, and the more human flesh they forced me to consume, the more I wanted to eat raw natural crops. I told Rosalita about my food cravings. When the Brothers weren't watching or at night, she snuck me large tossed salads like my mother made. She made the dressing with balsamic vinegar, olive oil, and mustard; my mother used peanut oil and lemon juice.

As I began to hang out in the kitchen, I became less lonely. I sat at her kitchen table for hours with soothing Pow Wow at my feet. During the day, she snuck me leaves of lettuce and chunks of apple. There was no kindness in the suburban monastery, except for Rosalita in the kitchen. She risked her life to bring me salads. My days were spent finding a way to eat real food, hanging out with Rosalita, making voodoo dolls, practicing the witchcraft my mentor Joseph, who was an advanced wizard, taught me, and soaking up Pow Wow's steadfast love. I could also reverse the witchcraft into white witchcraft and do good, when they weren't watching me and reading my mind. These were years when my non-cult contemporaries learned more advanced math, science, history of civilization, geography, literature. I learned only witchcraft. I had no tutor for academic subjects or even books.

The map room

The leaders decided to use my craving for fruits and vegetables to coerce me to do more psychic work. They started to withhold all food. They put spiders on my naked body. All I could think of was how to stop it. "Just kill me. Let me die. No one could live with this," I said to them.

"Just go through the door," Joseph said. "Go through the door into the map room. Into the nice map room. The Council is waiting for you there. Oranges, clean clothes, salads that Rosalita prepared herself—better than your mother makes. All you have to do is go into the map room and give us your intelligence." The Council, what Joseph called "the leaders of your division," were disguised men wearing robes, plus one woman. They wanted me to discern with my hands where they should strike.

The map room was ice blue and located on the top part of the monastery's tower. It had ornate wood panels, globes of the world, and world maps on the walls. Each session started with torture, putting needles in my gums as I lay on a leather couch and then spinning me in a leather desk chair. The spinning left me feeling as if I had a concussion.

"You will sit here and with your considerable sensitivities, you will tell us which parts of the world are most prone to accept Lucifer as their master." The woman spoke English with an accent, but I couldn't tell which one. "Put out your hands over this map and tell us where we are succeeding and where we should go." The men in ice blue robes nodded. I couldn't see their faces. I was required to put my hands over the globe without touching it, and I had to feel where the most spiritual energy came out, and tell them. They had divided the globe and flat maps into the thirteen satanic counties. One county might be huge; others such as Haiti were tiny. The population of a large county was not attuned to the spirit world, whereas people in the tiny counties were more spiritually alive. In terms of spiritual acumen, it would take thousands of Americans and Europeans to equal one individual from the Virgin Islands. The Philippines had two counties. They wanted to know the thirteen worldwide hot spots, which could be cities or whole countries. These spots were always

169

in flux, so they tested them over and over. Going to the map room was a monthly task.

Illuminati babies

These cults operate by destroying what is natural and whole. They want children whose minds they can shatter. A necessary condition of shattering a mind is creating an unbonded and unattached infant. They wanted an unbonded newborn from me but not one addicted to drugs or with brain damage.

Their plan was to shock the fetus through my skin and torture me at the same time, to ensure that I didn't stay emotionally and spiritually connected to the fetus. They put my feet in ice cubes. The medical assistants felt for the fetus' head and avoided it. During the shock, Philomena, who was me, had to go away, leaving the baby. I would not go away. With prenatal electric torture, if the mother stays connected, the mother–child bond is still intact despite the torture. They could not tell whether I left my baby or stayed connected. These were the moments of fighting them with everything in me.

"If these babies are born wrong, we will kill them in front of you." I was spun in a chair, and a vise squeezed my head. *Did I want a baby who would have the same life as mine or worse, or did I want a baby who did not belong to the cult?* They upped the electricity. If my children were born bonded and thereby deemed unprogrammable, they could be given a different role, adopted out, or killed. I could feel the babies growing inside me, kicking and being real. With them, I felt I would never again be alone and I could take care of them and give them the love I learned about from Daniel. If I didn't know what to do, he would come to me and teach me. I would fight to protect them. All the electricity in the world could not keep me from my children. Queen Philomena, this pregnant part of me, did not know of the babies we had already lost.

170

Melissa

One of the first memories I had when I started this trek into re-associating my tormented life came in a dream. In this dream, my one living child took my hand and led me over the hills to a grassy field. I thought the field was in Israel because of the programming, but it must have been in this suburb. There I saw a baby girl in a cradle surrounded by a circle of hooded chanting figures in charcoal gray robes. While I still lived in New York in the 1980s, this dream drew me to remember my four Illuminati infants. The first one, Melissa, looked like Eli, my cult husband. She was delicate, self-contained, and intense. Her soul shone through all her pores. After that breakthrough dream, I stayed shocked for a long time.

When my baby was born, the programmers still could not tell whether I had left the prenatal child emotionally during the electroshock torture. About a week after delivery, they tested the infant. They pricked the baby's left foot to cause pain, then tried to comfort the infant. If the baby accepted comforting, it was bonded. If its body stiffened and turned away in rage, it was unbonded. My Illuminati babies accepted comforting.

It was the first time the parts of me had someone to love since Daniel's death. I trusted the babies, they were all my insiders had, all I would ever have. And the babies trusted me. I didn't leave them for a second, not in the womb or outside. We were good mothers and loved our babies the way Daniel had loved us. We would gladly die for them. We put them on our heart. Their body weight pressed some of our pain away.

All but the third of my Illuminati babies were conceived through artificial insemination, and the first two were born on December 24th in consecutive years. A white-haired, thin man with a puffy face and eyes, in a hospital coat, performed the artificial insemination for each Illuminati pregnancy. His face looked as if he were drowning. They had me copulate during rituals but first they impregnated me with what they said was my cult husband's sperm. I was induced each time and given no painkillers during the labor. My cult husband was usually present for the birth rituals and was kind during the deliveries. He held my hands and head during the hard labors. An adult man was sacrificed during each ritual in which a child was delivered. They wrapped each newborn in the liver from the sacrificed thirty-three-year-old victim and paraded the child around to show to each member of the coven.

My firstborn was delivered on December 24, 1956. The ritual for Melissa's birth took place outdoors, probably in the enclosed back yard of the Holy Brotherhood of Priests. I had been so drugged, I didn't know where I was. The friars passed her around one to the other and put drops in her eyes during this consecration. They wore gray robes with yellow sashes. I wore a white robe with a pale blue sash. Afterward, they told me she had died and implied it was from the drops they administered because she was bonded, because I disobeyed. I never saw her again. It's possible that she was sent somewhere. It's possible that she is alive somewhere. They bound my screaming breasts after they took her away.

The Brothers sent me home for three months, and I attended school, but felt distant from the other students. While I was away, I missed energetic Pow Wow and compassionate Rosalita. At home I was not close to anyone. People walked past me as if I didn't exist. Outside, neighborhood passersby averted their gaze. Perhaps they knew.

Baby Daniel, the heir

My father took me out of morning math class at Oldtown Junior High School just before lunch. I hadn't expected him. My mother had a lunch ready for me, a tuna fish sandwich on wholewheat bread, carrot and celery sticks, a glass of milk made from Walker Gordon non-homogenized milk, and two Mallomars.

I changed out of my plaid skirt and put on slacks, a shirt, and a jacket. The doorbell rang. My father answered the door. Two men in overcoats entered, one carrying a black satchel. They took me under the arms, sat me in a dining room chair in the foyer. They filled a needle and plunged it into my right arm under my rolled-up sleeve. The gray walls spun. The ceiling hit the floor and the floor floated out the window and over the waterfall. Everything grew dark as my parents seemed to rise along the walls.

I didn't know how much time passed but I woke up, fell back to sleep, woke up, fell asleep. I felt bumped and jostled. My elbows hit wood. I felt a helmet on my head and noticed myself wrapped in a blanket with my knees up to my chest. It comforted me to hold my body so tight. I realized then that a box or a crate contained me and that I seemed to be in an airplane. The drugs wore off too soon. I shouldn't have been up. I overheard something about landing in a foreign language. No, I knew the language, French. They were shipping me back to France. I wondered whether my parents were happy that I was gone and whether my sister would miss me. My parents must have been happy because they let the men in. I must have fallen back to sleep, but my head banged as I landed. The men held me under the arms again because it was difficult walking after being cramped in a box.

I was in a limousine surrounded by large men, who gave me more pills to swallow. We were in Paris. I recognized the elegance of the streets and wildness of the traffic. The car pulled up to la Madeleine church. Looking back now, I am not sure whether they did virtual reality programming or only hypnotized me to believe it was Paris. They must have had crates in a warehouse and an apparatus to simulate a bumpy ride.

Joseph Jacobson, my familiar trainer, and Rosalita escorted me into the kitchen, and Joseph sent the two thugs away, *allez-vous-en*. I buried my head in Rosalita's bosom and shivered. I smelled the food on her apron but was grateful for the comfort.

She appeared happy to see me. Joseph gave me hot chocolate and croissants but I felt too blurry and nauseated to eat. I asked for an orange. Rosalita gave me a cold orange and kissed me. We heard scratching at the door to the basement. Joseph asked if I wanted to see my dog. Pow Wow raced to me, jumped on my lap, and licked my face. I cried and Pow Wow licked the tears from my cheeks. Until this moment, my heart had been a cold stone buried in a coal mine.

Rosalita led me to the small room upstairs. The bed had, as usual, very starched sheets that scratched. My elbows had blood on them. I slept a long time, a drugged sleep. I didn't yet know how long I would be there and still wanted to go home. Pow Wow jumped on the bed and slept by my side, molding his small body to my thigh, then hip and torso as he inched nearer my head. My arms remained crossed over my heart, in the same position as in the crate. I slept more.

As an adult remembering nothing of my past, whenever I passed a Westie on the street, a sense of love and joy exploded in me. Until now I didn't consciously understand why I was so drawn to this breed. *Perhaps it's the big round eyes,* I thought.

As soon as I was pregnant, I returned to normal school until I began to show. I couldn't concentrate in school or listen to the teachers. My mind was preoccupied with how to survive and keep my children alive. And all my induced learning disabilities remained active.

Much of this Illuminati group's imagery is a warped takeoff from Judaism and Christianity. For example, their targeting the second-born child to be the heir of the "kingdom" may be a reference to the Esau–Jacob story. The religious divisions of the cults believe in demons, spirits, prophecies, and worshipful rituals. But their god is Lucifer and/or Satan. Some religious groups worship one or the other. The group I was born into may have been the umbrella for the various occult religions, since this group worshipped both deities at different times or simultaneously.

My second Illuminati child was born on December 24, 1957. He liked to cuddle. I held him constantly. He slept on my heart, and affectionate Pow Wow was always stretched out by my side. These were excellent days for me. Daniel had dark shiny hair, not curly like the original Daniel, my friend. This infant had the prophecy on his head. The prophecy declared that the second-born Illuminati baby would grow to rule this part of the satanic kingdom. I didn't want that for him.

During the labor pains and delivery, my wrists were tied with rags to the headboard. Father Anthony stayed in the room, and one monk was on one side of the bed and three monks on the other side. No drugs were used. They didn't believe in painkillers. A monk said "Here it comes," and the baby and then placenta appeared. A monk held my baby upside down, and hit his backside. "It's a boy," Father Anthony shouted. One of the monks untied my wrists and another placed Daniel on my chest. We lived happily like that for eight days.

Daniel was the age when babies are circumcised. His consecration to Lucifer took place on a balcony inside this church. The Brothers wore white robes with red embroidery and cords and a black sash. I wore a white robe with red embroidery and a yellow sash. This was considered such an exalted ritual that they wanted some of the bloodline there. My parents wore black robes. The Brothers passed Daniel around. I didn't want them to touch him. The Brothers looked at him adoringly and patted him gently. They acted like new mothers. Some kissed his forehead and chanted softly under their breath. With their fingers they put an ash-like mark on Daniel's forehead, and little crosses all over him. Incense burned. They passed him around from person to person and chanted "Consecrated into our Brotherhood ..."

I didn't want my parents near him and felt as tense as a snapped twig. My father handed him to my mother clumsily. He had forgotten to support the head. My mother held Daniel well; her eyes became wild and she said, "This baby should be

Marlene's, not hers." My mother held the baby more tightly and suddenly threw him over the railing. A long way down. He splattered all over. His beautiful head separated and kept rolling away. All the mothers in me rushed together, all the bereft mothers, including the ones who had given birth to the babies in the brothel, whom the Illuminati mothers didn't yet know about. Even the mothers who had had their eggs scraped out ran there in that second. All those mothers gathered and flung themselves over trying to reach their Daniel. We threw ourselves over the railing of the balcony. It happened in less than the opening and closing of an eye. My head was aimed towards my Daniel, but then my body wasn't going forward but backwards. The priests grabbed my legs before I plunged all the way and drew me back up by my ankles. Milk drenched my white embroidered robe as if to nurse the dead. I ran down the side wooden steps and threw myself on top of the pieces of Daniel, his bones, blood, organs, tissue. I rubbed it all on me, smeared his blood and guts all over my face as if my skin could bring him back to life. An eyeball rolled to the side. I put it in my mouth and would not spit it out. I grabbed and held onto one of his leg bones, the femur. The pitch of my cry could have shattered the stained glass windows of Jesus healing children. That was the end of the scene for me but in the balcony, I heard rumblings and my mother screaming, "This baby belongs to Marlene!" as they took her forcibly away. My father at some point pontificated, "This baby was not allowed to be killed. We'll have to go before the Council. There will be trouble."

I hadn't wanted my children to live. I didn't want them to have a worse life than mine.

The priests who had caught my ankles pulled me away into the kitchen. Rosalita cleaned me up and I never saw the baby Daniel again. The Brothers had to tranquilize me.

Suppose you are in your car going to work and the car's upholstered seats start unraveling, and the frame crumbles, its motor self-chops into little pieces, its steering wheel cracks, and all its windows shatter as its gas spills onto the road. That's what rage that eats the insides of one's body feels like. They coerced me into doing voodoo curses on the vulnerable countries and had prayer teams of false priests chanting for Lucifer to sweep the nations. I didn't care about Korea or Ethiopia or the United States, the country that abandoned me, or even unfeeling suburban residents who strolled through the park without concern. I hated my parents and Joseph, and spent my adolescence planning or trying to kill them.

When I came to after being tranquilized, the Brothers were still in a tizzy. They had all changed out of their ritual garb and into their brown everyday robes. In the two years I was at the monastery, this was the most commotion I heard among the monks. They went from one private meeting to another. I overheard hushed debates about whether to execute or sacrifice Mother, but they worried that since I was missing for six months or longer at a time, it might raise suspicions about the family if she disappeared or died.

They had injected me in my own bedroom, where they kept me prisoner. When I came to, Rosalita brought me freshly squeezed orange juice, warm buttermilk biscuits she had just baked, and *café au lait*. They still pretended I was in Paris. When I sat up, I felt something hard under the mattress. Someone had put Daniel's femur there. It must have been one of the friars or maids. I still possessed complete memory of the night before. I placed his short, thin bone on my left hip under my underpants, got dressed and put on my coat, and went into the enclosed garden to a spot hidden from view. It became black like evil outside. The earth was cold and hard and I began scratching at it with my nails. I scratched for hours and my fingers bled into the grave and mixed with my tears and breast milk. The friars must have been watching me from a side window, but they left me alone. I kept scratching, bleeding, leaking, and drooling. Then I began humming. Sanity rode its sleigh slowly and kindly back into my fragmented, tortured mind. Halfway down, I found a rock and used it as a tool for digging. When the hole was deep enough, I slipped his bone in vertically and filled the grave with winter dirt. I did not place a marker but memorized where Daniel's bone lay. With the first light, I went back to my room. Later, I heard Christmas carols sung throughout the monastery. They invited the neighborhood to an open house that day. Rosalita had to bake cookies and make punch and eggnog. I cried in my room. Rosalita came in, washed and bandaged my hands, and bound my leaking breasts. I did not leave my room for two weeks. I sat in a chair crying, rocking, grieving, meditating on murder. Rosalita sometimes cried with me, which helped.

There were many discussions after Daniel's death. Joseph thought about sending me home for a while. The international leaders, who were involved in solving the problem of Daniel's having been killed, gave detailed instructions to my handlers about how to close me down. Until the close down, I remembered everything about those last days.

I have recurrent dreams of walking on a narrow path on a cliff that spirals up a mountain. If I lose my concentration for even a moment, I will fall off and plunge down the mountain. I think this is a dream of my fighting for sanity.

It felt like my heart poured out of my body but my heart had become coals, tar, and dust.

In 1968, I visited my mother in New York City when Ned was one and a half years old. Ned is my ordinary-life child, a cult baby but not fathered by one of their higher ups. Todd, my ordinary-life husband, had coerced me into conceiving so that he could avoid the Vietnam draft. I didn't have the electroshock torture during this pregnancy. During the visit, Mother took baby Ned to the open window in her bedroom, and both Todd and I feared she would throw him out. Todd didn't know the history unless he had my black book, and I was not conscious of my life at that time.

The leaders decided to hide the fact that their heir had been killed and wanted me pregnant again fast. They decided against getting a substitute baby and pretending that baby was mine, because they were quasi-purists and believed in prophecies. But they didn't order more of Eli's sperm because they didn't want the international community to know of the murder of the heir. So they let the Brothers impregnate me live. The Brothers lined up outside my door dutifully and reluctantly. Some of them were not able, but I became pregnant and delivered the infant privately, not in a ritual. Because she was deformed, they gave her away.

Then they sacrificed my last Illuminati baby, a boy, whom I named Matthew. The eighth day after his birth, the altar was prepared for Matthew's consecration. I sat at the round table in the kitchen with Rosalita. Joseph took happy Matthew into a side room and tested him. He returned and said something like, "*Il n'est pas programable.*" The ritual began with the chanting, prayers to Lucifer, incense. Only several priests were present. My parents hadn't been invited. Joseph lifted his left arm that held the sacrificial knife. I lifted mine and aimed my knife at Joseph's heart. He caught my arm midway, let go of his knife, and plunged my knife into Matthew who was in the middle of running with his chubby legs in the air while lying on his back. He plunged the knife into Matthew with my hands trapped under his. Matthew looked stunned and confused, and died instantly.

The morning after my fourth Illuminati baby was killed, I felt something hard under my mattress. I felt around and pulled out a bone, thin like Daniel's but about an inch and a half longer. It must have been Matthew's femur. One of the Brothers must have dissected it and brought it to me. That same morning, Rosalita let me keep a breakfast spoon. If the Brothers knew, they could have killed her for just this one thing. After midnight, I crept into the garden and found the memorial spot where I had buried Daniel's bone. This time, I dug with my spoon. I dug all night. I lay his bone parallel to Daniel's. I had made two graves for two brothers. I sat there all night and felt a force from above rock me softly and horizontally, back and forth, side to side. Sometimes this force stroked my spine. Slowly sanity slid back.

The cult world got wind of Daniel's death. Immediately my county plummeted in its standing in the international world. We were considered a county that had lost its power. A smile snuck onto half of my face. The right side of my lip curled and tears came only from one eye during my incessant crying. This half smile is the victory moment of these years.

The sacrifice of Matthew is one of the early memories I had in New York City about twenty-five years ago. In the 1980s, I got a coveted appointment with a therapist in this field, Sandy Flowers, and traveled to Virginia to discuss this memory with her. I didn't know whether it was true. Before I just thought I was a regular somewhat depressed and anxious person trying to get noticed in the big city. Now I was finding out ridiculous horror stories that couldn't be true. Or could they? I was sure they weren't true, but why did they pour out of me with recurrent themes and real emotions that came from a deeper place than my front person had ever known? What did I have to benefit from these memories? There was no benefit, only hardship.

Hatred

While at the monastery before my babies were born, I looked for help. During the day, I managed to take a walk outside. I still thought I was in Paris and tried speaking French to people. *"Voulez-vous m'en aider?"* They didn't respond. Then I noticed the street signs and realized I was in America. I didn't know I was in a suburb, but that didn't matter. I was used to their tricking me and making me think I was somewhere I wasn't, even on a different continent. I called out, "Help, help,

I need help." People looked away and crossed the street. I might as well have been speaking French or Greek. They could tell I was pregnant. In the morning, mothers and children were in the park. I was weak and hadn't eaten for about twelve hours, a long time for me. I should have asked Rosalita for a stash of food. "Somebody please help me with my baby." One of the women called a policeman, who returned me to the church. My hatred of people grew. The Brothers locked me in. I sat in my room rocking myself for a long time, holding my breath, not swallowing. No mother in me knew about the others, but all the babies were present with me. The rage turned to grief and whipped around me as if I had a prehensile tail.

Pow Wow

Valentine's Day brought a ritual. The executioner started skinning Pow Wow alive with a small knife. There was nothing I could do to stop them. They tied me on a wooden chair, and wouldn't let me close my eyes or turn my head. He whimpered and tried to get close to me, leaving bloody paw prints in concentric circles. Finally, he died, ending his merciless agony. It was a terrible end for the most compassionate and loyal of dogs. Shortly afterward, they sent Rosalita away. They lied and said she had committed a crime. I don't know whether they killed or deported her. Either they figured out that she had aided me or they wanted to torment me further. Or perhaps they got wind of a possible investigation. Honest police could have made Rosalita talk. She wasn't a mind-control victim. I lost what sanity I had left. My severe closedown followed.

A current friend who has a hard life but with no cult abuse says she would never write a memoir because she doesn't want to relive her life. If one is dissociated, one has to relive the events in order to get all parts of the brain to recognize one's life and one another. One has the choice of dying in denial or living with excruciating truths. One has to decide whether

181

knowing oneself and the truth about one's life is worth it. If there is a hunger to find oneself and take one's mind back from programmers, if there is a thirst to know one's life no matter how brutal the knowledge, then even a flash of freedom and knowledge is worth it. I have chosen to spend most likely the last decade of my life in this search. Knowing about my life lets me have compassion for myself.

A false memory, 1980

The memory appears early in my attempted recovery when I live in New York City. A nail sticks up out of the wood floor in my apartment near Amsterdam Avenue. I pound it with my hammer; rage pours out and a memory vaguely comes into view. One night after Joseph had killed my babies, he was enclosed in his bath. One part of me stole a hammer from the tool shed, another snuck down the halls and into his bathroom, and others pounded on his head. I hit him once with the full force of my rage. He became unconscious or died after my first strike.

Only rage could have made that force. Once you release rage, it keeps pouring out. Afterward, I feel a peace. It is as if the sea has opened and allowed me to kill. The memory is still hazy. By the time the nail is flush with the wood floor, I remember killing Joseph, but the memory is in pieces. I see a print of the 1793 oil painting "The Death of Marat" by Jacques-Louis David, and the impression of killing Joseph comes more into focus. In the painting, Marat lies in an old-fashioned bathtub much like Joseph's. Someone has assassinated him. He lies as if in a *pietà*, with his arm draped to the side like Michelangelo's "Pietà".

In 2013 I tell Alison about killing Joseph. She is shocked at my lack of remorse, and says my response doesn't match my reaction to my other crimes. When we investigate, it turns out that I don't have remorse because it never happened.

Finally my internal system flashes up the truth about killing Joseph. I see the scene. I was in the monastery cellar; the Brothers projected a slide of David's "The Death of Marat" from their slide projector. Marat, just assassinated, was in the bathtub. His arm hung to one side. The Brothers then projected a slide of Joseph's face, then a white closet door, a hammer, and a knife with a black handle, me walking in my long white nightgown, Joseph apparently dead in the bathtub. In my bedroom, my nightgown with splotches of wet hung on a hanger. "This is what happened. This is what you did. Link the pieces," the Brothers said. They played off my rage and sorrow about my children being murdered.

In my deepest mind, a core belief about myself formed: I believed I had killed him. The Brothers gave me the signposts in the slides. It was classical "false memory" programming, with the purpose here of making me believe I was a natural murderer. It turns out that I couldn't kill. When they started chopping ankles off one of their designated sacrifices or skinning someone alive, then I could, but only to prevent worse and inevitable suffering.

Chronic shock defines those 1980s days of breakthrough memories. I have to digest that I am a prostitute, breeder, murderer, bereaved mother. All that means that I am not a regular girl from Queens, or a regular dancer trying to create in Manhattan, or a regular person in any way. It means I am a freak of society and somehow have to come to grips, get a grip, swallow it. I fight with these memories, but don't even approach in consciousness anything about also being a kidnapper of babies.

Before I remember much, I go to Shakespeare & Company bookstore on Broadway and 81st Street and gravitate to the fiction, poetry, and self-help sections. After memories begin, I find myself looking at the true crime books. In the college I attended, no one reads true crime. It is like watching television and considered gross. But there I sit on the floor in the bookstore, examining these books that have more to do with my life

183

than any of the highbrow books. It is winter because my long black coat flares around me on the floor like a pool of darkness.

Ordinary, middle-class Jewish girl from Queens finds out she is a forced member of a secret, evil cult, that her parents, consciously or not, sell her into slavery. How do I do an about-face and accept who I am? Gradually. I combat shock and exhaustion. I decide somehow to stand by myself, no matter what. All the while, they torture me into submission and program my mind to forget what it recovers. This is truly a dance of one step forward, two backward, hand stands, tight ropes, and somersaults. But in some people, the need to know the truth can carve a path in ancient stone, can become a mountain stream in forbidding land.

Mrs. Twartski, Mengele, and my other programmers had put mind-control programs in me at an early age to perform certain tasks such as prostitute, accomplice, thief, and kidnapper. It was easy for them to call out the personalities who performed these roles, and for me to go into a robotic state, do whatever I was told to do and have no memory of doing it. It's good to know who one is but if one has had a life like mine, remembering can also eat one's bones up. I think one reason the cult leaders contaminate lives to the extent that they do is to encourage the victim/perpetrators they create to choose not to remember. They also up the torture to ludicrous degrees so that outsiders would not believe these stories—the same method the Nazis used. I have heard memoirists say they enjoyed writing their life stories. Writing this memoir is not enjoyable.

The Mafia side of the monastery

Assassinations

These "Brothers" must have been part Illuminati and part Mafia because we had to do many illegal activities, the kind of crimes the Mafia is known for. I had two cult accomplices, or rather I was their accomplice. One was Eli, the cult husband whose sperm fathered three Illuminati babies. The other was the man they would marry me to and who would father my child in regular life. As I approach these memories, the dental pain is severe. Every time I get close to a memory, I feel big needles going all the way down into my gums. The torture was to reinforce no telling, no remembering.

Eli and I were stationed near the church in a bar that had extensive wood paneling and rooms off to the side. I was between thirteen and fifteen years old, and wore very high heels that I could never walk in now, a red dress, and black underwear. I crossed my legs and swiveled from side to side on a bar stool as Eli played the crowd. Eli, four years older than I and a good manipulator, went around getting men interested in having sex with me and paying him in advance. Then he went up to a previously designated man, slapped him on the back and said "You go first." I proceeded into the room on the side of the bar with the targeted first man and once inside, started stripping slowly. Eli secretly entered from the other door. When my dress was at my feet, Eli stabbed the designated target in the back. Eli and I raced out onto the street before anyone knew what had happened. I had trouble running in my shoes, and he didn't wait for me. Separately, we returned to our hideout, the monastery. Another time I was already in the bed placed in the side room of the bar and with the designated victim on top of me, when Eli walked in and stabbed him.

After the men were murdered, we had to report to the police chief in his headquarters. There we received extensive programming not to recognize faces. A lineup of men sat on chairs and wore brown paper bags over their faces. The paper bags had a flap that opened and closed. Someone opened the flap so that we could see the face. A man in a police uniform asked, "Can you remember this face?" We answered, "No." "Is this what the face looks like?" was the next question. If we answered "Yes," we received two shocks of electricity.

When we answered incorrectly, we received none. Eventually, we were too confused about the truth to answer at all. They demonstrated later with white sheets of paper, and graph paper. They repeated this quiz until we recognized no faces and saw only brown paper bags or white sheets or graph paper.

Drugs

The monastery was also a cover for a drug ring. We delivered packages of drugs to a nearby schoolyard. For the drug sales, the cult used my to-be husband in ordinary life, Todd. Todd had grown up in Flatbush, Brooklyn and lived with his parents. He was also generational cult and one year older than me. The dealers put vials of drugs in my socks and in Todd's coat pocket. Somebody waited at a schoolyard for the drug packages. Sometimes Eli was used as well. I had a role even when my pregnancy showed a bit, usually in my fourth month. The male collected the money. When they had a huge shipment of drugs and an order, we took a baby stroller with a blanket covering it. I would pretend to be distracted and leave the stroller for a moment. When I returned, the stroller would be heavy with drug packages placed underneath the baby blanket. We pushed the stroller back to the monastery, where Father Anthony received and unloaded it. After that, I was not involved until the next delivery of drugs. These exchanges were somewhat less dangerous than the assassinations because no one got killed, and the planning was less extensive.

Kidnapping

Father Anthony, or one of the Brothers, showed me out the door. I left the monastery with the blanketed stroller. I wore a loose coat and a big floppy hat, which made me look older. A man was with me, Todd or Eli, occasionally a different Mafia gangster. We walked with this empty stroller. We passed a policeman who was in on the plan. We crossed the street by the school, and continued walking up the path and circling into the pastoral park. The man pretended to be my husband. We reached the water fountain. We passed somebody right near the water fountain—my cue. I said to the pedestrian standing by the fountain, "Could you watch my stroller for a second?" I went to get a drink of water. After I counted fast to ninety while drinking water, I returned to the stroller. When I came back, a baby was visible in my stroller. I proceeded with a heavier stroller, around the park and back the way I came. The male I was with took the stroller into the monastery. Sometimes I heard a baby cry. Father Anthony said to me "Go to your room" as he lifted something out of the stroller. Five times it was a baby. The other times, drugs were in the stroller.

I don't know where they got the babies. Either they stole them from innocent people or the babies were bred to be sacrificed at rituals and the parents were given money.

Knowing about these episodes crushes me the most. It would have been better if we were all killed. I will never know what happened to the babies, whether their parents searched and grieved for them, or what kind of life they were deprived of.

Closedown

Late in my recovery process, I remember this closedown. The awareness starts with body memories, stabbing and aching upper back pain that at first I think the rainy weather causes. I have headaches and a burning under my facial skin that I mistake for sunburn.

I lay stretched out, stomach down, on a stretching rack with my hands and ankles tied. The Brothers stretched me and threw babies and dolls at me. My upper back took the hit and my cheeks burned with shame and humiliation. I vomited as they stretched and spun me because I was already half unconscious and overdosed. They called out my most vulnerable

187

part, Baby Jane, who could tolerate very little. During the worst of this abuse, God or a compassionate force took me away from my body. He held me far away while the Brothers kicked and punched me and it felt good to be with Him or It. I was to believe that I had attended Oldtown Jr. High School and Pleasant Hills High School all these years, and that I was an average student and didn't have a boyfriend and wasn't looking for one. My sister was special and I was ordinary, my sister was beautiful and I was ugly. My parents loved me and I loved them. To make me believe these lies, the brothers tortured me. The methods of torture had been set up in the pathways and in Mengele's towers. The new programmers built on those and added stretching me on a wheel, whipping me as they spun me and peed on me.

When they poured blood over me and told me it was my babies' blood mixed together, some got in my eyes, and I screamed, breaking me out of the trance. They threw me on the spinner, tied my wrists and ankles, and spun me. God or a force of good came to me then and put itself between my spun body and dissociated parts. It said, "My beloved daughter." It felt like a field of wild flowers and I was not alone. Sunlight streamed into the damp dark basement tunnel. But does love keep you alive for a life like this?

As the memories emerge, the parts who hold them feel rage, then exhaustion during the day that turns into heart spasms during the night. Depression and anxiety hook elbows and dance in my brain.

"Now you are ready to go home. Nothing happened here tonight. You will remember nothing."

They expelled me wearing only a loose old coat and no shoes. My father's car waited outside. He got out of the driver's seat and opened the door to the back seat. He told me to put some clothes on in the back seat and he held a blanket over me. The clothes were too tight and the bra didn't fit at all. My mother hadn't realized how seven pregnancies in a row changes a teenager's body. I lay down on the back seat. My body had scratch and whip marks despite the Vaseline. My breasts leaked Matthew's milk.

My father drove to LaGuardia Airport instead of home. I had to go to Air France, walk back, pass a store, and buy a pack of Dentyne gum. The gum signaled to my chopped up, crushed brain that I was back in the States from France. I walked through the airport like a robot. It was before the days of strict airport security. I chewed the gum. My father then drove me back to the family apartment. I remembered the apartment and the hill it was on but nothing else.

I entered. My mother and I nodded to each other. I went to my bedroom. My sister's bed was empty. Her clothes had been removed. My father said she was at college. I was alone with my parents.

Once I returned home, a phase of my life ended. I remained a prisoner in their apartment until they moved to Long Island and I went away to college the following year.

The closedown the Brothers performed was so severe that I remembered nothing from this period of my life until I had a massage from a gifted physical therapist in New York City around 1992. She pressed on a swollen tendon on my left side of my breastbone and out came my fourteen-year-old head resting protectively over a small head. I burst into tears that were sealed away for about thirty-five years. I felt a baby's head nestling into me. He had black straight hair. I could smell him and knew his name was Daniel. I couldn't stop crying. Were it not for this tendon, I may not have ever rejoined in memories my babies born to the Illuminati and the kingdom of evil and shame.

NINE

A palace

I have absorbed emotional and cognitive impressions from the infants in me and am translating them into words. The adults in me are endowing what the infants and children communicate with some perspective. I will try to tell this inconceivable story more or less chronologically.

My handlers designated the thirteenth infant in me, who was really the fourteenth split, to be the queen of the Illuminati and transfer demonic power to world leaders. They used spinning and electroshock to split parts off from this original, pitiful infant. These splits live in rarefied air and are only for certain people to have contact with. Some of this mind control took place in one of the programming rooms in Pleasant Hills. Grandpa Max showed me the color ice blue, but its feeling was black. He put a tiny crown on me, and as I grew older, gave me a globe and a scepter to hold in each hand. The leaders' goal was to maintain the seed of power, and rule a new world, all for the glory of Lucifer.

As soon as I tell Alison these "secrets," I think I will be stricken dead. I am now lying on her black leather sofa, with her black and white dog that offers comfort at exactly the right moments at my curled-in feet. I have a visual of Lucifer extending his black claws. They showed many trick pictures during the programming. "These could be my last words," a child part in me says out loud. Lucifer extends his black claws. I am always stunned by what comes out of my mouth. Alison's dog raises his compassionate head. She replies, "Did you ever see Lucifer?" I say, "They showed me pictures of things like big black claws and dark smoke." She answers, "Just as God doesn't act in the world except through people, neither does Lucifer."

These memories did not slip out like a malted drink from a straw. A feeling would sting deep and hard. A dream would turn into a haunting nightmare. Body memories flicker in and out but are as severe as pain in real time.

My grandfather and uncles drugged, spun, and shocked me. I vomited. Somebody said, "She's going to be a government baby. She's going to get our monarchs to help us." My neck hurts. They had a vise around my head, squeezing it. My grandfather yelled, "You have to get used to a crown." He must have tightened the vise, because as I remember this initiation, my right eye feels like it's popping out. I have other body memories of chills. "We have to get her used to the freezer," and they wiped off all the goo from my body that they use for electroshock and put me naked into a little, old freezer. This second bedroom programming took place regularly.

The drugged monarch, 1943

I was in the back seat of a limousine. My grandfather held me in a white blanket. It was a long drive, and I slept most of the way. He folded the knuckles of his left hand and closely examined his polished fingernails. He had his usual self-satisfied, sticky smile. When we got to our destination, we went underground. Shadows were on curving-above-us walls and gray darknesses. Someone carried me a long way. It was bumpy; I thought the bumps were fun.

Once we arrived, it went quickly. Men took my clothes off even though it was chilly and wrapped me in a black blanket

192

and put a crown and blue cape on me. A man sat tied up in a metal chair that rolled. He was slumped over, asleep, and almost fell on me when they put me on his lap. He felt soggy. Two men held guns to his temples, one on each side, even though he was asleep and didn't know what was happening. A third much older man unzipped the seated man's pants, took out part of his body, and touched it to part of my body. He performed this task very politely as if he were serving lobsters at a dinner. "Long live Lucifer. Long live his kingdom." Other men said words out loud in a language I didn't yet know. Then they gave me back to my grandfather, whom people congratulated. He held me under my chest and thighs and flew me around the room as if I were an airplane, then he held me under my shoulders and legs and flew me again. It wasn't fun. He could have dropped me. Maps of the world hung on the walls I flew by. Everyone applauded and shouted, "Long live Lucifer, long live his queen of the twentieth century." Other men who wore white gloves dressed me, and my grandfather and I exited to applause, as if we were on a stage in a theater. We passed long lines of grownups; many had children with them, who were waiting to be blessed by the Illuminati leaders, who were the royalty from other counties. This county wasn't number one until the 1950s.

On the way out, we passed blond children in cages. They all had that Doris Day look—eager, scared, almost dumb, and pretty. We went past all the dark rooms with very low ceilings. Someone crawled as he held me. We drove on the bumpy road, onto the smooth road, and the bright stars, pale moon, and highway lights shone during the long drive home. *Why do they shine on me when no one cares?* I wondered.

The next monarch, 1945

I was much older when I returned to underneath this official palace, and which we were later led to believe was the White House. I was about two years old. We followed exactly the same

193

path in a black limousine. When we got to the man in power for whom we made this trip, they placed me on his lap, like the first time I was there, but he was not asleep and slumped over. He didn't feel soggy but hard and tight. He sat still, but was looking around alertly. I was surprised by how plain looking he appeared. I wore a crown and pale blue cape. Part of this man's body, the part that came out of his zipper, touched mine that was normally in my underpants but it had to be an exact spot. I didn't understand why we should have to drive a long distance for that. Men put me on a slab. Someone poured sticky stuff out of a silver pitcher over my front as other men said words in different languages. They rubbed it up and down me. Someone else told me it was semen and blood. I cried because the stuff they put on me burned my skin. Some leaked into my eyes. The pain of the skin irritation reminded my body of my Bear Mountain birth ritual. I had the same loop in my left nipple. The prayers asked for owning and conquering, world dominion. I must have been washed before the buggy ride, but my front still burned from what they put on me. I think they put a vise on my head again and turned the screw. If I ever told, they would make it very tight on my head and kill my parents. I also had drugs and felt woozy.

Queen or death

The torture for me, the master programmer's grandchild and the designated hidden queen of the Illuminati, started young to force me to choose between being queen and death. The fact that I am still alive might make you think that I fought for life, but I did want to die. I didn't want my life. No one would.

Earlier, and twice today in September 2013, I heard scream-ing and crying inside me, then it felt like a breakthrough and release. My left and right big toes hurt. Grandpa had put the needles in straight to the bone. He concentrated very hard on the torture, as if he were a painter and not aware of anything

194

but his canvas. When Mengele tortured, he was aware of the people around him, craved an audience, and was exhibitionistic. Mengele created dramas and liked to work with groups. Grandpa only worked on individuals in contained environments. He was a womanizer and a dandy socially, but when he worked he was entirely focused on his methodology.

This memory is coming in slowly. It drags its feet against my brain. I know I had the spinning, drugs from injections or rags soaked in gas or both, freezing, torture with a band around my head, and needles to the bones, but I don't know yet what more the queen had to do.

Grandpa Max asked my internal parts whom he made from the thirteenth infant, "Which one of you is going to be queen? I need a queen. We will keep doing this until you die, or agree to be queen. Everyone bows down to the queen bee. The queen killer bee. The child queen killer bee. The princess queen killer bee."

At exactly midnight, when I was three and a half, the queen's training began. Relatives gathered in the living room for my initiation. My grandfather took me into the second bedroom of his apartment. He started by shaving my head and drew sections on it labeled with numbers and letters such as A3, C6, J25. He hit specific parts deliberately with his hammer. Most of his pounding was on the right side toward the center.

I had to wear a head covering until my hair grew back. Then Grandpa spun me in the spinning chair, put needles in my feet, and whipped me. Afterward, I had to aim darts at the dartboard on the back of his door. No matter how dizzy I was, if my dart did not hit the target, he said, "You have to try harder, do better. If you don't get it this time, we'll starve you, shock you. Maybe this hit on the head with the hammer will make you aim better." Sometimes he used a rubber tipped hammer. When I was older, we had archery competitions to perfect our aim. Chaos thrives during rituals, but the leaders are supposed to be precise and accurate. Grandpa was preparing me for my role as a psychic killer. I had to reach the correct target. I had to be able to aim even if I had alcohol in me. Some of the killings would take place at political parties. Accuracy and security were always prominent in mind-control training.

In my grandparents' living room, the relatives enjoyed one another's company. They laughed, joked, told stories, imitated people. The air was electric with exciting energies. After I appeared, everyone was quiet in the living room. I could barely walk after the tortures. My grandmother directed me to her kitchen table. She showed me two tarot cards: a skeleton riding a donkey on the left, and on the right, a sun with a crowned woman sitting on a throne and holding a scepter and globe. I didn't know the word "tarot" yet and thought of them as picture cards. Grandma sat in a chair by mine and leaned over me, placing her weight on one elbow. "Which do you want?" she said as if I were choosing between an oatmeal and a peanut butter cookie. She explained the meaning of the cards, though I think I could have guessed it on my own. The sun and globe meant we would have world dominion. The crown and throne represented my role as queen. The skeleton warned that I'd be killed if I told or misbehaved. Even as a small child, it was clear to me that she asked me to choose between being queen and dying.

"Max, Max, she wants to die. Max, Max, she doesn't want to be queen. You hear that, Max!"

"Then we'll redo the torture until she changes her mind," he called out from the second bedroom. Blurry though I was, I consistently chose the death card. There were sighs of disappointment from the living room. My mother said that I was a disappointment, and now the family would think poorly of her. Grandpa said Mrs. Twartski would have to do some of the programming, that my grandmother wasn't productive enough. "He's just interested in having another affair," the adults whispered. My grandfather took me back to the spare room and hit me over the head to "clarify" my brain, but I kept choosing death. The needle in my left lumbar spine said, "You must be queen." Needles penetrated my feet, the torture for the program "You must never run away". The people inside who held the emotional pain, which stings deepest with clawing nails, suffered the worst.

The future

My Uncle Richard, the movie producer, took me into one of the programming rooms and showed me films of what he said were future events in the world. He claimed the prophets foresaw these events. Some of the events were ones that have now occurred, but not exactly as the films depicted. Since it was the 1940s, the films were black and white, and the buildings, cars, planes, and clothing were of that era. A few examples of the events are: a man tipping his top hat while being driven in a motorcade; a man in a different motorcade sitting doubled over, dead; a rifle sticking out of a window; buildings blown up; planes crashing into a building which looked like the Empire State Building; tall buildings crumbling and falling; a limousine crashing into a serpentine tunnel. There were other scenes that concerned more politicians, movie stars, and the financial districts. The people's faces were blacked out with a rectangle.

The film's soundtrack had commentaries such as "… and this disaster will occur …" while Uncle Richard made comments such as "It will be called 9–1–1." He didn't pronounce it "nine-eleven". This was before 9–1–1 was the emergency telephone number. Some of the events depicted, such as a stock market crash, have not happened, or have not happened yet. Uncle Richard insisted that they all would take place within my lifetime. At the end, the film spoke of "these accomplishments". Either the Illuminati prophets were particularly gifted, or the group actually planned some of these treacheries years ahead of time and caused them to occur. I didn't free myself of the belief in the Illuminati prophets' magical abilities until I retrieved these forbidden memories. Uncle Richard said that some of their prophets had predicted that I would be a traitor. In this, at least, they were correct.

Don't cry training

It's pouring outside today, and it's pouring inside me, but I have not been able to shed one tear. The program not to cry is that strong. When I was three and a half, I cried all the time, and overheard a conversation between Mrs. Twartski and my grandfather:

GRANDPA: "She's too delicate. We should have killed her when she was an infant."

MRS. TWARTSKI: "We couldn't because of the prophecy."

GRANDPA: "We can stop her crying, but I don't know what to do about her soul."

MRS. TWARTSKI: "She's a delicate flower. We already gave her the pillow suffocation to stop her crying."

GRANDPA: "We'll have to do the bathtub drowning."

MRS. TWARTSKI: "Where?"

GRANDPA: "Here."

MRS. TWARTSKI: "With who, me or her?"

GRANDPA: "You."

MRS. TWARTSKI: "What temperature?"

GRANDPA: "Lukewarm."

Mrs. Twartski filled the tub about one-third up. I saw her fingers feeling the water coming out of the faucet. Grandpa had a stopwatch.

GRANDPA: "I'll time it. Watch if the bubbles in the water become less. I'll be looking at the watch."

MRS. TWARTSKI: "Any time you cry, you will go under the water."

GRANDPA: "And one time we will forget to bring you back up. So don't cry too many times."

Mrs. Twartski undressed me in the bathroom. She put me in the tub and on my back, pushed me under the water. I couldn't breathe. I wanted air. Terror made me fight. She lifted me up. Eventually, I cried, and they did it again. They must have done this about ten times, but on different days. When they had finished programming me, Mrs. Twartski dried me off and dressed me in the bathroom. Grandpa told Grandma to give me some cookies.

"Feed her yourself," Grandma said, her blank blue eyes like knives as she slammed her bedroom door. The pictures on the wall shook. I didn't know why she was angry, but thought it might be because of me.

The sound torture's scratching siren blocked out memory. "No one will remember this event" was its purpose.

Some of the torture in Grandpa's second bedroom prepared me to be the masonic queen. Some divisions of the Masons are under the Illuminati, but Masons in the other divisions have no knowledge of these practices. He blew tiny hard black balls at me through a straw. They woke me up when I drifted off into sleep. Grandpa drew the masonic staircase up my spine, step one, two, three and so on to the crown on my head. He said, "The queen has to climb all these steps. You can't lead your people until you have achieved the highest order." He blew the hard little balls so that each one hit a certain vertebra in my spine that corresponded to the masonic step he worked on. "If you want to be queen, you have to kill with your own hands. It's an honor to kill and be queen. That's how you help your people. If you can't kill, you're no good. People who can't kill are good for nothing. You can't walk up the steps without killing. You have to climb all the steps. The top three are the Illuminati where you belong. Your mother is only at the middle. Your sister is at the bottom with your father, but you belong at the top, like me."

I notice that when I write about the masonic structure, my handwriting goes from large to minuscule.

Grandpa's face became almost all mouth, moving wide and rapidly. The clear brown skin, beady dark eyes, fierce concentration like a diamond cutter before the first strike—his concentration on pulling apart without tearing, and inserting without rupturing—all loomed. Maybe my mother objected so strongly to my dark complexion because it reminded her of his, though his had an undercoating of yellow and mine at that time had a foundation more of pink. Or perhaps Mother was just a common racist, like so many of her generation.

I feel hollow now with gashes of pain. Nothing hooked me to life.

The strongest split

I see myself climbing on the bathtub edge, opening the medicine cabinet, looking for a razor blade. I was three years old. Such a despairing child could attract attention. They used the old standby of trickery to attempt to strengthen me.

In the Pleasant Hills tunnel programming spaces, I saw six little dolls projected onto the wall before me. My grandfather and his projector were behind me. He said, "These parts all came out of you. I saw them leave. Let's see how brave each one is." He started at the right hand side and stuck a pin in the first one. I saw his very large hand projected on the wall. I heard a scream but didn't know where it came from. He did this to each projected image of a doll, with screams, and said, "I'm taking you," to the fourth doll that he said appeared the bravest. With his projected, enlarged hand like a monster's, he pulled that doll towards my body and threw away the other five dolls. "You'll never get them back, but you don't want them back, because they're weak and they cry. Whenever you cry, you'll lose another part of yourself." He squeezed my waist and ribs and said, "Now we've got the strong part in you for good." He put a cape, crown, and scepter on that imaginary fourth split, gave it a globe, and said, "Here's our county—this is what we have to rule." I was sucking my thumb.

"Now you don't have to die, because you have a much stronger person in you. This is the bravest, strongest part of you. Do you believe it came from you?"

"No, it came from the camera."

"For that answer, you will have to go back in the freezer." When I was gradually freezing, it was as if a large pendulum swung back and forth within my whole body about to erupt and shatter me into frozen chunks. When he let me out, he asked, "Where do you think that part came from?"

"From me."

"That's good. That will be your strong part, who will go to the monarchs and serve our lord and master." He kept building on an illusion, as all mind control does, but I couldn't stop crying. Uncle Sidney said, "We should give her a bottle." They did.

Grandpa considered himself a visionary, always charting the changing world and monitoring the density of evil. He believed or pretended that he could sense evil from that distance. World maps with colored pins covered the walls like in the basement programming spaces and in the monastery. Red ones indicated the countries these groups aimed at; black ones were supposed to be already dominated by evil.

The blue angel of mercy leaped into my mind like a loyal puppy. I could get away from all of this if I just had the angel with me. But despite all the suicidal programming they hounded me with, they wanted me alive. Perhaps that is why they sent Daniel to me at this moment. The tricks with the camera and projector couldn't strengthen me, but he could. My grandfather continued to do what he called work-ups. Twenty freezers were in the secret cellars where the endowment of the important men took place. He kept increasing my time in the practice freezers in the Pleasant Hills hidden tunnels to build tolerance. When I got back home from the basement tunnels, my mother offered me tomato soup with rice in it.

It surprises me that the Nazis treated their families tenderly as they destroyed many millions of others. The family knew what happened in my grandparents' spare room, as civilization knew what happened in the concentration camps in Eastern Europe. My grandfather travelled the world turning children's minds into fallow fields. He must have accidentally killed many, as he did in his hometown.

Refrigerators

It was a year later. I'd had a year of Daniel's love before they killed him. This scene happened after he was dead.

"Rosie, do you have the fridge empty yet?"

"It's almost empty, Max. Just a second." He dragged me into the kitchen. Grandma had the contents of the refrigerator sitting on the oval kitchen table near the window. "Look how you're inconveniencing your grandmother, making her do all this extra work, when she should be cooking dinner." He lifted my rigid body into the empty fridge, and closed the door. It was black and freezing. For a long time now, I had been used to the state of no comfort. My bones felt stiff and hard. There was no air to breathe. *If he didn't let me out, I would be another one of those tragedies found on the sidewalks of Pleasant Hills*, I thought. Every now and then, there was a child who died in our neighborhood. They were found in discarded refrigerators left out on the streets. The explanation adults gave was that the children played in them, the door closed, and then they were locked in and suffocated. People got fines for not taking the doors off their refrigerators. No murder charges. Whenever I heard those stories, or passed a discarded fridge, my heart would freeze. I passed out in this fridge. When he took me out and revived me, he said, "You must be one of us. You can't run away from being one of us. You have to be a slave like all the others."

"I don't want to be one. Let someone else be one. Let Rhonda be one."

"You both have to be one. I'm going to teach you a lesson until you want to be one." He kept freezing me until I relented. Grandpa timed me in the ice box. He went up to eighteen and nineteen minutes, but when he opened the door, I was unconscious, so he knew he had gone too far. My fingertips and ears were like glaciers. Grandma put earmuffs on me, but that made them worse. I thought my ears would fall off like icicles. My grandmother put cold compresses on me to thaw me out. My grandfather told me he wanted me to punish babies, to kill babies. If I didn't, they would kill other children by putting them in the ice box. That was one of the queen's "duties". *What should I do, Daniel?* My heart squeezed together just like it had when I had a heart attack on the sidewalk after Daniel died. *If I kill babies, babies will be dead. If I don't kill babies, children will be dead.* "You must kill babies, or you can't be queen. Our family depends on you. Our county depends on you. You must do it. Do you agree?" Grandpa Max asked.

At the masonic rituals, I had to kill. Blood splattered on the pastel walls, and on the black and white patterned floor. A man with leather gloves gathered my hands, and we stabbed. I made up a song:

> "Hush little baby, don't you cry.
> Even though you're about to die.
> I'll stab you quick, I'll kill you fast.
> I'm the only one who'll have a pain that lasts.
> Hush, little baby, don't you cry.
> I'll never never let them skin you alive.
> You're the lucky one who's going to die.

You will go to heaven with dry eyes.
When I look up to the sky, I will have to cry,
because now I belong to Satan."

The victim babies were not strangers to me. I was left in a room with them before the slayings. Daniel had breathed a conscience into me. I don't know whether I was born with one. I wondered whether my grandparents had had a conscience when they were young. Life for resisters within these groups meant trying to find the way of the least evil.

"I could always make another"

For several days, I have been feeling my vaginal wall. Then the physical memory returns. I was a four-and-a-half-year-old in the second bedroom, strung up in front of his dartboard, my arms tied to hooks on the door, ankles tied to a chair. Grandfather, who must have been in a particularly primitive mood because he wore his costume and devil mask, held a wand that conducted electricity. He placed it up my vagina, and I screamed from the shattering pain. He created internal Itchy-face-Frank, Change-subject-Sally, and Frozen-fear-Nellie, who would distract me should I approach remembering who I am.

My grandmother rushed in. "She has to bear children. What are you doing, Max? She's the Illuminati princess. You're going to kill her … the neighbors."

"I could always make another one. I could always make more," he shouted through the door. My mother, who sat in the living room, screamed, then wailed. I was still strung up, but I heard a blow. Later Aunt Eileen told me that my father had hit my mother. He was allowed to do that when she became hysterical. Something had really shaken the family. An invisible barricade broke. My sister kept saying, "What does that mean?" My grandfather left the room to yell at my grandmother. "You keep interrupting me. Now everyone has to be programmed not to remember this." Rhonda was two years old at that time, and the family discussed whether she could possibly know anything, and whether she needed programming.

I visualize what was going on in the living room. I see all my relatives sitting in Grandma's comfortable chairs aghast. I hear clearly the word that he could make more of me, or of what? I had thought my father was my father. *Who would want such a vicious, horrible man to be a father? If he was my father, then I am a double freak. Wasn't that against the law? Why would my mother have let out that scream? Such a piercing, tormented sound.* Sidney and Richard restrained my grandfather, who was wild and out of his mind. They pulled off his devil mask, and made him sit in the stuffed corner chair in the second bedroom. His eyes went to the side, and he looked troubled and distant, as if on the continent where he had been born, as if watching something in a dream.

My father and uncle unhooked me. My father shuddered when he saw me strung up. Didn't he know how my grandfather treated me? My mother put my coat over me; my father carried me out over his shoulder. I sobbed "Daniel, Daniel." People on this fifth floor stuck their heads out their front doors. My father said, "She fell off a chair," as my mother said, "She burned her finger." In the elevator, I turned my head around and saw my father give my mother an exasperated look. My mother looked down, as if she had done something wrong. I wondered whether my father blamed my mother for her father, as I blamed my mother for mine, or whether it was something deeper. Children with knowledge of sexuality and violence pick up the innuendoes of adult life, but I didn't understand what passed between my parents in the elevator. Marlene clung to my mother. We walked home. My mother went right to her room, and my father put me to bed. My sister stayed with my mother. I thought as I lay in bed shivering, shaking, still calling Daniel's name, that my grief for Daniel made my grandfather crazy, that all my sadness intoxicated him. And in bed, I cried out to God after having lost the only love that I will ever know. I cried out to him in the heavens who might or might not have been watching, "I cannot take a whole life of this." I felt Daniel rise from the newly dead, and lie beside me. He placed his hand over the opening to my frayed vaginal wall that steamed with the ravages of electro-shock. We breathed together, and I slept.

Choosing to be queen

These criminal groups think that victims need to make the choice to be evil even though they are coerced. A little while ago, I went into one of those faint-or-sleep states. I lay down and this memory leaped out of nowhere. When I was eight, my mother walked me to my grandparents' apartment. She had the keys. We entered, and I went ahead to the second bedroom. I was supposed to be there for a programming session. I had ballet twice a week; speech, piano, and mind control once a week. I looked in the second bedroom door that was open about one foot. My grandmother, who would have been in her forties, was strung up from the ceiling. My grandfather had his shirt off and held a whip. He waved the whip at me and said, "Get out of here." My mother grabbed my hand, but she had a slight grin on her face similar to how my grandfather chroni-cally smiled. Being hung and stretched was hard on a child's body. I think it would have been unbearable on an adult's body. My grandmother, while hanging, though she had her feet on a chair, looked at me with her shallow blue eyes and said "He's doing this to me because you won't choose to be queen."

That night we had a ritual in Old Pleasant Hills. I was in the center of a circle, and people threw pebbles at me saying things like "You're aggravating your grandfather," "You're making your grandmother be punished," "You're making us ordi-nary." I think that's when I said I would choose to be queen, but it wasn't a real choice. I just didn't want Grandma tortured though she was happy enough to have me tortured, even gratuitously and of her own doing. That's how children are. They love and protect anyone who gives them a homemade sugar cookie with an egg yolk glaze. I was that stupid.

The monarchs' slaves

Several years after they murdered Daniel in 1947, while my grief was still at its crest of desperation, my grandfather began splitting and layering to create and program slaves within me for servicing the monarch-type leaders. He created a line of white and black naked slaves, their supposed ages almost fifteen to twenty-six, although developmentally they were really young children. They wore iron necklaces around their necks, which were chained together. In mind control, the programmers create homes and locations where their newly created parts reside. They can't have personalities floating around like homeless people who won't go to the shelters. Grandpa constructed an internal well by just telling me it was there and torturing me into believing it. He put the electricity circuits on the soles of my feet. I was wearing an everyday dress, strung up on the ceiling, and when it hurt too much, he said "Who wants to come out and be a slave?" No answer. "Then you'll have to have more electricity." Internal people volunteered. He showed me pictures of African slaves all tied together. Was I willing to be like that? No. Electricity. Then yes.

In 2013, I dream that devil's horns grow out of my feet; I feel serious chest pains. In the morning, I wake with this memory: I was an older child, eight to ten or twelve or most likely all those ages. Grandma put me under her sunlamp in the master bedroom and said, "Now you are Negro." My skin became very dark. Grandpa and Aunt Mimi walked me into the second bedroom. Mrs. Twartski was there. They spun me in the spinning chair and injected me. Grandpa started to put a rag with gasoline over my nose, and Mrs. Twartski said, "Don't overdose her." I was relieved not to get the rag. They put me on the single bed by the window, where Grandpa often slept. He put a ring in my left nostril and another on the left side of my tongue. Mrs. Twartski asked why he passed over the nipple and vagina, and Grandpa said, "She's too prone to infection. No one will ever know." She put rings on both big toes and many very thin bracelets up my left arm. Grandpa handed her curved horn-like white pieces of bone. She glued them to the metatarsus on each foot. "These are your devil's horns, so that people know you're a devil-demon. You'll have to be very polite to the men who believe they will profit from the use of you. Turn her over. We need to darken her backside." Grandma paced the hall, banging things and making angry noises. Grandpa continued, "This is your costume. You will be dressed like this for eternity, even when you sleep in the well. Whenever you are bidden, you arrive wearing this costume, behave well, and do whatever they ask. Unless you are called out, you are asleep at the very bottom of the well. No one must know about you."

Through hypnosis, I had to walk down a rung ladder to the bottom of a well. The well went below the foundation, past Mengele's spider web, into the deepest part. My grandfather pushed me physically into the imaginary well he built. He pushed on the top of my head, pressing my neck down until my neck became a hand fan that could no longer open. "You have to go down, down deep into the structure; I am drilling a well right now. Now one by one go down there." The black slaves went by groups A, B, C, D … the white ones by alpha, beta … Greek letters. Each letter signified a different function such as sexual, criminal, blotting out memory. I imagine the programmers personalize the functions to the role of each of their victims. The white slaves in me existed to be used by elected officials, and the black ones were for top world leaders, also mostly elected. These men felt more comfortable degrading a black female. "Now you live in the well, and I and very official people will call you up when we need you, and you all stay down there unless we call you." When Grandpa tapped his foot, leaving his heel on the floor, seven times, or when Mrs. Twartski tapped a glass with a spoon three times, the black slaves would emerge. There are thirty-five of them in clans of seven. Grandpa would decide which one(s) to send by limousine or airplane to these important people. He tried to match the slave to the personality of the leader. The slaves were so well behaved that the handler didn't need to be present.

The monarchs who were part of this criminal group had the opportunity to order sex slaves from my grandfather. The butterflies were all female, but the sex slaves were both male and female and were designed to be older than the butterfly girls. The abusers' belief was that a true woman was a child in a woman's body. He advertised: "We create specimens who are pleasing to monarchs ... who can do any sort of trick for a monarch. Our specialty is form-fitting monarchs. We have girls in yellow, pale pink, light blue, green, violet, white. You choose the girl you want and we will form her to fit your needs."

For the female slaves, he pretended that he was supplying women's and junior's dresses. Customers could order size five, six, seven, eight, nine, and so on. Each size represented a certain sexual act. Various pastel colors also translated as code for an assortment of sexual acts. The assistants to certain monarchs ordered them in advance.

I don't know whether my grandfather invented this industry or whether he inherited it from a predecessor. He must have travelled the world creating these sexual slaves for monarchs. During a therapy session, we found these parts of me hidden internally in the corner of Grandpa's second bedroom. They huddled in shame and did not feel like human beings. Once we discovered them, they had a bit more trust in humanity than before. They no longer think all people are bad.

I read the word "brandy" in a book, and the slave parts got a craving for Harvey's Bristol Cream sherry and scotch. I think they're alcoholic. In the dressing rooms at this important American place, we were routinely shot up with something like cocaine to make us more energetic, numbed, and cooperative, and to help us bear the disillusionments and assorted pains. We never knew what drug they put in us.

My grandfather created an alternate black book that no one knew about, including Mengele. He said all of this was family business. He called two of his secretaries, who were his middle and youngest daughters, to record. My aunts left the second bedroom each holding a different "top secret" black book. Because of the torture, I had to give over my imagination also. Mind-control programmers usurp all the movements of victims' minds.

Transferring demonic power to world leaders

These groups flail about in archaic beliefs. One is that the queens pass on demonic power through their genitals. They hypnotized me into believing that drawers in the walls that resembled old-fashioned library card containers held "demons". They pretended to insert them with a long skinny rod, and told me I would always be demonized. The demons looked like black puffy smoke with blues in it, and had a bad smell like burning rubber. When they took the demons out of the drawers, their shapes were already fully formed, and appeared solid. They became looser as they entered me. They burned but not so badly as when my father put cigarettes out on my skin. The queens were sad and shamed, because they believed that they had demons in them and they had to go into a separate room with the monarchs. Unbelievably, my mother, sister, and some of the monarchs' wives were jealous of my position.

I had to remember how I entered these hidden rooms. You don't just breeze in. A long way from this underground suite of torture rooms was an entrance to a paved tunnel with sparse lighting on its walls. After the equivalent of several blocks, the road became unpaved. The drivers parked the limousines. Other men transferred the captive to an open car, like a buggy, and we proceeded on packed dirt roads. The tunnel became tighter and lower as the open car crawled along. After about another six blocks, I had to get out and climb through another tunnel using flashlights for light. Eventually, by crawling, I arrived at the secret ceremony district. World leaders and their wives, butterfly girls, and servants were already present. A trio of leaders of the worldwide Illuminati organization stood waiting.

Some of the butterfly girls were in cages, others hoisted on a conveyor belt. When the girls were strung up in hanging machines, sometimes upside down, the politicians serviced themselves. The "monarch" could choose which ones he wanted to play with sexually.

One time, while I was in an adjacent room, a monarch's voice boomed, "Flying girls, I want my flying girls." His wife was there holding a whip—a refined whip like people use on purebred horses. "Now don't make me whip you, gals. Don't make me hurt you pretty young 'uns."

Another time, a wife of a monarch did not have that down-to-earth ambiance. This one lined up the girls who had to "fly" by putting her right index finger inside the right side of the mouth of each girl, and pushed toward their right. She wore a plastic glove on each hand, because she didn't want to touch the air they breathed.

Escorts ushered me into the dressing room, where pleasant women prepared my body and hung up my travelling clothes. Wearing my cape, crown, and loop in my left nipple, I entered the alcove that held the sacrificial body, a baby, child or a thirty-three-year-old male. The three heads of the Illuminati and an executioner already filled the tight space. The executioner held my hands and killed the sacrifice as the men sang prayers in an inflamed manner. The executioner left and other

211

workers entered to excrete blood from the corpse. I had to sip a thimbleful, then the three men drank. All during this time, my feet floated above ground and I looked down on the scene from the low ceiling. The three men spat on me as I exited and walked down a pathway to a world leader. They spat because they considered it shameful that an Illuminati queen would not kill unaided.

The workers had gathered the blood from the corpse or pretended to. I had to stand in it as the world leader took a sip from an ornate goblet, which reflected his role in the universe. We both entered a tiny chamber the size of a phone booth, where there was a transfer, Old Testament style, from my clitoris to his penis, of what they considered demonic power. These groups had bizarre, ancient beliefs. Outside the booth, a man dressed in robes like a Vatican priest recited prayers in a language that sounded like half Hebrew, half Latin. I couldn't speak it, but someone in me understood:

> Hear, my children of divine majesty
> Hear O angels of the silver world
> Hear demonic forces of the golden world
> Lucifer's angels are gathered herewith
> All his children have their feet on the earth
> And their toes in Jesus' blood
> A river runs through
> Channel his power into this mortal man
> Channel Lucifer's force into this endowed leader
> Channel Lucifer's heart into the soul of the country
> Lucifer's queen is endowed with powers
> Lucifer's blessing is on this official of his own sovereignty.

Then my job was done, though I remained in a dense trance, part from drugs, part from shock. During these assaults, when I was a piece of cloth, with no rights or being, a veil descended

212

from the heavens and blocked their claws. They took possession of my body, but my soul hid insulated in a non-tangible substance that kept me from utter despair. The leader proceeded to the butterfly girls on the conveyor belt, and I returned to the dressing room.

By the time I was a young adult, they brought in another queen, but kept me at these initiations. Now there were two booths for the transfer of power: one for the new queen, Laura, whom they believed would cooperate, and one for the degraded me. "You're saving yourself, but now Laura has to do all the work. You care for yourself, but you don't care for Laura. The reason we have a bad leader is because of you." They put me on a little stage and the audience booed me. "You're a good-for-nothing queen, a blemish on your heritage, a stuck angel, a namby-pamby fallen angel." To be called "namby-pamby" in this vicious criminal world was meant as a huge insult.

Some of the leaders would not take part in these Illuminati rituals. One was drugged and kidnapped, another made a brief, angry appearance, others refused to participate. And some of the leaders wanted to be part of these grabs for power. Sometimes only the wife cooperated. The leaders of the hidden criminal world became nervous if a leader did not come from their organization. About such a leader, the visiting heads of this whole evil organization said to me, "We have another namby-pamby who's encroaching on us. This is all your fault. You punctured one of Lucifer's membranes. One of the seals isn't working, and it's your fault. You have interfered with our divine plan. You have not endowed our future. You have failed." The torturers threatened the world leaders who didn't worship evil and world dominion with killing their children if they didn't cooperate. Other men shook and strangled me. "If you ever tell what happens here, you'll be dead." As I go through these memories, the internal babies feel terrible anxiety. I have to hold the babies' heads close to my heart and rock them tenderly as I go about my day, and my life. "Ah, ah, babies, don't you worry, I'm here with you," I say to my selves.

This all happened in the forties, up to the nineties. My main goal in life was to make Daniel proud of me. He would most likely not have gone to college. He would have been a worker of some kind, making one woman extremely happy and teaching his children to be good citizens and spread love in their worlds. But the love that he gave me, the physical comforting during which I passed through catch-up developmental stages, his acceptance and understanding of me—took me out of this web of perversity and transplanted me. Almost seventy years later, my heart can still feel the thump of each beat of his heart, and the silent breath between them. One morning recently, I woke remembering his smell.

Government offices have their own closedown crews who performed the usual procedures expertly and extensively. The men didn't pump up their muscles like open peacock wings but were slim and tight in dark gray suits, white shirts, and skinny black ties. I wonder what these men dreamed about and how they treat their families.

The government cellar had about twenty spinning chairs in one place, and the men spun the butterfly people all at once. Projectile vomit flew like the fluttering wings of the butterfly girls. The government servants administered electroshock and tightened a head vise simultaneously, which made the tension level in the body enormous. Also we had to hold still or the guns that they held flush to our bodies might "accidently" go off. I heard shots through the corridors and in adjacent rooms. I don't know whether people were killed or whether they tried to scare us. Then came the whipping, kicking, needles in our teeth, more electroshock, always with guns pressed to victims' temples. In addition, they administered a series of six injections of mind-numbing drugs to help the brain not hold information: when entering, going into the booth, coming off the whipping stage, before closedown torture, after it, and as I returned

214

to normal life. When they put me in one of their freezers, I had to vow not to tell anyone, or they threatened they would kill any children I ever had.

Back to the normal world

When I was a child, the government men returned me to my parents' home in Pleasant Hills, and later Long Island. I remember three other dump-off locations when I was an adult. In the 1960s, I was discharged at Hiram College, Ohio, where I was a student. Young women in the dormitory accused me of spending the night with a college boy. "Which one?" "Do you like him?" "How far did you go?" "I was here, I was right here," my front person said to my dormitory friends. I couldn't understand why they accused me of missing last night. I saw their several peering faces, but a universe parted me from them. People without skin cannot communicate with those who wear skin.

I smelled a faint odor of Vaseline especially around my wrists. I didn't want water touching my body, the assault of water on decaying skin, but I had to make my odor vanish. I walked into the bathroom, away from my gaping dormitory friends, used one in the line of sinks, showered. The water hit my skin, pounding it to meal. I couldn't kill, it wasn't killing. It was murder. I couldn't do it. The Angel of Mercy scrubbed my back. Its giant golden wings filled the shower stall. "Come with me, my child." *Yes, yes, I will.* I sleepwalked half wet to the bottle of pills that only a few people inside knew about. There were only two left. Not enough. Someone must have been swallowing them during the night.

Everyone in the dormitory was rushing to class. I felt them swooshing past me. I had clean clothes. The pre-instructions were to make sure I had clean, respectable clothes for the next day. They were in my drawer. I needed food. I made my way to the cafeteria and sat at one of its wooden round tables. "Yes,

I would like two eggs, bacon, and toast." I wolfed it down, as if I had never eaten. The children wanted juice. My throat was sore, the chills rampant. My front person thought I had a fever. No one in the dormitory was sick. I made my way to math class; almost vomited in biology; fell asleep in French, my best subject; gazed out the window in religion. The professor talked about the prophets. I had a stirring feeling that there was no civilization, no hope.

After the classes, I floundered back to the dorm. Someone in me took the last little pill. The rest of us didn't see. Another inside person threw the bottle in the large can in the bathroom. I fell into a sleep of the dead. I felt the Angel's wings over my narrow bed by the window. A sophomore yelled to me that I had a telephone call. I kept sleeping. She said she'd tell them I was asleep. Some internal part of my mind knew it was their check-up call and that message would suffice. I thought I smelled blood, but almost all of my mind answered that was impossible. I began ripping hair off my body. The wings. Highway lights. Tunnels. I entered a deep, drugged sleep and dreamt of thugs beating me.

In the 1970s, while visiting my parents, I was dumped at their Manhattan apartment at 90th Street and Madison Avenue. One of the muscular escorts held me tight under my bent arm with our hips touching. I could feel his gun through our clothes. We went up the elevator to the eighth floor, and my father opened the front door. He had been playing solitaire at the dining room table. The escort immediately disappeared. I went right to my bedroom. My mother had put a fresh night-gown on my pillow. *Touching*, I thought. Some awareness must still have lingered up front in me. My father came in and asked me if I wanted something to eat. I had not eaten for a long time. The government doesn't feed you when they torture. My father brought me toasted corn rye bread from Merritt Bakery, and a glass of carrot juice.

In the mid-eighties or early nineties, an escort deposited me at my co-op on 108th Street and Amsterdam Avenue in Manhattan. The doorman who talked loud and incessantly was on night duty, but didn't seem to notice anything unusual. The escort held me in the elevator, opened my front door with a key he had and left. I was alone in my apartment with a head that already had forgotten everything. By morning, I would be another person returning to ordinary life, with my government robot switch on off.

PART II

THE WAY OF THE LEAST EVIL

CHAPTER TEN

Wife and mother

The last Pleasant Hills ritual, 1959

We all looked up at the stars. The night sky was black. Someone called out "Big Dipper," "Little Dipper". You would have thought it would make everyone humble. My clothes were cold. I couldn't stop shaking, sneezing, and yawning. I had spent hours here in the outside ritual site in Old Pleasant Hills. The ground was laid bricks, which looked hundreds of years old. They knew so many stories but kept their stony silence. The area was deserted. Even during the day, hardly anyone was here, blocks away from the busy Enterprise Avenue with its sub-way stop and shops, housewives buying, commuters rushing.

I came early with the set-up crew. Early but past midnight. My father walked me here, then returned home. He and my mother, sometimes my sister, walked here a few hours later. No reason for my mother to stand around in the cold when she had so much to do in the apartment. No one forced my father to come to these rituals the way they had to force others. He wanted to worship Lucifer with his whole heart. Mother didn't like the killings but enjoyed the sex. She always complained about father's being impotent so she needed the rituals to get satisfied. I hated all aspects of these rituals, which they also called worshipfuls.

My Uncle Richard used his organizational skills to get everyone going. Like my grandfather when he made women's dresses, Uncle Richard loved detail and exactitude. Every switch, plug, light had to be just so.

Mrs. Twartski talked with the other handlers of the neighborhood. They were comparing notes on how to structure people's minds. My cousins and school classmates arrived. Incense was lit. I hated the smell, others inhaled it lovingly. The altar was arranged. They used a low, stone wall that was part of this site and had been there for hundreds of years. That night there would be a sacrifice, a real one, not pretend. This part, plus the orgy, especially terrified the children. Sometimes an adult was killed but often it was children, both boys and girls though the group preferred boys, white ones. If such a child could be killed, any of us could be next.

I had a new job. I had to draw the designs that Lucifer craved on the bodies. Sometimes the person was already dead, and during the ritual they killed that person again for show. Sometimes the person was heavily drugged and would be killed at the ceremony or would wake up and be let go. Ever since my teacher said I had talent, the organizers had assigned me this job. Lucifer liked swirls in black and red, lines that never stopped zigzagging and curving. We only decorated the top part of the body and the parts that were exposed, such as the toes. The leaders said the designs enhanced the spirituality of the sacrifice to Lucifer.

Uncle Richard told me to hurry up. He said, "You are taking too long. You are dawdling." I was not dawdling. I tried to work in designs that dedicated this life, this body, that night this six-year-old boy, to God. On TV I had watched a contest. They gave you a form or a letter and you had to make a whole drawing that included that shape or letter in an unrecognizable way. That was when I thought I could write "God" on the bodies. I formed the "G" around the belly button and camouflaged

222

it so that no one could tell. If they discovered what I was doing, there would be two sacrifices and with no drugs for me. All the leaders had it in for me since I hadn't produced an heir. It wasn't my fault that my mother had killed baby Daniel, but they were angry that he and the others were born bonded.

Uncle Richard glared at me suspiciously. He didn't know why I was taking so long. He already wore his black hooded robe and eye mask. And the crowd was arriving. There were the Smiths, Joneses, Callaways, the Sheins, Olsens, Johnsons. Some of the teachers from Public School Number Three and Oldtown Junior High School arrived. There were the druggist and one manager of the grocery store, our dentist, and many women from Grandma's beauty parlor with their husbands and children, plus the women Grandma played canasta with. My parents and grandparents had just arrived.

The ink dried instantly and the carriers moved the body to the altar. A six-year-old girl who was being initiated stood there. It was her turn to do the sacrifice. The executioner stood behind her ready to use her hands. After her hands were used to kill, she would probably feel trapped, that she could never be free to leave. She would be so ashamed that she would stay in the only place where she would be accepted and where everyone was the same.

The lights blinked, the dagger went in, and lights on the side showed a soul being clutched in Lucifer's hand. The soul tried to slip through his fingers but couldn't. People watching believed in this afterlife even though it was clear that we were watching a movie on a screen. Uncle Richard directed it. Sometimes the adults were more naïve than their children. A robed figure stood to the side on the brick wall. He moved his left arm down sharply, which signaled that the orgy should begin. The orgy always began thirteen minutes after the only or last sacrifice. People were naked under their robes. They threw naked children up in the air and penetrated them. My father had an erection. He can only get one around children. My mother was looking for men.

Human flesh *hors d'oeuvres* were passed around. They had human meat in the kind of containers chicken salad comes in. Everyone had to have a chunk. It was not optional. We picked it out of the container with toothpicks. You had to chew it. You couldn't spit it out. It was cooked and had seasoning. Even if you got a piece with fat, you had to chew and swallow or you would be whipped right in front of everyone. The meat was stringy and lean. I hoped they were just pretending it was human meat.

About three in the morning, a whisper flashed through the site. A muted call sounded the alarms from the outer trees all the way into Uncle Richard's ear. The handlers stretched up their necks. The lookouts, who were perched in the tree branches, formed concentric circles around the site. The outer ones had a view of the nearby busy avenue. The most responsibility was on the lead outer person. The lookouts were usually older teenagers and young adults. They had to be able to climb tall trees, stay awake and balance for several hours on branches, and imitate bird calls that they had been learning since early childhood. They had to perfect low whispering because birds were asleep in the middle of the night. Just the cats prowled and owls were awake. That training was one of the fun parts of this life we all led.

The shutdown signal was given right in the middle of the orgy. If it had happened before the sacrifice, the child would have been killed anyway, probably in the truck. The robes were tossed into a large bag, and people scrambled back into their street clothes that they had placed carefully and in a deliberate order on the other side of the low, stone wall. Men quickly moved the corpse, paints, ritual dagger, and drugs into the parked truck. Everyone dispersed silently. We had rehearsed this time and time again, and this night we disassembled in seconds. Our secret religion depended on speed.

The first position lookout had spotted a lone police officer in uniform carrying a baton and wearing a gun in his holster while patrolling within blocks of our site. He was not one of ours. He was a new man on the beat. How had the police chief let this happen? He was supposed to let only our own patrol this neighborhood at night, especially on arranged ritual nights. He might be losing his authority. Our ritual site was wiped clean, but we could never return now. That is a fundamental rule: once a site has been invaded or almost invaded, never return. Fail-safe security is all-important. This event contaminated Pleasant Hills, as I had contaminated my coven and county's reputation.

When we arrived back in our apartment, my father was agitated. He was making phone calls and tapping on the table, more restless than usual. He couldn't even calm down enough to play solitaire. Within a week, extra programming began in the back programming room. My handler showed me pictures of a lone police officer walking. She said, "If you ever remember this ritual, you will go crazy." She shot me up with electricity and drugs. "If you ever report it to the police, you will present yourself as a babbling fool, a mad girl." They did this programming for months. All the drugged, spun children were shot through with electricity so that they would never remember and tell, even if cross-examined.

Meanwhile, my parents quickly bought a house on a wooded, hidden lot on Long Island. To walk near the wooded part, a police officer would have to walk on private property. For years, their hobby had been to take drives and look at houses on Long Island, where the middle class was moving. Now suddenly, they acted. They met with the builder every week while the house was being built. The Pleasant Hills clan dispersed and was absorbed by other neighboring groups. A new Long Island coven formed. The lone police officer never knew how close he came to being killed. Only the leaders discovered what had happened to the police chief's authority.

Marriage as punishment, 1964

Right before I graduated from Bard College, the young women in my dorm were breaking up with college boyfriends, getting apartments in the city, and jobs in large corporations like Pepsi Cola, continuing on in graduate school, planning on roaming around Europe. No one else was getting married and pregnant, and certainly not to a man she hated. The committee that controlled me found a male who was the opposite of me. We had nothing in common and opposing values, but we both lived in New York and my father was his father's lawyer. My grandfather as Wiezenslowski, a new woman who had taken over as "Mrs. Twartski", and some international leaders made this decision during my sophomore year of college. They ordered that I change colleges to be closer to my selected and future husband and next handler. I was twenty-one and wanted to romp through life on tiptoe, not be saddled with a taker.

Right before the engagement party in Todd's parents' backyard on Long Island, I stormed around my parents' Manhattan apartment, ripping my clothes and refusing to attend. My father gave me hand signals that got me into their car and to the dreaded celebration. I must have switched into another part when I arrived, for I danced under the canopy in his backyard by the pool that only my parents and I swam in. The lindy was in style then. I turned and spun and my dress flared. My mother whispered with other females including my future mother-in-law about my recent temper tantrum. Driving home, my mother said, "You wore the wrong slip which showed when you twirled around. You're wearing a polka dot slip and should be wearing a solid color. You made me feel ashamed." I wore an emerald green summer dress that had bold red and yellow flowers. A red slip would have been nice underneath. My mother had no way of snatching me and running away.

If only I'd had a protective part to help me escape or if only my front person had perspicacity, I might have changed my name and social security number, run to another country, and started a real life somewhere. I was twenty-two and didn't have the belief in myself or enough independence to make decisions. I had no memories or suspicion of my trapped underlife.

During another engagement-time trip to Long Island, I fought like a crazy cat not to marry and not to marry this man in particular. I was in a car with male programmers. They wanted me to marry Todd. Todd was six foot, thin, with medium brown oily hair, and pasty skin. He had a large nose, diminutive chin, and hazel eyes not unlike my mother's. A deadness and greed flowed from his eyes. He wore thick glasses that slid down his nose. He used the middle finger of his right hand to push them back into position. I screamed that I wouldn't, couldn't. Through drugs, hand signals, and threats, they subdued me and made me cooperate mindlessly. Even my mother noticed that this fiancé would try to keep me down. He was my punishment for not being one of them. His agreeing to marry me came with the deal that he could control me and I would support him through graduate school. Later they tagged on my having to have an ordinary-life child to keep him out of the draft. But the larger reason for this conception was so that my love for this baby would keep me compliant. *Run, Wendy, run before you give birth.*

The vanity, 1966

I pushed back the side mirrors of the painted vanity placed in the large bedroom with low windows that overlooked farmlands and the pond. The fields of this tiny rural town outside Rochester were filled with white, yellow, and purple wild flowers. Honeoye's soft hills felt like a melody and made me happy to be alive. I was twenty-three years old, teaching French in a country school, married to a graduate student. In the second year of our marriage, I still supported him while he sat in a recliner studying and daydreaming in the living room and

227

picking the hair off his right arm with his teeth and spitting it out. Though more ambitious than bright, he was preparing for a career in academia.

In the bedroom, I sat before the mirrors on the vanity which reflected back droplets of scars on the sides of my navel, not really scars but marks, whitish jagged colorations that looked a little like miniature people rushing to the subway, or the tips of waves about to break, or jagged clouds in the sky. I pushed the side mirrors in a quarter of the way, then back out a little. First they picked up the yellow flowers of the wallpaper on the side wall, cheerful and old fashioned. As I changed the angles, the mirrors reflected hieroglyphics even wrapped around my hips.

I stood in front of the painted vanity with movable side mirrors, wearing only my black bra. I had never before taken a good look at my belly, but that evening a curtain lifted or something shifted inside and someone younger inside me looked at my flesh and saw stretch marks, more on the right side of my body than on the left. I adjusted the side mirrors and looked at the stretch marks from different angles. *How do you get stretch marks that look like the skies after the rains? From pregnancy or obesity*, I answered myself. As far as I knew, I had never been pregnant. Or fat. I was skinny but loose skin girdled my lower stomach and hips, too loose for me to wear a bikini. When I attended Bard College, my friends and I had made a day trip to nearby Vassar College, and we had all tried on the bikinis in its campus store. Only I had loose skin hanging over the elastic. I was maybe nineteen at the time and a dancer. It didn't make sense.

I stood stunned, looking at my stained belly, stretching my neck as if it were a microscope to see the swirling lines. Dark theater curtains of my mind opened for a moment and I saw beautiful Paris and glistening babies and red. I saw Paris, not the Bronx. Or Brooklyn. Decades would pass before I would realize that Paris represented a programming ruse. My face and the pores of my skin became immobile, unfeeling, but underneath a torrential storm began. *Who was I? What had my life been?* I could not form the question of whether I had given birth to babies I didn't know about. I could not ask that question yet, or where they might be now. My heart spiked and receded, my brain spasmed, my breathing quickened. It looked as if the clouds on my belly would break into lightning. Perhaps I had a moment of lucidity because my husband was pressuring me to have a baby. I closed the mirrored vanity and my mind. My husband in the other room closed his book and wanted dinner.

I went into the small kitchen off the living room. We were living in a couple's finished attic, cheap, student-like housing. I warmed up franks and beans for dinner. Over the sink, a small table lamp stood on a shelf. Its cord went around the sink to a plug in the wall. No overhead light was in the kitchen. I leaned over to switch on the lamp and electricity shot through my body. I had another flash of Paris, and then I held my arm and realized an electric shock had ripped through my body.

"Why can't you be more careful?" Todd asked as he stood in the doorway to the kitchen. "I told you not to lean over the sink." In my awareness, I returned to Honeoye.

He began the refrain that had become his habitual dinner conversation. "If you are pregnant, they will not draft me. If you're not pregnant, they will draft me. They are drafting students, right now." My mind ricocheted between anger and guilt. I did not want a baby. *Was I just a breeder? To have babies for his benefit? If he were drafted and died in Vietnam, it would be my fault.* Once I repeated to our landlady what he had said. "Why does he think he is better than anyone else?" she answered. I had lucidity for one moment before the conscious part of my brain folded into the programming. I raced around town, even asking the family doctor where I could get an abortion. This rural physician looked at me as if I were a shrew. Instinct led me, not conscious awareness. And how could I have explained? My mind was scattered like dead people's ashes. But unlike ashes, the natural, organic electricity in the brain can bring it back to life.

Somewhere in the recesses, I knew. I knew what had happened to my sister and me.

The "expendable" child

Most of the experts who write about this abuse avoid the subject of the required sexual abuse of one's own children. Or perhaps they don't know about it because survivors are too shamed to disclose it. It's impossible to understand the full devastation of this planned destruction without acknowledging it. Writing about it makes me want to retreat to an island and never see anyone again.

The universal method of these groups is to let one child survive so that the mother can be controlled. This boy of mine who survived started out with a crisp, shining mind. He was born frowning though they hadn't given me electroshock during the pregnancy. He must have absorbed my emotions. As a child, his face lit up like a Frans Hals masterpiece, so full of life was he. His father was what they called a "commoner", which means not of a "distinguished" blood line, so my child was considered "expendable". I did what they told me in order to keep him alive.

Is it better to have your child slowly, tortuously killed or for you to rape him or her? They would not have killed us both together. I would have lived and he would have died. He was my eighth child. The others had all been murdered or abducted.

Their instructions were specific. All members of this kind of group had to abuse their children sexually at home and in rituals. Programmers don't call it sexual abuse or incest. They say, "You have to do this," and demonstrate. I imagine some parents were strong and wise enough not to. I wanted my boy to be alive.

My covering "front" person at that time knew nothing of this other life. Now I have many front people. They try to accept that I was a perpetrator but the despair is larger than they are. As one of them slips into almost suicide, another takes over. That's how I stay alive—by frequently changing. Why do I want to stay alive? I don't, but I must tell this story. These atrocities have to end.

My front person didn't yet know to talk to my insiders and find out about her history. She knew her boy had started out with an inordinate amount of devotion. My young son had looked at me with an idealizing, adoring kind of love. My inside people could hardly bring themselves to tell the others what had happened to this vigorous child. He had dark shiny hair that people wanted to stroke when they passed him. His hazel eyes were enormous and intelligent. His skin had an apricot tint. As a toddler, he concentrated as well as any adult. I sent him to a Midwestern university's school for gifted children. Their intelligence tests couldn't measure his aptitude for conceptual thinking. He could explain anything brilliantly. And he was so perceptive. I never knew what he would say and his comments took my mind to new places.

Once I took him to the planetarium. It happened that an exhibition of Taurus was showing. Just about everyone in the family was born under that sign. I asked him who the characteristics of Taurus reminded him of, thinking he could answer his parents, or half of his grandparents. He answered "Mayor Daley". He played the flute with such a perfect pitch, it made me want to start dancing again. He had empathy. We visited young adults in their first apartment. "They're lonely," he said. I had only noticed a vague uneasiness. When his father, Todd, from whom I was separated, told me he was living with someone and I cried, Ned put his head in my lap and said, "You're heartbroken". He had a logical, philosophical bent. One afternoon in Lincoln Park, I fell asleep. When I woke up a short time later, he was still sitting next to me. I said, "I fell asleep." He answered, "How do you know you were asleep?" He was six.

Why?

Why do parents have to abuse their children sexually? Some explanations are: to destroy bonding, to teach children that they are objects for others' use, to give them overwhelming physical and emotional feelings, to create familial triangles and rivalries, to teach them that they have to do what was done to them.

In addition, children at the mercy of groups like these have to be prepared for rapes that will take place during rituals, as part of programming. Trainers instruct parents in how gradually to stretch their children's orifices so that there will be a minimum of damage and tearing. Some parents cannot bring themselves to do this preparation to their offspring. Official trainers then step in. Ned's father was willing to stretch him so he wouldn't be injured. I couldn't, but they didn't let me off free. As punishment, I still had to abuse sexually, as did his father.

Sexual abuse punctures a child's relationship to the world and his or her own body. It teaches him that his body isn't his own, and that he is at the mercy of anyone who wants to violate him. It robs that child of the air and space around him. It cuts into his soul because our sexual life and the life of our emotions are intertwined and interwoven. It takes away the child's right to discover an enormous movement in his own time and way. When children are stripped of their sexual being, they are stripped of finding out who they are. A life-giving impulse is drowned by shame and discomfort.

We need water, air, food, touch, sleep; and we need boundaries. Boundaries to know where our limits are, to know we start and stop like countries. These groups destroy our boundaries before knowledge of them begins. They swallow our limits along with our concept of truth. Children in these groups live in a gray haze.

If my son hadn't been corrupted, he would have been one of the loving people in the world.

I hate genetic narcissism, the fact that people care mostly about their own, an extension of themselves. I fell into that same trap. These cults know that in the end what matters is the blood connection. We are wired for the preservation of family.

One of the mothers inside said to my front person, "I wouldn't touch Ned when he was born. They want the sexual stuff the second the child is born and I wouldn't do it, and then my sister wouldn't do it, and then another of us and another. Finally, the shocks became too much, and we gave out when they said they would start shocking him. Maybe they would shock a newborn, maybe they wouldn't. There's no way to trust them. We just wanted you to know that we tried."

If they would electroshock a fetus, they would shock a newborn. "Sister" refers to another part or personality within that section. In my journal, I wrote to the parts that knew of the sexual abuse of children. I wanted to know why they couldn't just fake it. They wrote back:

A MOTHER: "They did question Ned. They would have killed him if he didn't answer correctly."

ME: "We don't know for sure."

A DIFFERENT MOTHER: "I know for sure. I was there three or four times when they sat him on a chair and asked him whether his mother or father touched his penis, for how long, whether anything was put in his backside. He answered 'yes', he didn't know for how long and 'yes, things were put in his backside, fingers and sticks and toys,' he said. They asked, 'Did they

233

pat your behind at the end?' 'Yes.' 'Did they tell you to lie and say yes when the answer should be no?' 'No.'"

ME: "Where did they question him?"

A MOTHER: "When I was there, it was in the apartment on Oakdale, in Madison Park, and before then on Everett Place."

ME: "Could we have taught him to lie?"

THE FIRST MOTHER: "No."

ME: "Why not?"

THE MOTHER: "You would have had to use more torture on him than they did."

ME: "Would they have killed him if he said no?"

THE MOTHERS: "Probably."

Ram in the bush, 1972

In 1972, we were living in an apartment in the Midwest. Hours past midnight, there was a break-in, but someone had the key. Todd, who had recently left me, and two other men opened my door. I sprung up and heard Todd say, "Get the boy." My mind raced. *Do they mean Ned?* I thought. *How am I going to get to him? How will I fight off three men? I should have a gun!* As my panicked thoughts swirled, one of the men put a cloth over my face and I lost consciousness, but also heard the back door to the apartment close. Its thump sounded so final, inescapable. I was unconscious, but a part of my mind recorded, and witnessed. Even when put under anesthesia for major surgery, a part of the mind-controlled brain watches. I didn't know where my child was or what these men would do. I couldn't completely black out, and I was aware that it was right before his sixth birthday. Small Feasts of the Beast were being celebrated in towns across the world—not the twenty-seven year international ones, but still rituals to contend with. My bedroom clock said eight minutes after two. I was drugged and mostly asleep but still watching, remembering, calculating. It hadn't dawned on me yet that it was my thirtieth birthday. The men stood me up, held me under my sore armpits, and dragged me down the metal stairs. In remembering this, I wonder how many men have invaded my armpits. *How many fingerprints are there?*

The light on the steps looked mellow as if something sweet and festive were about to occur. We bumped into no one. I heard Todd say, "Lights out" from my apartment. He wanted me to hear him. He wanted me to think I would be killed or Ned would be killed, and terror swept me. I thought I heard him switch off the hall light and close the door. The rough men doing a job they were most likely paid to do pushed me into a black car still running its engine. *Where is my son?* I thought as I tumbled into the back seat. The mules in me rose for a moment because of the familiarity of this scene, but I was not aware of my inside parts and could not have identified them then. Todd had disappeared with Ned. *They had killed Daniel's sister when she turned six.* The drive along the water took less than half an hour. Few cars were on the road. The car sped, lights danced on the road like fairies. The pale moon and flat stars shone on the molten lake. Even when calm and mellow, the city has a razor edge. We parked in the grassy fields around the mammoth sculpture of robed figures. The men parked in the bushes close to the area where about one hundred hooded people had already gathered.

At the entrance to rituals, wardrobe assistants take your clothes and hand you a hooded robe. A woman at the entrance said, "Everyone has to be naked underneath for the movies." Those last words brought out an actor in me, one who was used to performing for cameras. I hadn't seen Ned since he left the apartment with Todd. Even the actor looked around for him. Everyone was rushing about, mumbling, dancing, chanting. I made out some of their words, "Ram in the bush ..." Black and white candles surrounded the ritual site but lights from cameras let me see well. Cameras shot the crowds and often panned on my face. It felt like a rape, even to the actor.

I saw the sharp outline of parallel altars, pale children placed on top. The altars had brought out a mother in me, which made the actor disappear into my depths of being. I thought I recognized Ned's profile on an altar. The moonlight and camera lights lit his body. I became certain that he lay on one of the two prepared altars. My heart froze and dropped. It was worse than my worries. He was motionless, probably not dead. A bomb of hatred filled my body. For a drop of prestige, his father would sacrifice him, like one of those Greek heroes. The other altar had a beautiful boy. People near me said it was John Lee, an Asian boy who lived in the same neighborhood as me. I did not know him. He was probably a better person than me or my son. The boys were naked; I wanted to cover them even with my black robe. The stars and camera lights glistened on their young limbs. Was John's family present? Were they members or had he been abducted? Flashes of Daniel's sacrifice ripped through my ribs. Daniel had been thirteen. There had been no escape. Decades later, there was no escape.

A tall man came up behind me, and I jumped. The crowds chanted "Choose who you will slaughter for Lucifer, praise his name." The Luciferians wanted the corruption of the soul; the Mafia, a snuff flick to circulate and sell. The man pushed his draped knee into my back and legs and walked me to the center of a circle. Hooded figures swayed and chanted. The candles flickered but the camera's lights projected harsh yellow. The robed man behind me drove with his knee. John screamed "Don't let them choose me, don't let them kill me," crying, gasping. I felt impressed that the child wanted to live. So many didn't. I hadn't. Daniel hadn't. I became paralyzed. I don't even think I blinked. Then I sobbed. The suspense built for the crowd as they chanted "Happy birthday to you, you have reached the age of treason, now all you have to do is kill your own boy—you don't even have a girl—or use your ram in the bush—a yellow-skinned boy. Happy birthday to you, you have reached the age of misfortune, now slay the ram and become of use, miserable queen, unfortunate queen, slay this ram and rejoin your fold." I couldn't choose. Ned screamed, "Just choose, Mom." His "Mom" made me break down further. They began torturing both boys, twisting their arms, shoving their heads back. They took out a razor as if to prepare for skinning alive. Ned must have known what was about to happen. He must have witnessed these scenes before. Someone inside me said, "Just take him," pointing to John. Ned screamed, "Don't do it." This child started out with great compassion. I heard Todd's voice and saw his face in the camera lights. He was talking to the camera and with a snide expression said, "I knew she'd do that." The crowd desired the torture.

I hadn't known this was a significant ritual. Little rituals took place at every holiday, at least once a month. They always found an excuse. The man standing behind me and pressing into me covered my hands within his black-gloved hands, and walked me over to the altar where Ned lay in agony. My heart felt as if it had a knife in it, the pain rippling to my arms and jaw. The man lifted my arms over my son, whose eyes were wild with fear but clear, not drugged. That gave me hope, since they usually drugged sacrificial victims. The cameras rolled furiously if silently, close-ups, panorama shots. The executioner's movement jarred me from ruminating. His right arm squeezed my intestines, his left knee jutted between my legs, as his left hand pressed a knife in my left hand, closed his hand around mine, and lifted my arm. It happened in a fast swoop. The masses chanted and hummed. The executioner abruptly as if following my mental order walk-dragged my limp body away from the altar where Ned lay as if dead, and toward the one where John lay as if dead. Someone shouted "cut," and the lights went off. It was black except for the flickering candles. The crowd continued chanting, "Ram in the bush." The wardrobe mistress entered from the side and slipped a

237

crown on my head. In the breath between seconds, with his gloved hands wrapped over mine, right after the blackout of lights, the executioner plunged the knife into, I thought, this beautiful boy John. Even now, I can feel the resistance in my arms, especially the leading left one, as a body memory. In the blackout, I felt a puncture of something soft but solid. I thought my hands had been taken from me and used to kill.

Blood spurted, the crowd cheered, and I felt a sinking fall as the crowd began its off-and-on orgy. When the ritual knife came down, my mind divided into two. One part was not sure whether John was dead and whether I had killed him. That part stayed in perennial searching for him. The other part saw that during the blackout, the stage crew removed John and replaced him on the altar with a raw sirloin tip roast. I fainted and vomited in my faint onto the meat. Part of the faint was relief. The snuff flick would be circulated. Part of my dizziness is from internal spinners keeping me from the memory, and part is from the anguish of realizing who I am.

I gained some consciousness, and the camera lights came back on for the next scene. When the crew's lights shone, casting a greenish hue on the hungry faces in the crowd, I noticed my parents for the first time. They lived in New York and must have flown in for this ritual. And I saw my grandfather who strutted about like the vain emperor with no clothes. He wore his Wiezenslowski mask, and smiled knowingly at the camera.

He was programming Ned after they removed him from the first altar. My grandfather held a gun to Ned's temple and said, "This boy is not allowed to love his mother. You will always despise your mother, and whenever you see her, you will remember how much you despise her. Go over there and tell her." My parents said, "Good boy." My mother kept turning her head over her shoulder to smile at the cameras, and tilted her head up. Her hair was newly dyed. Todd was about to be granted freedom from the marriage as long as he agreed to become "conscious".

A presence like a compilation of inside parts rises and floats above this scene. She is nine and a half years old, stretched out lengthwise on her side, leaning on her bent elbow and wearing one of the blue and white ruffled dresses my grandmother had brought back from Florida for Rhonda and me. She says over and over that she wants to die. She is comprised of many betrayals and was created when I was four and a half. Parts have to be established in the years before nine to hold their form. She is always there but not always visible like a cloud, a fox, or a suicidal thought. She guides me to the ritual site. The blackout occurred. John was removed from the altar. They lifted me from my faint and vomit, and placed me on the same altar that John had been on. Ned had been programmed by my grandfather. Now I was on the altar and they brought in a birthday cake for me on a silver platter. A dagger stuck out of the top of the birthday cake with black flickering lit candles. The crowds like a prophetic Greek chorus chanted, "I hate you, Mom, unqueened …" This leaning figure of parts of me pushes me forward. She will not let me stop writing. I want to have my dinner. "No," she says, "keep writing. Write." The executioner pushed Ned forward, lifted his arms with Ned's small limbs captured between them; the knife high, it started to move down—another blackout. The dagger had a rubber tip and was collapsible. It plunged into my heart that had already felt it had another kind of dagger in it. I was still alive, covered in my own vomit. Terrified, I was ambivalent about being alive. *I should stay alive to protect my child, but I cannot guard him*, I thought.

Ten days before the memory of this coming-of-age ritual presented itself, I felt exhausted and started thinking about a boy named John. I had a flash of myself drugged—the body memory of exhaustion may have been the drugged feeling. In the memory flash, I wore a black robe, was held under the

239

arms, and dragged down a building's front staircase by two men, one of whom was my estranged or ex-husband.

My nights were filled with insomnia. Finally, the memory crept out of my mind.

After I fainted on the second altar, they gave me smelling salts to bring me back. The camera panned on Ned's pained face, and John's terrorized but relieved face. Ned repeated as taught, "I hate you, Mom." He spoke his scripted words in that mind-control monotone. I felt myself crumble as if I had lost everything, and could never get any of it back. I felt that in my life I had just misery and hopelessness, and a child pressured to hate me who would eventually hate me. The chorus chanted, "He hates his mother," the cameras licked the words.

Taking advantage of this vulnerability, my grandfather in the center of a circle said "You think you have spine and are so fine like Bordeaux wine, here's what will make you shine," as he kicked my body, and invited the chorus to kick me. In the recall process, for four days, I have muscle spasms that I think are from lifting my dog too much. When I retrieve this last part of this memory, my back stops hurting. It is the beginning of October 2013 now. The real event took place in the fall around 1972. The mind has inner workings that push up anniversary memories, even forty-one years later. Afterward, in my ordinary life, I did not remember this ritual. But some part of my brain kept looking for John on the street, in the neighborhood.

After the ritual, when the two thugs dragged me back to my door, and dumped me in my apartment, I saw a bottle of pills—white round ones—that did not belong to me, spilled on my night table. Todd must have dumped the pills before he said "lights out." I took it as a message that he wanted me to kill myself. I became more depressed than usual. By now, my conscious mind didn't know a thing about John Lee, but my hidden mind thought about him constantly.

During these years of rituals and when they actively programmed Ned against me, only severe hunger would drive me from bed in the mornings. I would buy a fruit that I particularly desired and when the hunger pains mounted, I would drag myself out of bed and eat the persimmon or mango. That is how I stayed alive. Some of these feelings came back as I wrote this chapter. It felt as if my bones left my body. I had painted a mixed media canvas in the 1980s. I attached a doll that wore a starched white dress to a canvas of pasted-on strips of canvas in various shades of greenish black. The doll's bones were scattered over the canvas, though the doll maintained its prenatal position.

Rituals take a few hours, and mind-control programming sessions about half an hour, so the majority of one's time is spent in ordinary life. I had made one of the bigger accomplishments and one of the more significant mistakes of my still fairly young life in normal life. I sent my son to private school. His mind started working as if it didn't have programs in it. The true self is what the criminal cults want to obliterate. When my mother died and my program not to create was destroyed, I began writing and choreographing. Two real selves, my son and me. We had to be stopped. The long series of calculated moves to separate us intensified. Our hearts bumped and fled, knocked and hid, scarred bleeding hearts—hopelessness turned bitter.

When my son wasn't on altars or at rituals, he was a perfect student; I was a scholarship graduate student working toward a PhD, and taught modern dance classes to support us. Those parts functioning in the world knew nothing of the rituals and mind control. Absolutely nothing. We thought we were a regular person. The programmers used portable electrical gadgets to make us forget. "This ritual never happened. You weren't here. You were home asleep the whole time."

They sent away the parts of the brain that attended, and called out the unknowing, functioning personalities. With their electricity, they could accomplish almost anything concerning the mind.

241

There remained a bridge between Ned and me, but it was built of coolness, temper tantrums, and defiance. The programming remained hidden inside, unknown to the personalities living normal life, but affecting all actions and feelings. And underneath the programming was the abiding love that I have for my child, and I believe that he somewhere still has for me. On the surface, however, he opposed whatever I said, and I couldn't like him.

Alison said he opposed what I said because of programming, and he was afraid I would be hurt if we were close.

The rift, 1979–1982

This criminal group wanted Ned away from me permanently. A thug, an electroshock expert, and Todd had Ned and me sitting on two hard chairs that they took from my downtown loft. Tied to parallel chairs, we received electroshocks. Me, him, me—he screamed, "Let me go, Mom." One of their standard methods is to impersonate a parent so that the child thinks that parent is torturing him. They either use a look-alike adult or show a film and tell the child that the villain is his parent.

To get him away from them, I would send him to an excellent private school, I thought. I found a Quaker school that seemed wholesome. He would escape somehow. They separated us, but they didn't have to keep him. But the next week, his father took him away. I sat in the kitchen numb and immobile. I had turned to stone. Even electricity could not melt me now. While Todd packed up Ned's belongings, I did not think of my other stolen and killed children. These awarenesses were barricaded in recesses and caverns. I did not hear my son's logical, clear scream, "Let me go." It was not worth the struggle, we could not win, he was saying. I thought of my mother sneaking into my bedroom when I was three, or four, or five. She held a down pillow and placed it over my head. I turned and struggled. My sister in a parallel bed screamed, and my father rushed in, and

242

pulled Mother away as I gasped for air and knew my mother truly wanted me dead. I wished she had succeeded.

My son knew I did not want to give him up. He knew I had tried to find a better environment for him. Meanwhile Todd kept being promoted in academia, until he landed a national position. This kind of cult acquires positions like these through corruption and money, and rewards its most compliant members with prestigious high-paying jobs. It is one reason we find so many incompetent people holding positions of power. I was just a dancer and teacher. My son would be sent to power and money.

It was during the 1982 Feast of the Beast on Prince Edward Island, when the leaders tortured and pressured me the most to accept my role as queen and become fully conscious, that they cemented the rift. I was on a rack being tortured for my refusal to cooperate, when the slaves took Ned away. When he returned, he was thoroughly mind controlled against me, and probably fearful that if he was loving toward me, that I would be killed. That barrier never broke down. A tone of constrained disdain crept into his formerly loving melodic voice. Now he was on one side, and I the other. Never would he have chosen to be in this position of his own free will. One has to go through a life-threatening struggle for free will. It has not been a birth-right for us who were conceived within criminal groups like these.

ELEVEN

A mule's life

I sat in a big airplane. I didn't know how I had got here. Panic seized my throat. I receded, and another person came forward. In the time it takes to swallow or less, a person can emerge and recede. This new person was assured. She had instructions. Similar people came out with her, so she was not alone.

I was the one who emerged. I was a courier. We carried drugs and political documents from one continent to another. I walked through customs without expression. The inspectors did not look up my vagina, or into my rectum, or in any of my bras. I went by different names. I had been travelling since my late teens, two trips per year, probably a total of twenty-five.

Paris to Pakistan, 1972

The alarm clock rang at 3:45 a.m. I rolled over, pretending to sleep through the noise. Todd sat up in bed and shut off the alarm.

My clothes for this run were laid out on a chair: black trousers, new underpants, a brassiere slightly small for me, white socks, black loafers, a brown shirt. He must have gathered them after I fell asleep last night. He stored them in the narrow broom closet in the kitchen. The travel clothes would not attract attention. A "run" was when the internal couriers took something illegal from one country to another. I had many couriers in my system, but my other personalities didn't know about them. Todd pulled off my nightgown, and tried to dress me. I tried to bite his hand, but he waved four fingers on his right hand in front of my face. Something clicked in my brain, and I could not bite, kick, fight, or flee. My father had given him my hand signals as part of my dowry.

"That's good, darling girl," my husband said. "Just you lie there." He put on my clothes piece by piece, as if I were a child or a doll.

"Lift your arms through," he said. His voice went up and down, which meant he was not in a robotic state like me. I lifted my arms as if I were a marionette, just there to flop around according to someone else's wishes. Life can be taken away from you just like that. The childhood, teenage years, and now this expanse of adulthood. I lived it, but it did not belong to me.

My six-year-old ran into the bedroom. He wore his blue pajama sleeper, and cried. He ran to me, and Todd said, "Help Mommy on with her shoes." Ned pounded on my feet. He was a bright, intense boy who readily had temper tantrums. His mind ground out thoughts constantly.

Todd put on my brown parka that I wore only for runs, zipped it up, and put on my gloves. He forgot my hat and scarf. It was the Midwest in the winter, which meant brutal coldness. The building heat hadn't started yet.

I remained dazed, but parts of me floated above myself, and watched. These parts of my mind didn't like to go too far away from my body and the others. My son cried and needed his mother. So much of me wanted to spin out of this program, pick him up and tell him I'd never leave, but Todd waved the fingers, my brain pinched, and I stayed in the part of my brain that had been tortured into being a courier.

"Go back to your room," Todd told Ned. Ned didn't challenge Todd. Then Todd slipped his arm under mine, squeezed my arm through my parka, and walked me down the three flights of the row house in Old Town. I stepped over children's bikes parked on the steps. The new neighbors who had moved into the first floor let their children leave their bikes all over the public places.

I was sleepwalking and dull. Deeper in my heart were terror and grief that I had left my crying child, so connected to me that he woke from a deep sleep when I was forced to leave him. The robot part of my brain persisted, but the feelings from the other parts formed a halo around my brain and clamored. Some parts recorded the action so that one day I could tell what happened to me and at least thousands of others. I did this for the other mothers forced to leave their crying or sleeping children to make runs for pimps, runs that they would not be conscious of doing and have no memory of having done.

Two sedans were double parked in the street outside the row houses. They glistened in the dark like wet goose feathers. A man with a shiny leather jacket and a cap put his gloved hand under my free arm. For a moment, I was sandwiched between the betrayer-husband and the hired kidnapper.

"She's a wild fire. Don't trust her," my husband said, slipping his arm away, and turning quickly to go back into the warmer building. He wore his bedroom slippers. He knew the transfer would be swift and efficient. The front door to my building closed silently as the man opened the back door to the car, and pushed me in. I ducked my head, and he slipped in beside me. He pressed his hip into mine, pushed my back forward, clasped my gloved hands behind me, and handcuffed them. My heartbeat turned upside down. Sweat soaked my gloves even though it was freezing outside. He reached over me and pulled down the shade. I quickly looked up to my dark, shut third floor home, and my heart dropped. The man whose name I didn't know pulled down the shade on the other side. He told me to put my head down as he shoved it down. He pried open my mouth, and shoved a pill under my tongue. I felt ambivalent about the pill. If it brought me oblivion, it might not be so bad. He pulled out a handgun, and pressed it into my right temple.

The man cocked the gun and said, "I hope we don't have any big bumps or crashes." When I was a child in bed gasping for breath through my sobs, my mother had stood in the doorway and said, "If you don't stop crying, I'll take you into bed with me." I started to wheeze.

The car drove carefully through the narrow, dark streets. I imagined it went at exactly the speed limit. The street lamps glowed, but I couldn't read the corner signs. The program in me not to know my location was active. I fought to stay awake, but fell deeper and deeper into unconsciousness. Sometimes my head jerked up. I thought I heard Ned crying.

We arrived in the city's desolate outskirts. The driver shut the car lights off, but continued to drive. We crept slowly. Two men dressed in black, lean and quick, ran out of a warehouse. The man with the cap jerked me out of the sedan. The winter air splashed my face, and made me more alert. The two men from the warehouse grabbed my arms and walked me roughly into the warehouse, as the second sedan pulled up. Two men got out of the car. I felt the round head of a gun in my back. Even though a gun pressed into me, I could barely stay awake. My head plunged down and popped up.

Men lifted me onto an examination table. One warehouse man ripped my black trousers off. "Don't tear anything. She has to wear these clothes home," the other one said. *They didn't plan on killing me then.* He took the rest of my clothes off roughly, but didn't tear them.

A small, well-wrapped package sat on a side table. The leader man attempted to insert the package in my vagina. He couldn't get it in. I felt a faint pride that I had won that battle, if being naked in a warehouse and having dope inserted into you meant winning.

"We'll have to use the ass," he said.

Nearby a police siren blasted. The men froze, their muscles tensing like a mother deer spotting hunters. They darkened the room, swept the packages and clothing into a bag, and pushed me into a back room. Two men went in with me. They gagged my mouth, and held a gun to my throbbing head. My eyes looked around wildly. I feverishly wanted the police to find me, but even without the gag, I couldn't scream. I heard no knock on the door, or doors opening. The tendons on my neck jutted out brutally. Men outside whistled. *They must be lookouts.* After a while, the gun still held taut, a man outside whispered, "All clear."

They dragged me from the back room into a dirty, streaked bathroom. It reminded me of gas stations' bathrooms.

"Get on all fours," a man spit out. His saliva crossed the room. He appeared angry about the delay.

"She can't. She's in handcuffs," a chubbier man said.

The first man unlocked the cuffs, made a sudden, artful karate spin, and kicked me in the ribs to the ground. Another man filled the enema bag with water, and plunged the prong into my rectum. I then sat on the freezing toilet seat, shivering and having diarrhea. They used washcloths and towels to clean my legs, inserted the package in me, pried open my mouth, and forced me to swallow another pill with water from the rusty sink. They put a brassiere on me that had papers in between the material, and fastened a second bra on top of the first bra. They walked me into a wardrobe room. Closets stacked with clothes in the same style from sizes six to eighteen, and bras and underpants overflowed. Some had fallen to the ground. They chose a sturdy, inconspicuous outfit for me, similar to what I wore to get there. Hundreds, thousands of women must have passed through here. A men's division was on the other side. I felt like a cockroach.

249

They gave me a size eight. They tried on different pairs of shoes. None fit right. I had to be able to run if necessary. They let me wear my own shoes.

Birds outside chirped. I thought of mothers sleeping in their husbands' arms. Soon they would awaken contented, brew coffee, and boil oatmeal. Did I hear my child's crying?

The worker-man folded my clothes and put them in a black bag. He put my white socks on top and tagged the bag.

I became a mule in black pants. If I returned home and was not killed or jailed, then I would return to being a wife of an academic, making dinner parties for faculty from *Mastering the Art of French Cooking*, and the mother of a first grader, and a graduate student on fellowship. I remained so sleepy-doped that I could barely tell which man was which. They all scurried around as if a bomb were about to explode. The driver and my escort left. Other warehouse men controlled me now. They dragged me into an identical black sedan. Still dark, it probably was not 5:00 a.m. yet. Two men flanked me; each had a gun in my ribs. I felt them through the black coat they outfitted me with. With their guns cocked, these desperate men readied to shoot. *Do not do anything rash. Go along with them. What's going on here is bigger than one woman's protesting*, I said to myself mantra-style. Daniel had told me not to bring too much trouble onto myself. *Other victims must have tried to escape. Why else would they use two guns?*

A woman sat up front, next to the driver. I wondered how this middle-aged woman got lured into this business. *What could she get from it, or what was she preventing? She must have a child at home also*. We drove for a long time, though I kept falling asleep despite the guns. I had a vague sense of their giving me an injection in my arm as they dressed me in my uniform of another identity.

I saw light flickering in the distance, and signs for an airport. The car followed the signs to "International". Lights shone gaily. Midwest International Airport. The limousine pulled up to the drop-off section for Air France. The man on the passenger side took a small suitcase out of the trunk, and stood it on the sidewalk. He handed me a purse with my passport and ticket inside.

"You're on the 5:08 a.m. flight to Paris, France, flight 538. Our people are in front, behind, and on the side of you. Don't try anything. In Paris, you take another flight. We're watching your every step," the passenger-side man said. I walked toward customs and noticed a woman by my side, a man in front, and another behind me. They seemed to trail me. I opened my passport. My name was Sheila Richardson today. My photo was current. I couldn't remember when they had photographed me. My small suitcase and purse passed customs easily. They didn't search my body. I wanted to collapse right here on the airport's floor and go to sleep, but if I did, one of my stalkers would shoot me and flee. I believed that if I stated my correct name they would kill my child or me.

I started to come to when the woman by my right side waved four fingers on her left hand. The hand signal meant I had to stay in my stone-faced trance. The woman wore a pleated skirt and jacket. It looked like a dog trainer's outfit, the kind you saw on television during the Westminster dog shows. I passed through. I said nothing. I boarded the plane, and took my seat on the aisle.

One of the men had the aisle seat directly in front of mine, another man right behind me. I didn't know where or when the woman flanking me disappeared. Later I got up to use the bathroom in the back of the plane, and the man who sat in front trailed me. I closed the bathroom door, and noticed some of the enema had formed a skipping pattern down my leg like ants carrying breadcrumbs into a hole. I used paper towels and airplane soap to clean it, then pulled my pants back up. *You would think these men would supply pads.* I heard a tapping outside, not on the door but on some part of the wall. Two long taps, four short. My signal to hurry up. *If I was late because of cleaning up*

251

my enema, would they kill my son? At least I was wearing trousers this time. When they dressed me in tights and a skirt, it was harder to clean myself. I opened the door, and the waiting man tipped his hat to me, which meant trouble. He rushed in, probably checking to see whether I had discarded the contents of my inner bra, the one with the political papers. I couldn't take the chance, though were it not for my child, I wouldn't have minded provoking them to murder me.

I felt something desperate, or reckless and wild rise in me, something of my original spirit perhaps. A few hours had passed since I had received a hand signal, and I must have been coming out of my trance, slowly, leaving the world of mindless, programmed robot and re-becoming flesh and blood.

A nice man with a round face and soft eyes sat in the window seat on the rear left side of the plane next to an empty seat. I rushed into it. The nice man looked up surprised, as the man who sat behind me came over, bit his nails into my shoulder and said, "Miss, you were sitting over here. You got confused." He took me by the arm, jamming the nail of his thumb deep into my arm muscle. Squeezing my arm more and more tightly, he led me back to my original seat, smiling pleasantly at the passengers who watched him.

The next day when I was home again with my child, I would look at my arm and see a sprawling black and blue mark like an octopus shooting out feelers, seeking help. The guard-men were not supposed to use force in public, or leave marks that could jog the memory. I have to thank this bruise for getting me to this memory over four decades after it occurred. A present-day bruise with a similar shape led me right to this forbidden awareness.

Back in my seat, I wondered why the nice man with soft eyes didn't suspect something foul. *Couldn't he at least have reported a problem to the flight attendant?* "Miss, may I help you with your bag?" the front man said. The men formed a team, but from their dress and manner, one would never guess. The back man

252

acted like a businessman with his gray suit, tie, and briefcase. The front man seemed like a hippie in his blue jeans, cap, and wrinkled shirt. I got simultaneous hand signals from front and back—"Stay in trance, don't speak, don't attract attention, one wrong move and we will kill your boy."

We proceeded to baggage claim as an unknown man in casual clothes approached. His skin was dark, and he didn't seem to speak English. He handed me another valise, and slipped a purse onto my left shoulder. I felt myself fold flat.

The two men kept aiming me down the jammed corridor with noisy people and foreign language signs that looked like dancing scrolls. They sat me down in a waiting room, the new purse on my shoulder, and the valise by my feet. I received a hand signal to look inside the purse. I found an American passport with a photo of me—for this leg of the trip, Sandra Daniels was my name—and tickets to Pakistan. Just then a man asked in foreign English if this seat was taken. He sat down, and I knew he was my next escort. Formally dressed, he had an inconspicuous manner. The other man sitting across from me wore gray chinos, and a blue open shirt.

I didn't have to think. They pulled the strings. The casual one waved his four fingers, thumb tucked, and I plummeted back into the trance I had just begun to emerge from. I noticed a Pepsi next to me. It must have been for me to drink. Drugs must have been in it. I would rather not know what would happen next, so I swallowed it. The man across smiled slightly, the man next to me sighed with relief. Pretty soon I would be at home with my child, figuring out how to kill my husband, if I returned.

An announcement was made in what I thought might be Pakistani, then in English, to board the plane. I didn't recognize the names of its destination cities. I didn't know where Pakistan was. In trance, I boarded the plane to Pakistan. A suspicious-looking, all-covered-up woman sat across the aisle, and eyed me through her peripheral vision.

After we landed, I stood up to get my coat, but a different coat occupied the overhead compartment. I took it, and carried it over my arm.

"Have a nice day," the cheerful flight attendant said to the guard in front of me.

He nodded his head and tipped his hat.

"I hope you enjoyed your trip," she said to me.

"Thank you," I answered sweetly.

"Have a nice day," she said to the kidnapper behind me.

"And to you," he answered, and turned stiffly.

I saw that one man carried my first coat over his arm. He stopped, and emptied the pockets. Later he threw the coat in a garbage pail.

The men flanked me, but pretended they didn't know me. My head wouldn't stay steady. Everyone thought of Todd as a hero. He was chair of a department, and he sold his wife into slavery, and told my agents not to trust me because I was a spitfire. *When I get home, I could castrate him in his sleep, or put poison in his hamburger. Couldn't these people tell how drugged I was?*

I walked obediently as if in a dream into the trap of customs. I pulled my body through the airport as if it were a reluctant dog on a leash. I felt a rumble of terror like the sounds before a thunderstorm peaked. I could move, I could walk, but the terror played a roll call under my heart. I didn't think that I could contain it. It crescendoed when the officers took me into a back room and closed the door, click, click, double lock. I didn't know the nationality of the men who followed me and were now locked out. Inside here in customs, they were all Pakistanis. The men wore official uniforms, the woman a purple silk robe that brought out the blue highlights in her heaps of black hair. She translated into a distorted English.

"Leave down on the table."

They left my loafers on.

Right now in the present as I remember, my inner skin turns red.

They ripped me open the way eager adolescents tear open their Christmas gifts.

"Look for the bra," the woman translated.

They ripped off the inner bra with document padding.

"Get her off the table," the woman translated.

The men talked fast, sometimes at the same time. The woman in silk didn't translate everything.

"Maybe we should keep her. Why send her back?"

"She doesn't have a contract."

The fear I'd had since my first run took hold of my throat. Worse than killing me, they could keep me as a sex slave. "Look at the boobs, big," the woman translated.

"Nice boobs, bigger than our women's."

"No, they have stretch marks."

"We don't like stretch marks."

"We could do better. American boobs could be better."

"We have better right next door."

That poor woman, I thought.

"She's no good."

They slapped my face with the outside part of their hands, punched me in the stomach, kicked me until I buckled in two. *This dialogue must have been scripted.*

"Let's see if we got everything out. Maybe she's hiding something from us."

A familiar loneliness seized me. I couldn't live in this world, with people. I thought these four men, smelly, unwashed criminals in uniform costumes, on government payroll, planned to re-explore me, but that was their signal for rape. The smell of fermented urine and dirt rose. Once I started vomiting, I could not stop. It was as if the vomit became my anger.

Behind the rape room, the men pushed me through a hidden door in a brick wall. It opened onto another square room with a familiar-style black chair. They threw me on the chair, and tilted it back. A man who wore a turban traced the blue veins on my throat with the tip of his knife. *These men wanted something*

255

more from me. There was a reason they would not let me pass. A man with a turban began: "Who would think there was bright red inside these blue veins? It's as if the blood were wearing an overcoat. If we took the coat off, a lot of blood would come out—that would be a shame. That's what will happen if you disobey again. Like when you sat in the wrong seat next to that man. You don't want us to kill an innocent person. Some nice, innocent person. You don't want to force us to kill that person. If that person had helped you, he would now be dead. You don't want to force us to kill your little boy, who is at home now wondering where his mother is. It would be a shame if you didn't return to him, wouldn't it? All you have to do is behave. Sit in your right seat. Make the deliveries on your own. Go where you're supposed to go.

"We are going to give you the opportunity to redeem yourself. We don't usually do this."

Was this all they wanted, I think, *just to punish me*? The man with the turban started using hand signals. He said: "You will go on your own. You will travel all over the world being our mule, our puppet. If you ever disobey, remember, or tell, we will kill your boy that day."

This was what they wanted, for me to travel without the plants. I burdened their finances by needing escorts. They wanted more from me: "You will take another flight, change planes in Copenhagen. A man will take you by your left arm. You will not look right or left, just straight ahead. You will have different names. They will be on your ticket and passport. You will get your new purse when you land in Copenhagen. You are our courier girl. You have to regain our trust."

They electroshocked me as they gave me the information again about flight numbers and names. A series of songs ran through my head. I heard the melodies, but not the lyrics. As they electroshocked my nipples, they said: "It would be a shame if we didn't let you return home to your little child. It would be a shame if we had to keep you here for ever and ever. But maybe you would like living in Pakistan in one of our clean brothels, or maybe one of our not-so-clean brothels where the girls have many diseases. You can live a year or two with syphilis, before we put you out on the street. We have Americans in our brothels. Big, powerful America, and we have their girls. We could keep you here. If you disobey again.

"We would not want to have to kill him, take him out of his private school if you disobey." *So they knew where he went to school.*

"If you try and escape, don't do your assignment, remember or tell. We would hate to have to kill him, your boy." They spun me, then stopped the spinning abruptly, jarring me, and shook me roughly. If that happened to me at the age I am now, my bones would dislocate.

The female translator cleaned me up. She made my hair neater, and told them that I needed a new coat to cover me. The customs men had torn my clothes.

I was released from Pakistani customs. Then I could escape, but where to? Where to in Pakistan? I might have tried something in France, but not here. I would end up in a brothel, which would be full-time work.

My first run came in 1962, when I was in college. After that, I made one or two runs per year. In 1966, when I was twenty-three and pregnant, my controllers used me again. Todd walked me to the gate at La Guardia Airport. I was wearing a medium blue dress with a large bow on the bodice, the pre-feminist maternity style of the Sixties. I had a container in me within a leather pouch. Someone in me ran into the bathroom. That part didn't know what was about to happen, but knew she had to stall for time. She couldn't figure out a way to escape, so she started tweezing her eyebrows in front of the bathroom mirror. She stayed in the bathroom for a long time, tweezing. When she emerged, Todd said, "You took so long. I almost came in after you."

During the later runs, my anticipation to be home was ecstatic. I would see and hold my child, even though he squirmed and hit. I could eat fruit and a salad without fear of moving my bowels and being killed if I could not retrieve all the dope. I could shower and wash feces off my legs, and practice sanitary ways of cleaning. I could breathe in fresh air with the windows open, and not the braided smell of urine and semen. I could go back to school, and fall into the role of an ordinary person and faculty wife. Perhaps Todd would be repentant. Other abusers offered a short-lived consideration phase. I craved being soothed and sanitized.

After one of the runs, when the limousine with my driving escorts pulled up to my home, I got out of the back seat. The front-seat man handed me my original purse and keys. He separated the key to my front door, so it stood out like a telephone pole. I walked up the three flights of steps, opened the door, and walked past the marital bedroom. It was early morning dark, maybe 4:30 a.m. Todd was in bed with a woman, probably one of his students. The girl had long, straight, blond hair, the kind men love. Her skin was anemic-looking, and she was ultra-thin. She was probably a freshman at the university. Todd was on his side of the bed with his hands folded under his head. He smirked and pretended to be asleep. I walked past this bedroom, down the hall, through the kitchen, into the back bedroom where my son was in too deep a sleep. I felt his pulse, and put my ear on his chest. He was alive but drugged. I lifted his arm, and it fell heavily. I lay next to him and held his pudgy hand with long fingers. Todd's fingers. *How to escape? Was there a way to save Ned? I couldn't kill my husband tonight because of the poor used girl next to him.*

* * *

It is a typical night in 2013. I sleep for a few hours and awaken with a thrust, my jaw clenched, my teeth notched like antique drawers. Another memory arises in my consciousness. An older courier went through customs stone-faced, and no one suspected her. No one peered up her vagina. She said that she took a plane with her body empty to a stopover country, which could have been Holland, France, or anywhere. She went on command into a bathroom and a woman, a native of that country, in the next locked stall, climbed underneath into hers and inserted a package of dope that had a white string attached like a tampon. If customs searched, they would think she was menstruating. The foreign native woman climbed back to her own stall, unlocked the door, and exited.

I feel my inner face underneath my skin turn scarlet. The parts of my brain, the personalities within, turn scarlet with shame. It is one thing to be a willing criminal. It is another to be an unwitting slave.

After another run, when I picked Ned up from school, Sharon the teacher said, "We missed you yesterday. Ned was upset, and not getting along with the other girls and boys." I didn't know that I had missed a day. Ned ran up to me and pounded my legs, then bit me through my gray flannel slacks and socks. I started crying. *What have I done to my child?* I thought. I sat down on the floor, pulled my knees to my head, and cried. Perhaps it was the teacher's kindness that set me off, someone who seemed to care. I didn't know whether I was having a nervous breakdown, or just crying out of hopelessness. As children, my sister and I would cry only when someone was kind. My back was pressed against a bookcase filled with children's books. Toys were scattered on the floor. The teacher Sharon never would have believed where I had just been. Sharon said something to Ned, and I was able to hold his hand and take him out.

When I got home, if I got home from a run, I could tell the woman who had a child my son's age. I could tell her during one of their play-dates. I would then never hear from her again, and Ned wouldn't have the play dates. There were others I could tell, and never hear from again. So my life was surface normalcy interrupted by criminal activities that I

259

didn't remember, and if I happened to remember enough to tell someone, I would be marked as crazy. The world colludes with crime.

Courier training

Being a mule wasn't punishment for disobedience. My training started young, in the bathtub. My father, with his hand on my left shoulder, said: "Let me see you be the little girl who spreads her legs."

"Let me see you be the girl who lifts her behind. Let me see you be the girl who has packages put in her poupee and behind."

While my father bathed me, first he pulled out different parts by talking, then giving hand signals. We rehearsed this every Saturday night. This was not part of the sexual training. It was the training to be a mule, what they called a courier.

I would come out of the bathroom after having been run through my exercises, and my mother and sister would be busy with something in the next room. Neither one of them would notice me. My sister would go back to our bedroom without looking into my eyes, or even at me. My mother would be like an invisible person for the rest of the night. My father looked flushed with accomplishment.

"Now we're going to create an idiot girl who people won't think is very bright. You don't have a mind, you're just a body. You can't think, you just follow directions. Whatever anyone tells you, you do, no arguments, no kicking." Mrs. Twartski and Wiezenslowski spoke to me in the room behind the laundry room in Pleasant Hills. I wore a helmet, and sat in the black programming chair with electrodes over my naked body. They spoke to my part named Mary Jane, who was created when I was five. Mary Jane wore Mary Jane shoes, and white anklet socks.

"If we say go here, there, you don't fight or complain. Whenever we press on your nose, you're a windup toy. When we press your nose down, your job is over."

When I was seven and three-quarters, drugged on the black chair with electrodes over my naked body, they called Mary Jane out by pressing on our nose. I had to walk little steps with a bottle in my vagina.

"Walk over there, turn around, sit down, Mary Jane." They spread the cheeks of my backside and fit a package in it.

"Do you like the way that feels?"

"No," I answered. They shoved it further in.

"Do you like the way that feels? This will be your life from now on. This is what happens to all little girls in the world, every girl you see in California, Mexico, Paris, Italy, Spain— every little girl everywhere—it's happened to them. Don't tell anyone."

It is 2013 and I drive to the airport and experience an eruption inside of fear. I ask who feels such terror, and find the mules. They are afraid of airports. Later they will have to go through customs. We who have not been mules rush to them. We travel because we want to. We have no drugs or political papers on us. The mules agonize. The rest of us console. We will care for you, protect you.

The little boy

Ever since I started remembering decades ago, I had an impression of my entering a doorless department store with a wind wall at its front. I saw myself in my twenties, my hair in a French roll. I wore a leather skirt, like a rich American. I thought I was in Paris. The store resembled Bloomingdale's. As the years went on, the memory filled out. I had the impossible impression I had gone into the store to find a child. I was on the main floor, where they sold perfume. A little booth was to the side of the counters and a man in a robe, similar to the Brothers at the monastery, handed me a seven-year-old white boy with freckles, greenish eyes, and red hair. The man's hands were darker than mine. The signs in the store used a different alphabet; it looked like figures dancing. When I told her about this, Alison pulled up examples of South Asian languages on the computer. I recognized one of them, Urdu. I took the boy's hand and walked him out to the waiting limousine. Men sat in the front seat. The man on the passenger side held a gun in the opening between the seats. He pointed the gun at the little boy. We drove through narrow, winding streets. The little boy, who seemed experienced, and I both knew what the gun meant: one wrong move and the men would shoot this little boy. That meant if I bolted from the car, they would shoot him. The little boy knew not to talk or cry. He sat rigidly and stared ahead. He had pants and a short-sleeved shirt on. We were both robots in this hot country. His hand was on the seat. I reached for his hand again. He had short chubby fingers. I felt his heart and his breath through his fingers—beats of sadness, more sadness than fear. He might have been drugged. I let my hand tell him that I was with him, that I could not save him but that I could feel him. This boy whom I didn't know will be part of me always. This boy who was probably stolen and would eventually be killed. I sent as much of myself to this child as I could. The men in front did not feel us, but the gun kept pointing.

"Get rid of her now," a man said. They pulled over. "Get out of the car," the driver said in a heavy accent. I held onto the child. In my mind, we would both get out of the car. "Leave him." The other man cocked the gun as if to shoot the boy. I left the car. The boy was not with me but the boy was with me. The road went down sharply. Little huts were everywhere. Someone came up to me and said, "Come with me" in an accent. The car was gone. We went down a path to a hut. A woman inside the hut gave me comfortable clothes and a purse. Another car drove me on the highway to the airport.

What if they were bluffing? What if I hadn't left the car? Maybe the boy would not have been killed.

Earlier, my grandfather and father refueled a pre-existing program. We sat at the dining room table in my parents' New York City apartment. I was home from college, perhaps summer break. My grandfather, wearing his Wiezenslowski mask, put down a Jack of Clubs, Jack of Hearts, and Ace of Clubs, cues that called out my mule parts. "We have an assignment for you and you have your choice. You're going to Pakistan. You could either take a child, or transport a child, or kill a child. You'd better transport the child because you're not a good killer. Since you're a wimp and a sissy, that will be your next assignment."

Thinking of this little boy cuts through my extensive programming not to cry. Remorse fills the tears. *What would have happened if I didn't take the boy out of the store or leave him?*

The red-haired boy may have been one of the children bred to be used for these purposes. Then his parents would have received money or some privilege, and a slashed conscience. Or his mother might have been a brothel girl like me, who grieved his loss and yearned for him all her life. The world will never know whose little boy it was and what happened to him. Children are being used as he was right now.

TWELVE

Beginning to come alive

Creativity regained

These groups are expert at assessing infants' potential. Always on the lookout, they had spotted my creativity fast. In early childhood, my drawings, interest in color, expressive movement, and struggle to find new words and the right word tipped them off. In my ritual abuse cult, you are not allowed to do anything that lets you come close to your core self. That self, they believe, belongs to them. So my handler and her assistants used drugs, torture, threats, and extensive electroshock to command me never to be creative again. But during a programming session, my father added, "Leave all the creating to your mother and sister." The program not to create stayed put in my splintered brain until around 1978, when my mother began her last phase of dying. In my literal child's mind that held this programming, I thought if my mother wasn't going to create, then that program was defunct. I couldn't leave the creativity to my mother and sister if my mother was dead.

I began creating in my mid-thirties. I saw dances in my head, put them on paper, and then transcribed them to space. I would notate the dances on graph paper with squiggly lines that reminded me of a movement, a color for an emotion, and words that described the movements, stage direction, interactions, and place in the score. Film, costumes, setting, and music were woven into the conception. That first year after this program broke, I choreographed seven or eight long dances and wrote over one hundred poems. I started a dance company to perform the choreography.

I had zero awareness of my true life then. I hadn't even remembered the incest. My dances were about life in general, not that I really understood what life was supposed to be. I was no longer a dead robot. The air was sweet, the sunbursts golden, the blue curtain of sky clear harmony. My cracked, tangled heart spread and opened and breathed. I felt solid.

But while I joined this artists' world, forces were against me, conspiring my recapture. And parts of my mind were against myself, as was preplanned. After all, I was a manufactured robot. Some inside parts smelled something fishy. These parts existed in my internal ghetto city and had the job of reporting to my handlers what was going on in my life. They had learned through heightened torture to obey and not question and above all not think. It takes a world of electricity to stop the brain from thinking. They told the abusers what I had done.

Reporting and recall

One internal reporter telephoned my father in New York. She told my father that I was about to mount a performance in the theater-loft I had just opened for my new dance company. I don't think my handlers ever found out why this program had broken, but they were swift to act on its demise. This father who could not care less about dance or art or me was on the next plane to the Midwest.

My inside reporters patted themselves on the back. *We have done well*, they thought. My front people who knew nothing of the reporting on myself were impressed that my father was travelling to see my work. *He really cares*, they thought. My more aware insiders screeched "Traitor, betrayer." The creators

266

screamed, "All our hard work for nothing, to be ruined, you fool."

I refuse to be angry at myself, even though it eviscerated these years of my life. Those parts were tortured beings just doing what they had been tortured into believing they had to do. But here comes despair from other parts, ones with a wider view of my interior. Yes, I did this to myself. I got some creativity back, but at what cost?

Overnight, I became dead again. Electricity and rape punctuate programming. My performance's opening was that night, and I could hardly rise from my bed. My father sat in my apartment, expecting me to serve him food. He was like a black pit sucking out air and cleanliness. He was a dark hole of perversion. After the portable electroshock and the rape, he delivered the command: "When your sister telephones you, you must return to live in New York and leave the Midwest." After the opening night performance, I had to drive him to the airport. A friend in the audience said later, "You were so filled with life and energy. What happened?"

Seasons later, his telephone call came. He put my sister on. She delivered her command: "You don't want to be a bad mother, and they'll kill Ned if you don't come." My father returned to the phone to make sure I would be obedient. "We will kill him." I returned to New York as ordered. Ned didn't want to leave me and live with his father, I didn't want him to leave. I clung to him, but I had to push him away to save his life, or so I thought then. My son would stay with his father. He never came back to me.

My conscious mind knew that I had been living in the Midwest, but my father had wanted me to return to New York. I couldn't consciously remember that his reason was to keep an eye on me, or that after Mother died, he had called me back, though I knew she had died. I knew I had begun creating, but didn't know it was not allowed, or that they had had to tighten the reins, get me to behave, tweak the programming. I thought

267

I was back in New York because my father had had a heart attack. It did not help that my father and my new assigned handler, my boyfriend Eli, kept torturing me to get me to obey and stop creating. I was breaking the rules and following the rules. I was creating, which was breaking the rules, and reporting on myself, which followed the rules, but I couldn't hold it all together in my head.

Once a program breaks, it's difficult to put it back in. My front people were on one track, and my insiders couldn't stop them. Had my front people known how much the internal ones and my body suffered, I think that they would have ceased their work. But they were oblivious to the other side of my life. Even though the subject matter of my creations was still vague and abstract, the family attacks on me were vicious.

I arrived in New York in 1980 and immediately began looking at what others were performing and began auditioning. Being in New York had its benefits. A new form of art called "performance art" was buzzing. It suited what I was doing because it didn't require balletic technical skill, used multimedia, and was expressive and socially aware. The choreography I had been doing easily transformed into performance art.

First memories

One afternoon when I was walking to the Star Health Club to go for a swim, I vomited into a corner, outdoor, city trashcan onto empty cans of Tab and Coke. In my head I saw babies, one being thrown, another being stabbed. *What was the matter with my mind? Why was I seeing violent, vicious scenes?* More memories began to erupt. There would be no going back.

I took a class from Elaine Summers in what she named "kinetic awareness", a body technique that helps defrost frozen tension. People would lie down on rubber balls from a toy-shop and suddenly have breakthrough memories. People who had spent their adult lives in therapy would do one session

268

of kinetic awareness and recover a lost part of themselves. I was one of the dancers who lay on blankets in Elaine's huge loft, moved our bodies internally from our joints, then placed six-inch rubber balls under our necks. Instantly an image of my mother peeing on me appeared. Shocked tears drenched me. That was my first memory that came straight from my body, not a typical incest memory, and it hinted at something even more ominous. Memories that come from the body are compelling and easier to believe. From there, incest memories charged out like bulbs in early spring.

I was closer to my real self than I had ever been, except for the year I had spent with Daniel, when I experienced love.

Twelve-step meetings for sexual abuse

We rushed straight from our jobs without eating to the six p.m. meeting. We sat in a large oval on collapsible chairs, our feet rubbing the spilled-on basement linoleum floor of a midtown church. To open the meeting, one by one, we iconoclasts went around the room and in shame and victory confessed who our perpetrators were. Some people had always remembered the incest although they hadn't spoken about it before. More were like me, remembering only that very week or day yet another betrayal and trauma, and in the throes of absolute early shock. The group whispered fathers, stepfathers, sometimes mothers, often neighbors, siblings, teachers, religious leaders. I had always remembered my paternal grandfather's sexual abuse. Each week, I added to my personal list. Mother came first, the other grandfather, uncles, grandmother, and sister. Finally, I got to my father, who I thought had loved me, and who had protected me from my mother's rages. My outer world smashed, and each piece had a bold black line around it.

One week, I added Bambi, our miniature Doberman, and the group of comrades and strangers gasped. Shivers went through the group meeting. Eli let out a horrific scream. When I heard the scream, I thought *How nice that he cares so much about what happened to me.* I later realized that he was warning other cult victims not to dare follow in my memory path. I couldn't name it yet but my consciousness had entered the realm of ritual abuse: the extended family incest, bestiality, and people close to me masquerading as helpers but really blocking my path. I had a vague impression of shadowy meetings outdoors with robed figures. I had no notion yet of the mind control, but I knew I was following a stormy current in a shifting raft through dangerous waters into a disallowed unknown.

Some of us in the Manhattan 12-step support group for sexual abuse earnestly worked on excavating our treacheries. My front person scratched and dug into my brain with all my energies, gathering all my strength to endure the horrendous scenes unfurling from my mind. I would see them as if watching a movie, then record them as accurately as possible in my journals. In the morning or waking up from a nightmare, I would plow through emergent memories. In the afternoon, I would encourage the children in me to draw what they wanted to tell. I always had art supplies on hand. The children could sit on the floor and draw what they didn't have words to say.

But at night, cult-loyal perpetrators would abduct me and warn me not to believe what came out of me. The double agents in the 12-step meetings used their internal memorizers to report what survivors said. They shared experiences that reflected what was already known, pretending to disclose their deepest truths. Consciously, I didn't recognize my slimy, handsome boyfriend Eli as the main plant in this territory, but my inside parts must have known. Why didn't they warn me? Maybe they thought something worse would happen if the outside me knew. But also the nature of dissociation is for parts of the mind to endure distinct lives and not communicate with one another. A huge disconnect existed between the outside me who lived my life and the inside people in me who knew about the cult abuse and mind control and didn't tell.

Trying to help survivors

I entered the training program for kinetic awareness. Survivors came to me for sessions, and I tried to help them. At the same time, I thought I needed clinical skills to manage people's huge reactions to knowledge about themselves. Like so much of my life, I thought it was my decision to get further training. I didn't know I was programmed to go to school and become a therapist instead of an artist.

I studied and received a master's degree from Hunter College School of Social Work in 1993. Soon I had a full-time clinical practice, and many of my clients were mind control and ritual abuse survivors. Some found me honestly, but many were sent. Wherever there are mind-controlled clients, there will be plants and trespassers. They reported knowing one another from rituals. They would get some clarity in their session, but that night or week, they would be reprogrammed. Professionals didn't know how to treat them at that time.

I wrote about my experiences with my clients and my own attempts at healing myself in a clinical book. Despite the threats, I continued writing this book to expose the abusers' practices. However, a few chapters of the otherwise helpful book took an oversimplified Christian approach that I had been programmed to include. A Christian publisher gave me a contract, but when the False Memory Syndrome Foundation took hold of this field, saying that all these memories were implanted in clients and suing earnest therapists, this publisher withdrew its contract.

I also curated art exhibits on ritual abuse, which launched me onto a more serious hit list, especially after publicity. I started a lawsuit for sexual abuse against my father and an uncle, which was eventually thrown out of court because of the statute of limitations. Some of my internal parts remained fearful, others intractable. I didn't care if I was hurt. I just didn't want others to be. I gave lectures to New York City professionals and survivors on incest and what we then called satanic ritual abuse.

I depicted my incest memories in a mixed media performance piece called "INCEST: Remember & Tell," urging the survivor audience to cut through dissociation, find their true selves, and speak out. This performance was well received, well attended, and reviewed even by major papers like *The New York Times*. Arlene Raven chose it for her "critic's choice" for *Village Voice*. The performance was funded and toured. We had sold-out audiences. After each performance, there was an open audience discussion. Women poured their stories out. Some had never told anyone before. Some of their utterances weren't completed because survivors broke out in staccato sobs. They cried "My father …" "My brother …" "My uncles …" "My mother …" People were just beginning to speak about their mothers raping them. The play started with a scene of an actress-dancer raping a naked doll. A shudder went through the audience. The audience members were very supportive to one another. Sometimes they sat in silence when the pitch of emotion reached the theater-loft's rafters. The evenings felt holy. Men were present, but I can't remember any talking about their own abuse. A woman who directed a nursing home was in the audience and said, "Now I understand why children are so mean to their elderly parents."

Multiple personalities

I had discovered all these memories, and had focused on helping survivors, but I didn't yet know the most important part, that I was multiple.

Some moments in a life are indelible and do not wash away no matter how many years have passed. These moments derailed the stream of my life and put me on a different path. I was in my bed, about to go to sleep or wake up, when a curtain ripped open within me. Many people inside came to the surface—I think now it was my Council, the leaders of my internal world—and told me they existed.

"No, I am not multiple," the surface me or me's screamed back. "Others are multiple, not me. Multiplicity is a hoax," I flailed, contradicting myself. The force of my recoil from my own being alone could have right there shredded me into fragments. I realized that I wasn't one piece but had parts to my brain that alternated and rotated and carried either shameful acts, or scenes of atrocities, or programs not to remember. I did not want to bite into the apple, but I did want to bite. My integrity and also curiosity and desire for truth urged me on, despite my recoil. The shame overwhelmed.

It took me time to yearn to be with every single part of my assaulted mind. I had continued interference not only from the inside but also from outside me. Slowly, breath by breath, thought by thought, eyelash by eyelash blink, I accepted my selves. I didn't know them yet. That would take years. But I came to know that my mind was a tangled web of despair and the condition serious.

While I was lying on my good Stearns & Foster mattress and propped up by delicious down pillows in my apartment on 108th Street and Amsterdam Avenue, either in the middle of the night or early morning, hundreds of scenes squeezed out of my constipated mind. Each scene was held by different parts of my brain, different personalities. I had to face that multitudes lived under my surface reality and I had to meet everyone. That moment was the worst and the best moment of my long life. Despite my initial revulsion, I learned that the parts I avoided are the real me, and the strongest.

Even as I had these pivotal memories that led me to the heart of ritual abuse and eventually mind control, I didn't know that each program or command to do a task was held by a different part of my brain. Nor did I realize that these parts were not random and free floating but were arranged in strict hierarchical, chronological order. Although I, like all humans and animals, was born with a natural brain, programmers hijacked it and rendered parts of it servants of evil purpose.

THIRTEEN

Trapped in therapy

The first plant—a psychologist

Elaine Summers' advanced student, Annette, referred me to a New York City psychologist to help process my budding memories. Sheila Lesser, Ph.D. had long blond hair, a child's bookworm face, and legs that seemed to go in opposite directions. Her specialty seemed to be giving practical advice, which no one needs in therapy. I imagine she did this in order to distract me from the search for traumatic memories. Although Sheila seemed to view me as a specimen, she appeared interested in my theater work and encouraging. My front person did not know that she, Eli, and a major traveling mind controller trained some of my inside parts in her office.

"Roll up your sleeve," the international programmer said and gave me an injection. "Follow my fingers. You will remember nothing more of incest." An electroshock.

"You will forget the memories you have," Sheila Lesser said. "You will tell no one of these memories; you will stop your performances about incest …."

"Upon penalty of death," Eli continued in his heavy Israeli accent while twisting my left arm backwards to almost breaking. Twice a week, I went to this therapy and about

275

once a week, I had these anti-therapy sessions. While I was quasi-satisfied with therapy on the outside, the colonies of my insiders raged.

A warning

An inconspicuous car pulled up as I walked down McDougal Street in Greenwich Village. Eli and another man pulled me in. The man held my arm behind my back and one hand over my mouth, while my boyfriend slit my nose with a razor and said, "Stop before we kill you." They dropped me off in front of a hospital downtown, giving me papers that identified me as Madeline Smith. The Emergency Room doctors sewed my nose, asked Madeline no questions, and discharged her. The outside me didn't notice the scar on the strip between my nostrils, or the pain. The inside me's fumed.

The cult handlers pulled me away from Sheila Lesser because she had not managed to quell my memory process and productivity. For a while I remained without professional help, which in my case meant cult help. Even though I was better off, I felt adrift. When swimming in a sea of sharks, one needs the illusion of a raft if not a lifeboat.

A bright survivor, Denise, who frequented the 12-step support meetings for survivors of sexual abuse, where Eli recruited people, called and told me of a pastoral counselor who helped survivors by doing short-term walk-throughs or visualizations of hidden memories. I felt intrigued but cautious. That night, a call woke me up and a male voice called out my scheduler. "I want to talk to the person who schedules Wendy's undercurrent life," the voice said. *It sounds like Eli*, I thought. Then that part of my mind receded and another part received that information. The voice gave this pastoral counselor's phone number, which I didn't have to write down, and instructions to call her. She had an out of state area code.

The second plant—a Christian pastoral counselor

This pastoral counselor, Catherine Carter, gave in-home seminars to educate survivors, and she happened to be giving one the following week. Denise and I took the train to her town. Catherine's neighbor, a popular pastor of a large local Presbyterian church, picked us up at the station. They lived in suburban split-level homes. The pastor, Cliff, in his late thirties, had red hair, was pleasant and accommodating, in good physical shape, and over-energized. Catherine was about ten years older and overweight, used a walker to get around, and often had life-threatening asthma attacks. During her seminar, I was in a hyperactive mood, asking too many questions and responding too noticeably. My front person was not in control.

Afterward, we went from Catherine's den to the pastor's living room in his identical home across the street. Cliff, his wife Liz and her mother, Catherine and her live-in mother, Mrs. Landon, gathered around Denise and me. Mrs. Landon grabbed my wrist, put a razor blade on my wrist's veins, and said "You do what I say or else." Mrs. Landon was a short, stocky woman with dried-up skin holding together a body that appeared empty. She had cunning and alertness but resembled stale, crumbling leaves in late fall. A lifetime of worshipping evil depletes the body of blood and life. The tip of the razor penetrated my skin. She called out the slaves my grandmother had created when she slit my scalp with her razor blade. All adult programming is grafted onto one of the personalities or a group of them that was created in childhood. Mrs. Landon got out a vacuum cleaner. "We're going to burn you at the next ritual and vacuum up your ashes unless you obey us." Liz's bent-over mother carried the electroshock kit to the pastor, and Mrs. Landon gooed us up and injected Denise and me. Drugs carry one away from terror into a blurry compliance that can be felt as a relief.

Cliff asked Denise, "What do you want to be?" She answered, "An investment banker." "You are not permitted," he told her. "Wendy, what do you want to be?" I answered, "Just what I'm doing now." "You may not do your book, choreograph, paint, or write, and you have to withdraw your lawsuit. You can be a therapist or a secretary. Denise, you can't even work." He looked at me and said, "She's sleeping over." Looking at Denise, he said, "She's going back to Manhattan." Denise looked worried, more for me than for her. To me, he said, "We're going to work you over," and about Denise he said, "Get rid of her."

Liz drove Denise back to the train station, while Mrs. Landon continued working on the obedient child slave parts of me she had called out, using electroshock and other torture. These parts were supposed to live eternally in cages in the closet in my grandfather's second bedroom, even though he was long dead. Now she wanted them to live in cages in the closet in her guest room. "Your job is not to remember," Mrs. Landon said to them. "If you remember, we'll make you into ashes and you will go into the vacuum, your leftovers into the garbage disposal." She injected me over and over, and the drugs made me foggy, and nauseated. Afterward, she showed me boxes of Goobers chocolate-covered raisins and peanuts, and told me that eating them would make me not remember anything. During recent therapy where I retrieved these mind-controlled-away memories, Alison said to these child parts, "It was the drugs that made you forget." Mrs. Landon placed an upright vacuum cleaner right by the head of my bed in the guest room, as a reminder or cue.

My front person thought *They must really like me, inviting me to stay over, and such knowledgeable folks too. They must be good people, because they are Christian*. My internal people blindly followed orders and had a deep sinking feeling. In the corners of my mind, I see hand signals going wild. Trapped again, others in me thought, and terror seized me. Before I left the next day,

Mrs. Landon opened the sliding closet door, and I saw cages on the bottom. "This is where you will live for eternity," she said to my child slave parts. She put a lock on the closet. My child parts shook with fear, and my internal adults didn't know how to reach them.

Catherine took me into her grip with weekly counseling sessions during the day and mind-control programming and rituals at night. Before each ritual, Cliff administered electroshock and drugs. The outdoor night-time rituals took place in a deserted field. The participants, naked under their black robes, danced wildly around a blazing bonfire. Cliff had a penchant for immodest exuberance when he was not playing the role of the restrained Presbyterian pastor. During the flamboyant ritual, he said, "Is anybody here not Christian? Anybody who is not Christian is going to be thrown in the flames." He turned to me and called out Queen Philomena. "Are you going to be Christian or will you be thrown in the fire?" "Yes, I'll become Christian." Queen Philomena had to protect her people within. Afterward, they dumped me at the train station. In the middle of the trip home, when I had to change trains, I made my way to the candy bar station in the middle of the two train tracks and as directed bought Goobers chocolate-covered nuts. They allowed me to choose between nuts and raisins.

I thought becoming a Christian meant going to church. For a while, I attended this pastor's church, but they said they wanted me to have a church closer to home. After the command and assault, I walked around the city wondering which Manhattan church I was supposed to attend. My inside parts were confused. I was being sucked into evil, and no one on the other side helped me pull against the current.

After a ritual with torture, Cliff said "We have found a home church for you." Interspersed with electroshock, they gave me the address of the Acres of Grapevine Church in Manhattan and instructions to go there on Sunday "because you need Jesus for protection".

It is the end of 2013. For days I have coaxed out this 1990 memory, clearing a path through my brain, reassuring the children who hold this memory in the cages of the locked closet that they are safe enough now to tell. The memory unfurls. The terrorized children huddled in the closet in Mrs. Landon and Catherine's guest bedroom. Small, terrorized children who trust no one shoot me images as if in a film, then talk.

In a private ritual in the pastor's living room, Cliff called out Queen Philomena. He required that she put on her cape and crown, and hold her scepter. In real life, I was practicing kinetic awareness with incest survivors at that time. Referring to my clients, he said, "You will lead your people into church and Jesus' blood. You will tell them that Christianity is the way to heal, tell them to go to church, but one of our churches. Then we will send them to our line of Christian therapists trained and ready to close them down. You will go to the Acres of Grapevine Church and lead your clients there. This is the work we have cut out for you," he said.

Queen Philomena in me didn't want to lead people to Christ, or what these abusers considered to be their Christ. She threw down her scepter, flung off her crown and cape, and had a queenly temper tantrum with spitting and stomping.

"Then every one of your clients, past and present, will be sacrificed. We will start by chopping off their left ankle and proceed to skinning them alive. If you prefer that to happen, then disobey us." If you have ever seen someone's ankle chopped off while they lie on an altar or the start of a skin-alive, you believe these threats. "You decide. You lead people to the churches we tell you, or you indirectly kill your clients. It's up to Queen Philomena. They are her subjects," the pastor roared.

"You will persuade your clients that they are demonized. You will tell them the only way to be free of demons is to have deliverances in one of our churches. We will stop this movement of knowing and remembering. You will be instrumental,"

Cliff said. For security reasons, they would not have killed my clients, but my drugged, terrorized parts didn't know that then.

That Sunday I took the bus to the Acres of Grapevine Church. The second I entered, a beautiful and wholesome-looking woman greeted me. Grace stuck to my side and became a friend and companion to me. Only now do I realize she was a handler.

My programmed inner parts became a member of this church and also attended the small neighborhood home groups. Going to this church had some positive effects. The music inspired and took me out of the earthly realm, a feeling of being in a family comforted me, the Bible teachings taught how to live and values, and at times I could feel what I believed to be the Holy Spirit. At this church and others like it, anything that popped into your head could be the voice of God. I took communion each week, but had convulsions right afterward. There were so many sick and injured people who attended that I didn't attract too much attention. I had experienced belonging and community in my cult life but not in real life before. My outer mind didn't hold any awareness that this was cult life again.

I am Jewish and had never considered becoming Christian until I was ordered to. Two of my cult survivor Jewish clients followed me to this church. This was before the rules against dual roles for therapists, and in any case mind-control programming supersedes generalized codes of ethics in strength.

I continued trying to do authentic therapy with my mind-control clients, kept creating, and also writing a clinical book.

Punishment

One winter night in 1990, I left my computer running, grabbed my giant study Bible, and hurried to the bus stop so as not to be late to my prayer group. The bus driver did not lower the

281

bus steps, and as I descended, I stepped in one of the many cracks in the sidewalk and smashed my ankle. My front person thought I had the worst luck. I didn't think there was anything more to it. But there was.

Two mornings before, in the early hours, Eli, Grace, and my ex-therapist entered my apartment with a key. I sat up in bed as they streamed into my bedroom. Sheila brought in a chair from the main room. They tied me to it, while Eli pressed his gun to my head. On the outside, I showed only stunned silence. Inside, where no one could hear, were sobbing screams. Sheila did hand signals in front of my face.

SHEILA: "Wendy dear, you have misbehaved again and evoked a great deal of anger, wrath, from very high-up people who think you are not as controllable as we would like."

GRACE: "It's Monday night now. On Wednesday night, you will go to home group. You will not walk there. You will take the bus."

SHEILA: "You will exit the back door, look up, and see a man giving you directions. You must follow them."

They recited lines as if they were in a high school play, I thought. Eli pressed the gun in further. Two other men entered, whom I recognized as Stan, the pastor of the Manhattan church, and the higher-up pastor, Ralph, from the other location who had sent me the client. *Of course.*

I thought I smelled alcohol on Ralph's breath. "I want all these art supplies cleared out."

ELI, WITH THE GUN: "I'll take them away. I can use them."

RALPH: "Bitch, no more painting, writing, dancing. You are through as an artist. We're about to send you away for good."

282

Stan shoved a gun into my back, right behind my heart, which seemed to have stopped. With one gun pressed in, I felt as if I were hanging on a mountain. At the moment, Eli seemed aware of himself, but at any second he could fly into his demonic-style rage. Ralph spit foam. With two guns pressed in, I was floating with clouds, not sure I would land anywhere. My body was far out the window in polluted air and fragmented with hundreds of pieces going in disparate directions. Ralph grabbed Stan's gun, as if to say his violence wasn't enough, and moved it from my back to my crotch. I heard a click. "No more expressing yourself. Don't forget to take the bus Wednesday night."

Over a decade after this "accident" occurred, it pushed its way out of my closed-down mind. I had told Alison about the bus accident during one of our therapy intensives, about what bad luck I had with all these accidents, but she thought I might have had some signal to fall, since I'd already told her I had inside parts who were trained to fall. My mind was a blank. But months later, as I walked to the post office during a lunch break at work, I envisioned a man in a suit with brown hair and a pleasant face. I didn't know him. He made circles with his hands and arms, which were bent at the elbows. He directed the hand signals to my internal parts in a deliberate way, staring into my insides. I looked more closely. He looked like a businessman who had just finished work for the day, and stood outside the back bus door among the other passengers waiting for the bus, but slightly to the side. I had a clear view of his body and hands.

The bus driver hadn't lowered the high bus steps. I carried my heavy study Bible. A girl in me began stepping down the rear exit, when someone else inside me looked up and saw this man's hands. A boy inside me behind her pushed another inside person, and the girl fell down the bus steps onto a highly cracked sidewalk. The toe of my shoe caught in one of the cracks, and I spun and fell. I lay screaming on this spider web of cracks and splits in the sidewalk. My ankle broke in three places and had a double closed dislocation. Even shots of morphine in the Emergency Room didn't take away the pain.

About ten waiting passengers observed the fall at the bus stop. The bus driver quickly lowered the bus steps, then called for an ambulance. A would-be witness slipped me a piece of paper with his name and number printed neatly on it. He told me he would witness that the bus driver hadn't lowered the steps. The front person who received the paper didn't know that this witness was the same person who had given me the hand signals.

One of the home group's members visited me at St. Luke's Hospital, and confessed in private to my front person, the queen in me, and anyone else who was listening, "All together the support and prayer group threw curses at you. We were disappointed and thought we hadn't coordinated the attack well enough. We had to keep trying." She delivered the message that they had been trying to kill me, but they had probably just been scaring and warning me. If they had wanted me dead, it would not have been difficult to accomplish.

"But I am so injured and in a cast up to my hip for months," I said to her.

"But we didn't kill you, so we failed."

They wanted me to believe it was their curses that magically broke my foot, rather than my inside people obeying hand signals they had been taught in childhood.

In real life, despite my injuries, I continued doing the kind of therapy work I wanted to do. My clients, who must have been programmed to be in therapy with me, still made progress and became increasingly aware of who they were. Even though becoming a therapist wasn't my idea, I found the work rewarding and enjoyed helping people in despair. Perhaps we were all getting too close to the truth.

I had just about recovered from the bus accident in 1990, when another occurred in 1992. A giant man crashed into my

284

head as I was swimming at the Star Health Club. When questioned, he blubbered, "I did not see her" and continued swimming. He dislocated my vertebrae and gave me a concussion. I lived, but it was another two decades before I understood what had happened. In therapy in 2013, I hear the words: "You will go to the Star Health Club. You will swim the crawl forward, then back. A large man will crash into your head." My memory followed these words and discovered the voice of a therapist I believed was a friend. She also used hand signals. I didn't know she was a cult member and handler. I don't think the swimming pool crash was a homicidal attempt. It was another warning and branding of ownership.

Later, I was drugged and kidnapped from my Manhattan apartment and taken to the main branch of this same Christian church. A mob of people I knew, plus one international programmer, mauled me.

"You will be one of our line of therapists. When people have memories, you will erase them. You will tell people that demons are causing their memories. You will be part of our Christian army of therapists who will close down this chaotic movement to know what's real. You will become the enemy of anyone who tries to lift our veil and expose truth." They wanted me to have credentials. "You'll go to Hunter so we can keep tabs on you. You'll be a B student there, not an A student. Then you'll be one of our gals." They meant Hunter College School of Social Work. At least they sent me to a good school.

Slowly I began to remember these church leaders at satanic rituals. The leaders of the main branch of this unconventional church sent me a member of their congregation, who had just started to remember ritual abuse. I believed that this church was offering me a practice treating its congregation. The new rememberer sat on the sofa tense and ashamed, her arms and legs tightly crossed, not able to make eye contact. I told this young woman to reject this church and go to a safe, clean one, because this church was part of what she was trying to get away from. She left aghast and that was the last I saw of her. As soon as I remembered the pastors and congregants at rituals, I told my clients, and they and I left the church. The walls of my life recollapsed.

Ritual abuse experts

Still trying to get free and thinking I was acting on my own initiative, I got a coveted appointment with a pioneer therapist in the deep south, Sandy Flowers. Hardly anyone could get an appointment with her. As I explained myself, she stopped taking notes, circled around me as if I were an interesting antique piece, and said, "Do you remember being in a black chair? It looks like you've had black chair programming."

I hadn't heard of black chair programming but my inside people sprung to attention, both those who wanted to be free and those who had the job of preventing freedom, and also those who were not up for any more torture.

"I'm not taking any new clients," she said, smiling. She looked like a youngish but middle-aged Southern belle. She referred me to Judith Peterson or Ann Wilson. Why I chose the Christian baffled my front person. Had I learned nothing from the "pastoral counselor" and "evangelical church"? My front person did not know Ann was part of this cult or of the programming.

Decades later, the parts inside who held this memory all gathered together and told the front person the bad news that would lead to healing. I was back in Catherine Carter's guest bedroom still in the early 1990s. I was only partially conscious. Catherine said about me, "She's having good memories. She's close to a total breakthrough."

CLIFF, THE PASTOR: "We'll take her off your hands. We'll send her to our old standby." (Cliff pressed his thumb hard into my third eye.) "Juice her up."

Mrs. Landon, Catherine's mother, lifted my left arm and injected it. My heavy arm fell back down. She put goo on me.

Cliff called out the little girls whom Mrs. Landon had put in cages in her closet, and ordered everyone else in me to go away. Mrs. Landon punctuated his orders with electroshock. I felt like a cut-up chicken under cellophane in a grocery store.

MRS. LANDON: "I'm putting a piece of paper with a name and phone number in your purse. Tomorrow you will call her and make an appointment. No one else inside you can know this information. She will be waiting for your call at 3:00."

I went south to Sandy Flowers' office as directed, returned, and found myself again in Catherine's guest bedroom, flanked by my programmers and handlers. Cliff told me that I would go to Ann Wilson, and would not return. "If you remember what happens in Ann's territory, we will kill your son," he said. He told Catherine she was rid of me. Eli added, "If you remember and tell, we will skin him alive," as he waved the index finger of his left hand in front of my drugged body, while shoving a tarot card of the hanged man at my face. Motherhood is particularly charged for people of this lifelong abuse. The mothers in me blocked the knowledge that I had fallen into yet another trap and was being closed down.

I left New York City and moved to the rural town Ann lived in. Instead of getting to mind control programs, parts, and structure, Ann focused on Jesus, demons, intruding human spirits, and spiritual warfare. Ann performed "deliverances" as she moved her hands back and forth spiraling upward—hand signals that meant, "If you ever tell, we will kill you or worse."

In regular "therapy", parts in me came forward and spoke. They thought it was real therapy and their chance for freedom. When a part is first coming out, it feels like a wave rising, almost like levitating. Ann persuaded me that these were not parts of myself but human spirits and demons or demonized human spirits, people who had at one time lived in the real world and had now become spirits invading my body. To rid me of these supposedly supernatural beings, she verbally bound all the demons and commanded that the demons and human spirits go to the throne of Jesus for judgment. Then she symbolically put Jesus' blood on any openings that might be left in me, to seal them and prevent them from being redemonized. She made a mob of hand movements, and I felt a movement and an eruption within me, followed by exhaustion and a need to eat protein. I thought I had been delivered.

Some of these hand movements were to get rid of my front person, who fell into a coma-type sleep while still in her office. Then, without my being conscious of it, Ann called out personalities within me and directed them to caves, caverns, closets, drawers, drawers within drawers, wells, freezers, internal coffins. Some she dumped in the rivers running through my system. Crucial parts of my existence became locked away in the recesses of my mind, and I didn't know it. She closed down the courageous parts of myself that had tried to come forward and speak. She banished my internal Council. By the time she had finished with me, all the inside parts who knew their and my story had been locked away, and my outside, everyday life person thought that I had been mostly filled with evil entities. My front person thought she had sent away the evil spirits; my inside parts knew that they had been locked away into internal representations of actual containers.

Ann convinced my front person that outside forces caused all my problems and conflicts, that I was a mere pawn in the universe. I began seeing life and the gray skies as filled with demons and demonized spirits. During the programming sessions, her Christian music played in the background, but it rendered disguised mind-control messages. She said it did spiritual warfare for her. She recited many Christian prayers using words like demons, human spirits, authority, pathways,

288

portals, channels, protection, broken, armor, weapons, vexes, hexes, curses, vows, fallen angels, astral projection. She taught me how to handle spiritual attacks, which were really only insiders telling me the horrible truth about my life. I was to pray that the demons and curses be sent back to whoever sent them and up the chain of command threefold in Jesus' name. When I complained that that was overkill, she said, "It's what God wants." I had to say "the Lord rebuke you" whenever I felt such "spiritual attacks". In that way, I silenced the lucid truth seekers within. She gave me Christian books to read that held the same beliefs.

Ann's closedown of me was systematic. Drugs and torture take away the ability to think and have a will. Because she had possession of the volumes of my black book, Ann knew how to draw out and intimidate vulnerable pieces of my dissected brain. "You will never remember, tell, or write about what we do, or we will kill your only living child, of that you can be certain." No one in me doubted it. In retrospect and without the drugs or concussions, I can see that it is doubtful they would have taken the chance of killing my son. My protective acts were most likely for nothing.

Christian therapy for the cult

During week-long intensive therapy, Ann's assistant Marge brought me drugs to sniff. Marge's husband Lenny hit me over the head with the handle of his gun. A hit over the head feels like sliding down endless winding steps on one's back. During a concussion, it's impossible to connect thoughts. Concussed thinking is like trying to knit with one knitting needle. Ann said, "This is how you close people down. As soon as someone has a memory, you know there's an alter there. Most people have been trained in hand signals. First your alternating hands pull out the alter as if pulling on a rope. Round up all the alters, put them in a chamber (your hands go down), then use words,

289

tell them they're in a cave, etc.—you can improvise what. Tell them they'll be there forever and put Lucifer's stamp on them so they're encapsulated, like a pill in plastic. The right fist comes down before the left. Now you will go back to New York and practice on your clients." Marge sang "O beautiful for spacious skies" and a medley of other songs. "Whenever you hear one of these songs, you will remember what your job is, why we made you into a therapist." That was lesson number one.

Lenny performed lesson number two during a different trip while I was still commuting from New York City. "Everyone has human spirits and demonized human spirits in them. Your job as a therapist is to have long conversations with these human spirits, to bind the demons, and send them to the throne of Jesus for judgment. You do rope pulling hand signals to pull them out, then flick your hand outward to send them to the throne of Jesus, and use your fists to communicate to go to the throne for judgment. With your mouth you're saying Jesus but your hands say Lucifer. Then give the hand signal that the ordinary life parts will remember nothing of these commands. Hand signals override words."

Ann continued, "Make people dependent on you, make them think the only way to get rid of these spirits is by having you do deliverances. Persuade them that they are filled with demons. You will go back to New York and practice on your clients, then move here and be part of our practice."

"Lesson four, you will hand in all information on your clients."

"Lesson five, you will tell us immediately if anyone is close to breaking free."

"Lesson six, you will go into supervision with Jennifer Winters." Jennifer Winters was one of the better-known psychologists working in this field and extremely well respected.

"Lesson seven, if Jennifer Winters tells you to send someone to a hospital, you will. She will tell you which ones."

I foolishly believed that if my clients weren't closed down, they'd be killed. The cult would not have killed them all, but

I thought they would kill at least one. So I had to tell them they were filled with demons and distract them from the truth of their lives by saying they were subject to spiritual forces outside themselves. I had to tell them they were just a pawn in a battle, instead of focusing them on their thousands of inside parts. I had to make them believe that feelings and wishes cause things to happen, and that they could do horrible things to people with their minds, rather than that programmed people respond to pre-arranged signals because of mind control. Somehow no one in me was scared enough to use the hand signals. Meanwhile cult handlers most likely tortured these same people, who wanted to be free, in rituals and programming sessions. Back in New York, as I was giving my clients misinformation, thinking I was saving their lives, these clients were triggering me with hand signals, probably thinking also that they had to do it to prevent something worse happening to me. Evil thrives on victims' goodness.

I commuted to Ann's town every few months until I received another command: "We do not put you in a position to help people get free. When we give you an order, it's not for you to do what you want with. It's for you to do what we want with. You're going to close your practice and move to where Ann lives. We will keep a closer watch on you."

After seven years, Ann and her colleagues deemed that I was sufficiently closed down and were disgruntled that it had taken so long. She needed my space for other unwitting survivors making progress in their quests for freedom, and was anxious to discard me to make sure I could not influence any of her new victims.

Right before I was sent away from her rural town, Ann drugged me and Lenny put a head vise around my now fifty-seven-year-old head, squeezed it more and more tightly until someone agreed to be a seven-year-old girl who was in charge of a whole schoolroom of internal children.

291

"All the children have to be told there's no point in seeing other therapists because they are all Ann. If you need a therapist, you have to go back to Ann. You must never tell anyone about Ann." They were sure they had sealed me off for good.

They went through my black book, step by step, identifying the important personalities and enclosing them in storage containers. They repeated all the original tortures which these internal people had experienced, to emphasize that they must remain locked away and never disclose their secrets. They read that my grandfather had put me in freezers and when he separated out the black slaves in me, he had tortured me in a human-sized freezer. Ann then bought such a freezer and put it in a room adjacent to her therapy room. She called out these slaves in me, put my body in there, and told them they were stored permanently in her freezer. They are now in my internal safe house.

She told me what to say if anyone wanted to know why I had stopped therapy. "You are bored with therapy, bored. Ann, me, doesn't want you to, but you are so bored that you have to stop."

If you are a survivor who has been closed down, go back to the closedown memories. They will tell you who has been frozen off and silenced. Then rescue those parts of yourself from storage. The mind and heart want to be whole. Your yearning for your full self will help you find what they took away. Their closedown is a road map to what is missing in you, a shortcut to self-awareness and rebuilding the self. It also will validate your memories.

Hiding a piece

The head programmers must have taught the underlings that traumatic memories resolve only when victims bring all pieces to consciousness. The closedown specialists planned to take pieces of crucial memories out and block them, so that I would never be able to complete and therefore resolve certain dissociated sequences. Ann would call out a part of me that played a role in that memory, torture and shock that part, and move it into storage in what she called a "morgue". There the parts remained in cold storage, separated from the other parts of me who had participated in the experience. In my last session at her counseling center, Ann asked for someone who could withstand the ongoing spinning and burning to come forward. The threat of more torture hung in the air.

A heroic four-year-old came forward. "This is your assignment—when there's a painful event in your secret or outward life, you split off a small part of the memory and put it in this box. It doesn't have to be the worst part of the memory, but it has to be a part of it. Now you will leave here and will never come back for therapy but will report back to me every six months, sooner if you do anything not allowed. Go in peace, forgetting everything. Move to Baltimore, and we don't care what you do or become. Just remember nothing."

During this castration of the self, the universe delivered a moment of joy.

The day I became a horse

Couples and families with invigorated children sprawled on the hot mustard sand. Radios and six-packs of coke and beer held down the corners of their striped, frayed-edge blankets. I was alone and needed a place where I wouldn't be crowded. I scanned my possibilities. I stepped onto the orange sand, and carried my beach chair to the water's edge. Drip castles dotted the dark wet sand. I felt disappointed not to see the wild ponies at Assateague Beach. I needed to feel close to something untamed. Perhaps they were sunning further down the shore.

The beach smelled pregnant, the color of inner grass. A few yards from the low tide, I dropped my chair, pulled off my beach robe, and put on my large straw sun hat decorated

293

with clusters of artificial fruits on top—a banana, green grapes, and plump peaches. The breeze sculpted my mouth into a smile. I spooned my feet into the sand. My toes popped out like spring buds. My spine sank into the back of my low beach chair. My breath skimmed the green gray ocean. I exhaled into the rhythm of the vibrating waves. My pores opened and yearned for the thinnest air.

I smelled horse. Pungent, stinging. A wild pony lay down on my right side. Brown and white, slim and muscular with an eager look, it lay parallel to me, like a puppy. I was tempted to stroke its spine but it was wild. And it had fleas and flies. A fatter gray horse slid from behind and lay down on my left. I was snug tight in the middle. Two pets. A cozy living room in the center of the beach. A third, tan and delicate, approached gracefully and lowered on its balletic legs behind my chair. The brown and white one lifted its head, then rested its chin on the sand. The gray horse swished its tail. I absorbed its happiness. The tan one edged in closer.

A calm encircled me. At last, I fit in. I belonged. A community. The wild horses with fleas chose me above all the other beachgoers. Who was the leader of our pack? I wondered. Perhaps the more muscular one. My soul had no borders. It floated on the calming waves. I was with my own kind. I was chosen. I looked around for a photographer from the *Baltimore Sun* to record our family. The breeze enveloped my limbs. The sun became a torch above me, blazing a path. The scalding sand formed diamonds and sapphires, and I tasted salt and the richness of creation. The earth. I breathed into my part of the universe as if it were my husband. My nostrils turned inside out. Calm, calm, endless calm. A hedge of stillness held us and sealed me into their world.

I heard a rumble and felt a jolt, like the first quiver of an earthquake. My right eye's peripheral vision caught hooves a half inch from my scalp. A fourth beach pony, darker tan, fought for the spot to my right. Hooves, legs, manes, flying, neighing. On my stomach, dragging my sandals in one hand and my hat in the other, I inched toward the tide, like a crab, creeping low so as not to distract the ponies from their playing or fighting. In case of a stampede, better to be in the water than on the burning ground. Moments before, the other beachgoers held one eye transfixed and with the other shot darts of envy at me. Now some laughed. Two ponies were still butting and neighing in our nest. The sand singed. The orange and brown resonated and danced in the wind. All four ponies sped off in the same direction. My former gang flew way down the shoreline.

"A male," a man called out. "Two males were fighting for the females."

Maybe the beach ponies thought I was a horse. Maybe I had been in a harem. My legs reared up on the relenting sand, my arms stretched into other legs with hooves. Orange turned burgundy, and the wind waved my mane and suspended me. My spirit galloped and galloped with belonging and through the crashing waves leapt into my future and past.

* * *

I could not live as a corpse, molded into my abusers' conception of a human being. Something in me stirred, then fought to know the truth. I refused to abandon myself. All I needed was a little support and help and when I found that, I began the more targeted search inward. I had not suspected there would be so many caverns in my brain. No matter how many or how dense, I plan to travel through them all and find the captured parts of my mind. I yearn to be who I am without the programs.

FOURTEEN

A glimpse of freedom

But first another punishment marriage, 1998

I had thought that Darlene, the woman Ned married, was from the normal world. But at the wedding, Ned's eye twitched faster than a hummingbird's wings.

Three women flew to his wedding with me. Two stayed in the hotel, and one with her daughter who lived nearby. I saw Ned for the first time at the rehearsal dinner. He looked handsome and accomplished. As I rushed over to him, instead of rushing to me, he looked at a woman I didn't recognize. She nodded, moved both hands as if to shoo away a pesky animal. Only then did he approach me. He needed her permission to greet me! Then she came over to me, stuck her face in mine, and put a closed hand out for a shake in my face too. I said "Who are you?" and she said "Cindy, Todd's wife." I had seen her only once, years before.

I remembered all this clearly. Then there was a big blank, and I didn't pick up any narrative until the next morning when I went to the continental breakfast in the hotel, after my two friends had already eaten. I had slept later than they had. When there's a blank and your life disappears from under you, then you know something is amiss. I had to go to therapy to retrieve the lost narrative.

297

In the hotel, everybody was asleep. It was after 2 a.m. My son and one of Darlene's brothers came in quietly. The brother injected me, and they silently dragged me out of the room in my nightgown. I thought about holding Ned as an infant pressed against my heart, and realized that I had led my friends unknowingly into danger. In my mind, I gripped a thick rope that sunk into a pure, olive-colored ocean, then all my thoughts suddenly froze. The men forced me down wooden steps and into a parked car, which sped along a steep driveway like a garage ramp. I felt jostled in the car, sleep-driving to somewhere. We drove a long way and arrived at an indoor banquet hall. People gathered at long rectangular tables with white tablecloths. Darlene's family dominated the head table. This could have been a fairy tale like *Alice in Wonderland*. Darlene and her parents and sister and sister's husband and sons were there with Todd and Cindy, the stepmother who had stuck her face and hand in mine, my former in-laws and crowds of people I didn't know. They were all drinking heavily, especially Cindy's alcoholic father, who was the most boisterous. I still wore my nightgown. Some man was kind enough to put his jacket over me. It was June 1999.

They sat Ned and me on straight chairs in the middle of their circle, tied us both up, and circled us, chanting. The crowd at the secret middle-of-the-night banquet chanted:

> Stolen from the nest
> Stolen from the nest
> He'll never rise again
> This boy of yours will never rise again
> Trapped in a marriage
> Trapped in a marriage
> Your punishments again
> He'll fall from grace, amen

"My punishment again." *Yes, just like in my own marriage.* Ned must not have known that he was kidnapping his mother only to be electroshocked himself.

Taser blasts assaulted both of us. In therapy, Ann instructed me never to remember this. They bounced the Tasers off me and Ned, as they chanted:

TO ME: "Let him go"
TO NED: "You'll never be free"
TO ME: "Your boy is doomed"
TO NED: "Your fate is sealed"
TO ME: "It's all because of you"
TO NED: "This is punishment for you"
TO ME: "Look at your deeds"
TO NED: "Now you're stuck"

The circling and drinking crowd sung "Booby prize …" which was insulting to Darlene, but she didn't seem to notice. Maybe the insult made her hysterical, unless she was that desperate for a husband. Then the orgy. Darlene wildly copulated with every male, while her father chased girls. Ned and I were tied up on those chairs and drugged, through the chanting:

> Poor boy, poor boy
> Undone his life
> Poor boy, poor boy
> Trapped underground for life
> No more hope for him
> All because of his sin.
> Poor mother,
> Poor mother
> No rescue possible
> No heritage possible
> All her efforts naught

You're punished, you're through
There's nothing more to you
There's nothing more for you to do.

If he had done something they wanted to punish him for, if he were sufficiently rebellious for them to give him an inappropriate marriage, then he must still have a conscience. What I want for Ned is not to be one of them. He resisted. He was punished. He is holding his soul as best he can. I soar. I see light, as if from Mr. Jacobs' apartment, streak the darkness.

These drunken cultists were punishing him as they had punished me through a degrading marriage, twisting and thwarting him like a bonsai tree. I don't know what they were punishing him for—perhaps not being willing to kill. Maybe my parenting had not been for naught.

At the end of this wedding-ritual humiliation, they untied us, drove me back to the hotel, and cautioned me about not forgetting to lock the door. "It's a dangerous world out there." Drugged, I slept for hours. When I woke up, my friends had already had their continental breakfast downstairs.

The day after I processed this memory, in the late morning, something else crept out of my mind. Some part perceived an action, a silent movement in the blackness, out of my peripheral vision. Another man had entered the room before Ned and the brother. He glided to the bed closer to the window, where my friend Amy had wanted to sleep. I saw a handkerchief flash in the dark. Silly of them to use white handkerchiefs. Then he snuck to the other bed between mine and Amy's but by then, the other two men had me sleepwalking to the door. The first man in raced through the hotel room pushing open the bathroom door, looking in the wardrobe alcove. Ned must have told them I had three friends. He hadn't known one would be staying with her daughter. It had never occurred to me that non-cult people would be drugged. In the morning, when my two friends had just returned from breakfast and I was just

waking, they looked at me suspiciously. Everyone's unconscious mind must have been rattling, but nothing had slipped
into consciousness yet.

During the night and for weeks afterward, two simultaneous rhythms pervaded my heart. It was sinking, and in its
middle, it burst like an overripe fruit but with sadness. Soon
I would be in my front person, not knowing I had endangered
my friends who had just wanted a fun trip. After the enforced
wedding, I wept through the night silently. Almost all of me
realized that he had married into cult and that we would
remain separated. Before his wedding, now and then there
would be a word, gesture, or sigh from my son that recalled
our connection, but mostly there was only ice with barely a
crack. After the marriage, another layer of thickened ice set
over the winter landscape.

The closed-down years

I remained hollow and unknowing for thirteen more years
after Ann closed me down. I managed a little bit of a life. I still
worked as a therapist for people who were in emotional pain.
I bought a house in a suburb of Baltimore, decorated it and
created a garden, made some friends. I walked around as
if something huge was missing, like the inside of me. I had
fewer memories than before and did less creative writing.
I performed activities to absorb my anxiety. I cleaned, dusted,
washed, ironed. I knitted and went shopping. I cooked dishes
that had to simmer for hours, like chicken paprikash. I couldn't
figure out why I had so much time for cleaning. I didn't even
know that the missing me was gone.

I spent more hours at my job. As soon as Ann discarded me,
I reverted to doing good therapy with clients and did not put
forth any of Ann's pretend-beliefs. For me, much of being a
therapist is feeling what the client is suffering. Having someone
else holding their feelings lets the clients see their situations

from a distance. Objectivity can set in. Changing angles frees them for a moment to transform themselves. They can then go back to their sorrow with a new perspective. My life remained stagnant until a handful of my sister's hair, a towel's fall, and a doctor's comment restarted my search.

Ned lived a short plane ride or a day's drive away from where I lived in Baltimore. I was invited to visit every couple of years. He visited me maybe twice in a decade.

I endured the insults of ordinary life without knowing about the real trespasses. I am afraid that every one of my visits coincided with a pre-planned ritual. During these rituals, my grandchildren were programmed against me, and the leaders threatened their lives as a snare to get me to kill. As I got older, I must have become more immune to their ways, because I continued to refuse, and my grandchildren were not killed. But, like me and Ned, they were raised in the cult. And I could do nothing to rescue them.

One of my first intensive therapy sessions with Alison was spent discussing how to make a child abuse report. I had called Child Protective Services and ascertained that they took out-of-state reports anonymously. They would go to the school and question the children. The children had already been mind controlled to deny. I retrieved in therapy how to signal children that it is all right to talk, as if they were reporting to a master in the cult. But the twenty minutes the worker would spend with the child could not counteract the mind control not to tell that they had received from birth on. When the parents found out, the children would be double programmed with a stronger lid. The system was not sophisticated enough, and the workers would be too naïve. I didn't know my daughter-in-law very well, but the man my son was in these rituals was not the person he was in ordinary life. Alison and I concluded that the only way I could help my grandchildren, and all children, would be by writing this memoir.

There was a death warrant on me. I was supposed to go to the 2009 Feast of the Beast, an international ritual dedicated in part to the transfer and promotion of leadership. There I would have been forced to "fall on the sword", the ancient way of suicide, which was how my ancestor King Saul had died, my ancestor according to this group. My body would have been cooked and eaten. At my home, the forgers would have left a suicide note. The cult relies entirely on its members' obedience. If you don't report what you're doing, they won't know. If you're not where they want you to be, they may not come after you.

These groups usually have a fail-safe plan. Since I didn't attend the last Feast of the Beast ritual to be forced to kill myself, then when I am seventy-two, they will send people—most likely family members—to escort me to another ritual where I will be required to "fall on the sword". I have written letters to the police and left them with lawyers and doctors. The letters state that I am not suicidal or psychotic, and give the names of persons to investigate should I have a serious "accident" or die.

My son and his family visited me a few years ago, before I remembered the rituals in New England. Darlene took the lead in hurting my grandchildren and torturing them into believing their punishments were because of me. My remembering this visit is why I left Baltimore and am in hiding. I have no contact with my family. My grandchildren have probably been programmed to believe that I don't want them in my life. I care enough about them and all children to have written this book.

The tide, fall 2013

I'll have to hide. I will get in the car with my clothes and files, computer and dog. I will drive a long way. Like the bride whose train covers the ground behind her, like the snake shedding its seasonal skin, I will take steps away from my known world. Unlike the cicada that returns every seventeen years, I will not return.

I take steps away shedding love, friendship, family, money, the known world. I step into a tide, lie on my back and float. *Whyo, whyo, whyo*, the waves murmur. The silken sky covers me. The green ocean becomes an inflated raft. A rip tide erupts and floats me far away. I don't fight it this time. My elastic body folds, suspends.

At my first week-long intensive therapy session with Alison in 2012, I spoke about "running for my life". I heard myself say those intense words with sincerity, but I hadn't a clue what I was talking about. I accused myself of being melodramatic, looked at myself from a distance and didn't understand the urgency of this belief. I would have left my home and arrived across the country before those parts of me who spoke these mysterious words identified themselves.

I abruptly closed down my life in Baltimore. I gave two months' notice at work, but it still felt like a sharp, unquiet end. People grieved my leaving. Of all my clients, only one understood that something was the matter and that's why I was leaving. The others said, "Enjoy your travels" and thought I was abandoning them. But an injured roofer with a frozen shoulder who had a mild mental handicap said, "Now I will have to worry about you." He knew I wouldn't leave my practice unless I absolutely had to. This morning, my first morning in my new location, where I fled to, I am crying for the clients I left behind and didn't see through to the end. Before I left, I told a few friends the real reason. One said I was just upset and making up stories; another said, "I'm worried about you," implying I was insane. Leaving my clients, and the hope that my family would come around, hollow out my heart.

Epilogue

My grandfather was once a scared little boy in Galicia until they forced him to decide to be evil, this grandfather who attempted to destroy so many young minds. My mother was like a firefly closed in a glass jar with only one hole punctured for air. Even when the firefly changed colors fast, it remained lidded and caught. My sister was afraid. My father was still a child doing whatever he could not to be a victim. This next generation is under the lid of this oppression.

I had a year of a boy's love. Sixty years later, I had a friend who nurtured. And another friend who cared enough about me to point me to someone who could help. Alison cared that I become free. People cared. A small amount of love can undo what man has connived from the beginning of time. Love is that potent.

Even seeing some of my mind's barriers dissolve affirms this laborious process. Even a moment of not being surrounded by satanists makes this trek through awareness worth it. The unspeakable purity of freedom is like breathing the cleanest ocean air.

Despite every day that I had expected to be my last, I have grown into an old woman. Being alive allows me to honor those who were killed or driven crazy. It allows me to remember and tell.

Today, in another country, I walk through a wooded area with my West Highland Terrier, and by chance an old man using a thick cane walks his large black dog at the same time. He tells me the herons have flown to another park because of a hawk. Multitudes of empty nests crown bereft trees.

ACKNOWLEDGEMENTS

Without Alison Miller's clinical support and steadfast encouragement to tell my story, this memoir would not have been written.

I want also to thank Baron Wormser, Eugenia Kim, and Kim Dana Kupperman for their interest, guidance, and concern.

The names and locations have been changed to protect the innocent and consequently the guilty. My name is real, as are those of Alison Miller, E. Sue Blume, Daniel David Baker, and some others.

ABOUT THE AUTHOR

Wendy Hoffman is a survivor of criminal abuses and has been a psychotherapist for over two decades working in general practice and the field of recovering dissociated memories. Her MSW comes from Hunter College School of Social Work in New York and her MFA from Fairfield University in Connecticut. She has done performance art and given multimedia art exhibits in NYC, on tour, and in Chicago. Her writings are published in *Passenger*, *The Healing Muse, Jewish Women's Literary Annual*, and other literary journals.